THE COMICS OF ALISON BECHDEL

David Ball, Series Editor

THE COMICS OF ALISON BECHDEL
From the Outside In

EDITED BY JANINE UTELL

UNIVERSITY PRESS OF MISSISSIPPI / JACKSON

The University Press of Mississippi is the scholarly publishing agency of
the Mississippi Institutions of Higher Learning: Alcorn State University,
Delta State University, Jackson State University, Mississippi State University,
Mississippi University for Women, Mississippi Valley State University,
University of Mississippi, and University of Southern Mississippi.

www.upress.state.ms.us

Designed by Peter D. Halverson

The University Press of Mississippi is a member of
the Association of University Presses.

Copyright © 2020 by University Press of Mississippi
All rights reserved
Manufactured in the United States of America

First printing 2020

∞

Library of Congress Cataloging-in-Publication Data available
LCCN 2019034414

Hardback ISBN	978-1-4968-2577-3
Trade paperback ISBN	978-1-4968-2578-0
Epub single ISBN	978-1-4968-2579-7
Epub institutional ISBN	978-1-4968-2580-3
PDF single ISBN	978-1-4968-2581-0
PDF institutional ISBN	978-1-4968-2582-7

British Library Cataloging-in-Publication Data available

CONTENTS

ACKNOWLEDGMENTS
IX

THE WORKS OF ALISON BECHDEL
XI

INTRODUCTION
Serializing the Self in the Space between Life and Art
JANINE UTELL
XIII

I. IN AND/OR OUT: QUEER THEORY, LESBIAN COMICS, AND THE MAINSTREAM

THE HOSPITABLE AESTHETICS OF ALISON BECHDEL
VANESSA LAUBER
3

"GIRLIE MAN, MANLY GIRL, IT'S ALL THE SAME TO ME"
How *Dykes to Watch Out For* Shifted Gender and Comix
ANNE N. THALHEIMER
22

DISSEMINATING QUEER THEORY
Dykes to Watch Out For and the Transmission of Theoretical Thought
KATHERINE PARKER-HAY
36

BECHDEL'S MEN AND MASCULINITY
Gay Pedant and Lesbian Man
JUDITH KEGAN GARDINER
52

MO VAN PELT
Dykes to Watch Out For and *Peanuts*
MICHELLE ANN ABATE
68

II. INTERIORS: FAMILY, SUBJECTIVITY, MEMORY

DANCING WITH MEMORY IN *FUN HOME*
ALISSA S. BOURBONNAIS
89

"IT BOTH IS AND ISN'T MY LIFE"
Autobiography, Adaptation, and Emotion in *Fun Home*, the Musical
LEAH ANDERST
105

GENERATIONAL TRAUMA AND THE CRISIS OF *APRÈS-COUP* IN ALISON BECHDEL'S GRAPHIC MEMOIRS
NATALJA CHESTOPALOVA
119

THE EXPERIMENTAL INTERIORS OF ALISON BECHDEL'S *ARE YOU MY MOTHER?*
YETTA HOWARD
135

INCHOATE KINSHIP
Psychoanalytic Narrative and Queer Relationality in *Are You My Mother?*
TYLER BRADWAY
148

III. PLACE, SPACE, AND COMMUNITY

DECOLONIZING RURAL SPACE IN ALISON BECHDEL'S *FUN HOME*
KATIE HOGAN
167

FUN HOME AND *ARE YOU MY MOTHER?* AS AUTOTOPOGRAPHY
Queer Orientations and the Politics of Location
KATHERINE KELP-STEBBINS
181

INSIDE THE ARCHIVES OF *FUN HOME*
SUSAN R. VAN DYNE
197

SERVANTS TO WHAT *CAUSE*
Illustrating Queer Movement Culture through Grassroots Periodicals
MARGARET GALVAN
214

FRAMING COMMUNITY FROM INSIDE OUT
The Information Worlds of *Dykes to Watch Out For*
DON L. LATHAM AND JONATHAN M. HOLLISTER
230

CONTRIBUTORS
245

INDEX
249

ACKNOWLEDGMENTS

This project has been a collaborative effort from the beginning and has benefited enormously from extensive support and encouragement. First and foremost, I must thank David Ball, series editor for Critical Approaches to Comics Artists. His encouragement, his humor, and his intelligence make him the ideal collaborator and interlocutor; it has been a privilege to participate in his vision for the series and to reap the benefits of his keen critical and editorial eye. Vijay Shah at the University Press of Mississippi has been a great supporter of this project, and Lisa McMurtray, who is entirely delightful to work with, has ensured that every stage of the process has gone smoothly; I am grateful to them both. I am grateful, too, to Pete Halverson for the wonderful cover design and his work securing permissions. Thank you as well to the anonymous peer reviewers, particularly for feedback on my introduction. I would also like to thank, at the outset, Alison Bechdel: it has been an honor, and terrific fun, to engage with her work in these pages.

I owe a debt to James Phelan and Frederick Luis Aldama, leaders of the Project Narrative Summer Institute at Ohio State University. My time there in 2011 first prompted my interest in Alison Bechdel's work, and I am most grateful to them for their guidance. James Donahue, Jennifer Ho, and Leah Anderst (the last in addition to being a contributor) have been supporters of this project from the start, and I am most grateful to them for their friendship. Sarah Copland, Brian Cremins, and Ernesto Priego facilitated work on the book in its early stages, and Daniel Worden has been a great help throughout (indeed, I find his work in this series to be a model). In addition to being a contributor, Susan Van Dyne has been a valuable resource on Bechdel's work as well, and I thank her. Thanks are due to all the contributors; each has been an exemplary colleague and collaborator, responsive to deadlines and requests at every point, and generous with their enthusiasm for the project.

Special acknowledgment must be made to Thomas Sokolowski, director of the Zimmerli Art Museum at Rutgers University, and Amanda Potter, curator of education and interpretation, for providing the opportunity for me to meet Alison Bechdel as part of the opening of the exhibition *Self-Confessed! The Inappropriately Intimate Comics of Alison Bechdel* (September 1–December 30, 2018).

At Widener University, thanks are very much due to my colleagues in English and creative writing and beyond. Kenneth Pobo has offered ongoing support and interest, as have Michael Cocchiarale, Annalisa Castaldo, Mark Graybill, and Kate Goodrich. I am grateful for the support provided in the form of a sabbatical leave to complete work on the book, and for this I thank the Widener University Faculty Council Faculty Affairs Committee, the Office of the Provost, Mara Parker in her role of associate dean of humanities, and Scott Van Bramer in his role of acting dean of the College of Arts and Sciences. Many thanks are due to the staff members of Morris Library at the University of Delaware and Wolfgram Memorial Library at Widener University, particularly the interlibrary loan staff of the latter, and most particularly Susan Tsiouris. I owe a great deal to my students, especially those in my course on graphic narrative, for their insight and conversation.

Finally, as always, my deepest gratitude goes to my family for their love, patience, and enthusiastic support. My sister Tracy Farber is always there with encouragement tempered with humor, as is my brother-in-law Glen Farber. My parents, John and Linda Utell, have been steadfast in their support, for which I am most grateful. My gratitude to John-Paul Spiro is beyond words.

This book is dedicated to my amazing niece Abigail Lindh Farber: may she always have all the love she deserves—and what she deserves is boundless—and more.

THE WORKS OF ALISON BECHDEL

Abbreviations used for frequently cited works:

AYMM   *Are You My Mother? A Comic Drama.* Mariner, 2013.
Essential *The Essential Dykes to Watch Out For.* Houghton Mifflin Harcourt, 2008.
FH   *Fun Home: A Family Tragicomic.* Mariner, 2007.
Indelible *The Indelible Alison Bechdel: Confessions, Comix, and Miscellaneous Dykes to Watch Out For.* Firebrand, 1998.

INTRODUCTION

Serializing the Self in the Space between Life and Art

JANINE UTELL

Alison Bechdel has described her work as "inappropriately intimate." She suggested the phrase for the title of a 2018 exhibition spanning her entire career, and it captures the transgressive and sometimes playful nature of many of her comics, as well as the demands she places on her readers as they enter her world.[1] Bechdel has used comics to explore multiple versions of her most private selves. In her work, we are invited into a world where the messy feelings of difficult and deep relationships are sounded and where things that challenge our ideas of what should be represented are, in meticulous, sometimes graphic, detail. At the same time, entering into that world is itself challenging. Navigating the private histories of others, seeing the losses and traumas of others, bearing witness to their essential humanness: these are challenging acts artistically, narratively, and ethically, but they are what Bechdel calls on us to do.

Bechdel is preoccupied with intimate lives, including her own, and with making varieties of intimacy visible, in a variety of narrative forms. In the many interviews Bechdel has given about her life and her art, and in her own writing about her work, such as that collected in *The Indelible Alison Bechdel: Confessions, Comix, and Miscellaneous Dykes to Watch Out For* (1998), she offers herself up for scrutiny and continues to probe what drives her to represent her most private concerns.[2] Her major works—the long-running comic strip *Dykes to Watch Out For*, and her two critically acclaimed memoirs, *Fun Home* (2006), which has also been adapted into a Tony Award–winning musical, in addition to receiving numerous accolades, and *Are You My Mother?* (2012)—bring us first into the lives of a lesbian community, and later into the lives, past and present, of Bechdel herself.

On first look, it might seem that the trajectory of her work has taken a swerve. *Dykes to Watch Out For* (*DTWOF*) ran from 1983 to 2008 and launched Bechdel's career. The strip serializes the stories of a group of lesbian friends and lovers as they go through romantic entanglements and the arcs of long-term relationships, consider marriages and have children, struggle with careers and health crises: in short, live entirely ordinary lives with all the humor, pathos, and anxiety of any ordinary person. It is the very ordinariness of the intimate lives of *DTWOF* that makes it such a significant moment in comics. Bechdel, who has been out as a lesbian since 1980, committed herself to representing, to making visible, the lives of individuals in her community, even if sometimes she depicts that community as being more utopian than seems quite possible. In *The Indelible Alison Bechdel*, she writes of early *DTWOF* cartoons: "The quality of the drawing and writing was wildly uneven—more often than not the cartoons weren't even funny—but lesbians were so desperate to see a reflection of their lives that it didn't seem to matter much" (*Indelible*, 27). *DTWOF* speaks to the need of people in a subculture to see themselves reflected back to themselves, something Bechdel believes helps members of that subculture "reach [their] potential" (Critchfield and Pula, 400). Bechdel, along with other gay and lesbian comics artists from the 1970s through the 1990s like Mary Wings, Roberta Gregory, Howard Cruse, Diane DiMassa, and Jennifer Camper,[3] created a space first in underground comix and then more widely in comics culture for previously invisible members of the community to be seen, and to see themselves.

DTWOF is concerned with community, and with the intimate relationships that form and develop within the networks and bonds of that community. It imagines, even idealizes, what it means to be out, to live openly and free from shame and prejudice. *Fun Home*, published in 2006, and *Are You My Mother?*, published in 2012, seem to turn from the outside in. Layer by layer, the two memoirs delve into Bechdel's relationship with her parents, the first focusing on her father and the second on her mother, moving backward and forward in time. They cross the boundaries of multiple spaces as they move further inward toward deeper, more intimate parts of Bechdel's many selves. Bechdel the artist deploys "Alison Bechdel" the narrator, who tells of "Alison Bechdel" the character, who herself changes as she traverses the spaces of home and therapist's office, the interior spaces of psychic life and memory, the textual spaces of family photographs and books, all nesting (not always comfortably) within each other. All of Bechdel's work, both the cartoons and the memoirs, should be read as concerned with relationality, with representing the intimate spaces of the self, and that self in intimate relationship with others. Whether she is drawing the dykes of *DTWOF* sitting around a kitchen table drinking wine and talking politics and lovers, or drawing herself sitting in her therapist's office describing a dream, Bechdel makes visible the self out in the world alongside the inner world of the subject.

Bechdel's Life and/as Art

Bechdel's world started out rather small. She was born in 1960 and grew up in Beech Creek, Pennsylvania, a place where, she says, "the pressure to conform was savage" (*Indelible*, 20). Bechdel began life in a rural setting, raised Roman Catholic by parents who were forced to move back to the United States from Europe, where her father, Bruce, had been stationed in the army, to take over the family funeral home—the "fun home" of the celebrated memoir. Bechdel and her two brothers grew up in a Victorian-style house that was the object of Bruce Bechdel's obsessive attention. Bruce Bechdel, who worked as a high school English teacher in addition to being a part-time funeral director, lived as a closeted gay man. Helen Bechdel, Bechdel's mother, acted in local theater and, according to the accounts in her daughter's memoirs, was aware of her husband's sexual orientation, including dalliances with underage young men. The tensions created in the family by the closet—shame, silence, fear of exposure and disclosure—profoundly influenced Bechdel's work.

It was living with such tension, such shame, that led Bechdel to come out as a lesbian at the age of nineteen. Shortly thereafter, Helen Bechdel decided to divorce Bruce Bechdel, and subsequent to (perhaps as a result of) this series of events, he stepped in front of a truck as it barreled down a Pennsylvania highway not far from the family home. This is the catalyst for *Fun Home*. Was it the daughter's act of coming out that led to the father's suicide? Was there something in their relationship, some shared connection, that might have saved him? How had the daughter been able to choose a different path?

Dykes to Watch Out For: The Making of a Lesbian Cartoonist

In an interview with Terry Gross, the host of National Public Radio's program *Fresh Air*, Bechdel says:

> In many ways my life, my professional career has been a reaction to my father's life, his life of secrecy. I threw myself into the gay community, into this life as a lesbian cartoonist, deciding I was going to be a professional lesbian. In a way, that was all my way of healing myself. ("Lesbian Cartoonist")

Bechdel had been drawing since she was a child, but becoming a professional lesbian cartoonist did not happen immediately. After graduating from Oberlin College in 1981, Bechdel moved to New York and began applying to art schools; she was roundly rejected. Around this time, she started doodling dykes in letters to a friend. The oft-told story of the genesis of *DTWOF* is a sketch of "Marianne, dissatisfied with the morning brew: Dykes to Watch Out For, Plate No. 27"; Marianne is depicted nude, standing crane-like on one foot with a coffeepot in her hand, the grimace on her face haloed by frizzy hair.

Becoming a lesbian cartoonist *was* easy for Bechdel, she writes in *The Indelible Alison Bechdel*, insofar as others had paved the way. By the time she walked into the Oscar Wilde Memorial Bookstore in Greenwich Village in the early 1980s, she writes, "There was already such a thing as a lesbian cartoonist. I didn't have to invent it, or fight for it, or suffer over it. I just did it" (*Indelible*, 10). The challenge for Bechdel at the start was drawing *women*. Since childhood, drawing men had been a way for her to work through strategies of representing gender and sexuality and a means of practicing her craft, but she came to see it as neither personally nor professionally fulfilling. Early on, attempting to represent women had proved an obstacle, even as being out as a lesbian and becoming more committed to a highly politicized feminism led Bechdel to see the necessity of drawing women. She writes:

> As I grew more and more politicized, it began to rankle that my sketchbooks were devoid of women. . . . To draw a woman involved not just a change of subject matter but rewiring the circuitry that seemed to run directly from my subconscious to my pen. (*Indelible*, 24)

We find here Bechdel's ongoing concern with, and belief in, the power of representation, but we also find her struggle with finding and wielding that power in a heterosexist and misogynist society (including, possibly, some of the underground comix world, as might be seen in the work of figures like R. Crumb, influential as such figures have been for Bechdel herself).

For much of Bechdel's early life, being a woman meant conforming to conventional stereotypes of femininity and experiencing shame attendant on the female body. It was not until Bechdel realized she could draw women *as lesbians* that it became possible to handle the female form, and thus possible to tell women's stories through comics (*Indelible*, 26). A well-known scene in *Fun Home* depicts the young girl character Alison in a diner with her father; the two of them see a bull dyke walk in, a moment the Alison narrator describes in gutter text as "unsettling." Bruce asks, "Is **that** what you want to look like?" The Alison narrator reports in gutter text, "What else could I say?" and the Alison child character in the panel replies to her father, "No" (*FH*, 117–19).[4] This sequence becomes the powerfully moving scene "Ring of Keys" in the 2013 off-Broadway musical adaptation by Jeanine Tesori and Lisa Kron (moved to Broadway in 2015), and it speaks to the significance of representation and the force to be wielded by signifiers of transgressive gender performance. The ring of keys on the bull dyke's belt is a small visual detail in the *Fun Home* panel, yet it gathers meaning and affective force in the theatrical adaptation, allowing for the transcending of the shame the girl Alison feels in that moment. Through its use of the "portrait of the artist as a young person," or *Künstlerroman*, genre, *Fun Home* shows the origin of the circuitry that led to shame and discomfort with sexuality, and the work involved in "rewiring." Both *Fun Home* and *Are You My Mother?*, moreover, elucidate the ways in which Bechdel, throughout her career, has imagined that direct line from her subconscious to her pen.

Finally, then, here was Marianne; Marianne was joined by Twyla, and Madeleine, and Bechdel's friend receiving the doodles in the mail suggested the dykes be sent to the feminist periodical *WomaNews*, which Bechdel did in 1983. At first the cartoons were single panels with a bit of wry, dry wit. In 1984, Bechdel began producing *Dykes to Watch Out For* in serialized strip form, and in 1987 the central characters of Mo Testa and Lois were introduced. By this time, *DTWOF* was appearing in publications beyond *WomaNews*. Bechdel would go on to self-syndicate the comic strip nationwide and release eleven collections of *DTWOF* cartoons, with titles like *Spawn of Dykes to Watch Out For*, *Unnatural Dykes to Watch Out For*, and *Hot Throbbing Dykes to Watch Out For*, as well as assorted merchandise such as calendars and mouse pads. (These were in addition to the design work she was doing for gay and lesbian activist groups, creating posters, T-shirts, and the like.)

Until Bechdel ended the strip in 2008, with the occasional revival after the election of Donald Trump to the presidency of the United States in 2016, *DTWOF* followed the lives of Mo, Bechdel's alter ego; Mo's lovers, first Harriet and then Sydney; Jezanna, the owner of the independent feminist bookstore Madwimmin Books, where Mo works until a "Bounders Books and Muzak" puts it out of business; Sparrow, a bisexual woman who winds up having a baby with the very progressive and mild-mannered Stuart; Clarice and Toni, long-term partners (until the arrival of Gloria) who have a little boy, Raffi, together; Ginger, a PhD candidate in English who often finds herself unlucky in love (including a long-distance relationship with Malika, whom Ginger meets at a lesbian conference in Atlanta); and the polyamorous genderqueer drag king Lois. The strip responds to current events, satirizes women's studies programs and queer theory, pokes gentle fun at Pride and vegans, and in general gives a clear-eyed, generous, and often hilariously particular insight into a community of lesbians. One notable exception might be "Real World," the strip Bechdel produced after 9/11. Entirely wordless, a sequence of eleven panels shows the responses of each of the main characters: reading the newspaper or watching television, meditating, holding each other. The prioritization of relationships and the deploying of private intimacy in the face of public trauma are clearly signaled.

DTWOF took for its material Bechdel's own experiences living in such a community (though perhaps not as ideal in real life) in Minneapolis, where she moved from New York in the mid-1980s. The strip is also the source of the famous "Bechdel test." In an early episode titled "The Rule," which ran in 1985, two characters are trying to decide on a film to see. One character explains her rule: the film has to (1) have at least two women in it, (2) who talk to each other, (3) about something besides a man.[5] The wide recognition of the Bechdel test, way beyond the readers and fans of *DTWOF*, is the result of greater cultural attention to women in media and reminds us that representation, visibility, and identity are central to *DTWOF* and Bechdel's work.

DTWOF followed the contours of changing attitudes and ways of thinking about gender and sexuality over the course of its entire run, showing through meticulous and cleverly chosen detail, and a great diversity of characters, what these look like in lived experience. As Lois says in "Au Courant," published in 1994, "Love is a many-gendered thing" (*Essential*, 125). At the center of it all is Mo, with her signature striped shirt and spiky hair, round glasses, neuroses, and righteous indignation. Often seen holding a newspaper and alienating people even when she doesn't mean to, Mo judges her friends for looking at beautiful women in the midst of a protest against the First Gulf War ("Dancing in the Streets," 1990; *Essential*, 63). The introduction of Sydney, a gender studies professor, affords the opportunity for much satirizing of academics, as well as for working through the political disillusionment that came with the first Bush administration in the 1990s; suddenly, Mo's righteous indignation seems impotent. Sydney is a complex figure. Snarky and cynical, Sydney left another character, Thea, when she found out she had multiple sclerosis before her involvement with Mo; Sydney also cannot quite keep herself from creating erotic entanglements for herself over the internet. Yet one of the especially emotionally resonant story lines of the strip is Sydney's diagnosis with, and treatment for, breast cancer, which unfolds in parallel with Clarice and Toni getting pregnant and giving birth to Raffi. Bechdel's strip speaks directly, and intersectionally, to the collective experiences of contemporary women from the highly singular points of view of diverse individuals.

In this way, *DTWOF* approaches a kind of universality that Bechdel perhaps did not expect when she began the strip. Bechdel's website, dykestowatchoutfor.com, still attracts thousands of visitors who comment on and celebrate the strip through its archives, even as updates on the blog have become more sporadic. On the occasion of the comic's twentieth anniversary, in a 2003 interview with Teresa DeCrescenzo for *Lesbian News*, Bechdel said, "I kind of half-seriously miss the days of being invisible. I wouldn't really want to go back, but it has been hard for me to watch queer culture get systematically deracinated and assimilated and depoliticized over the past 10 years" (25). And while early on the cartoonist did claim that getting some space in the *Village Voice* would be a professional achievement, she refused any move that would seem to be allowing the appropriation by, or pandering to, the tastes of the mainstream (Bechdel and Thomas, 14). When she was contacted by Universal Press for syndication in mainstream newspapers in 1994, on the condition that she produce a strip that was "less political," Bechdel said no: "I have less than no interest in speaking to the mainstream. I mean, if my works ever got banal enough to make it into a mainstream newspaper, I hope someone would just put me out of [my] misery" (Rubenstein, 34). Nevertheless, as issues important to LGBTQ folk have themselves become more mainstream, and as prevailing attitudes have changed—as the binary of "closeted" and "out" has ceased in many ways to be the dominant means of imagining gay and lesbian existence—Bechdel's work has found new audiences. One might even suggest that *DTWOF* itself played something of a role in these cultural shifts. In 2008 a substantial collection, *The Essential Dykes to Watch Out For*, was published with the subtitle *The Lives, Loves, and Politics of Cult-Fave Characters Mo, Lois, Sydney, Sparrow, Ginger, Stuart, Clarice, and Others*. By 2018, the *New York Times* had named *The Essential Dykes to Watch Out For* one of the fifteen most important books by a woman in the twenty-first century (Garner, Sehgal, and Szalai).

Fun Home and *Are You My Mother?*: Comics, Coming Out, and Self/Knowledge

It is *Fun Home*, published in 2006, that has garnered Bechdel international accolades. This memoir of Bechdel's coming out and her father's suicide has been honored as *Time* magazine's Book of the Year and won an Eisner Award for Best Reality-Based Work. It was a finalist for a National Book Critics Circle Award and was named one of the best books of the year by sources ranging from the *New York Times* to *Entertainment Weekly*, and it is regularly assigned (and sometimes banned) on college campuses as a first-year common reading, including at West Point. The recognition of *Fun Home* has brought Bechdel more mainstream success, as well as greater attention from academics and acknowledgment of the significance of her work from mental health experts and LGBTQ activists. *Fun Home* has been adapted into a musical, first off-Broadway in 2013 and then for Broadway in 2015, where it won numerous Tony Awards: Best Musical, Best Actor, Best Score, Best Book, and

Best Direction. Notably, Jeanine Tesori and Lisa Kron, the team who brought *Fun Home* to the stage, are the first all-women team to win a Tony for Best Score. Bechdel was named an artist-in-residence at the University of Chicago in 2012 and received a MacArthur "genius" grant in 2014.

Much of the work on this groundbreaking book began during the run of *DTWOF*. While the memoir is more explicitly in the mode of what is recognizably life writing or "autography," to use Gillian Whitlock's term,[6] the continuum of interests in selves and the nature of the subject—queer and lesbian identity and sexuality, gender performativity, the nature of embodiedness and relationality, and shared or troubled epistemologies and subjectivities—extends from *DTWOF* through *Fun Home* and *Are You My Mother?* In *Fun Home*, Bechdel sought to enter into the selves of her father as well as her own subjectivity. This process took a uniquely bodily and multimodal form: Bechdel posed herself as every subject and took photographs for every panel in the book, drawing from the digital images.[7] Over seven chapters, each opening with a re-creation in black-and-white cross-hatching of a family photograph and each drawing on an intertextual relationship with books and authors most appreciated by Bruce Bechdel (especially James Joyce and Marcel Proust), *Fun Home* moves recursively through nonlinear temporality across multiple versions of Alison Bechdel.[8] Bechdel the artist appears in its pages, merged with her character-self and narrator-self, via the drawing of a hand holding the drawing of a photograph: the notorious and compelling centerfold image of her babysitter Roy, presumed to be an object of erotic attention by her father (*FH*, 100–101). Bechdel as the character Alison appears as a child, a college student, a teenager, a child again. And Bechdel as the narrator appears in text boxes and gutters, drawing our attention to the spaces between past and present perceptions and subjectivity, between what is said and unsaid, between what is real and what is remembered.[9]

Fun Home takes as its subject not only the death of Bechdel's father. Central to the narrative is her development as an artist and her defining of herself as a lesbian, processes that unfold as inextricably linked. In chapter 3, "That Old Catastrophe," the character Alison is depicted at her typewriter in a panel using an over-the-shoulder view. We cannot see the words on the sheet of paper, but a text box with an arrow pointing to the paper and lettering drawn to look typewritten fill us in: "I am a lesbian."[10] The text in the gutter, providing telling by the Alison narrator, fills in a further gap, one of temporality as well as knowledge: "Only four months earlier, I had made an announcement to my parents" (*FH*, 58). The image is repeated, fragmented this time, in the final chapter, "The Antihero's Journey." In a much smaller panel, juxtaposed with another smaller panel so that the two together take up the same amount of space as two other panels in the tier they share in the middle of the page, a close-up on the "n" key of the typewriter completes the this time partially viewed sentence on the paper itself unmediated by arrow and text box: "I am a lesbia [. . .]." The panel underneath, depicting Alison's hands putting the letter to her parents in the mailbox, shows the completion of the moment and the act of coming out to the family (*FH*, 210). In the earlier iteration, the words narrated tell us the significance of the typewritten sentence, and the image of the typewriting is in fact a flashback, conjured by the narrated words. In the second iteration, no words are necessary. We already understand the significance of the moment as we re-see it, the image repeated and the moment replayed and drawn out by the infinitely suspended "n" over the page, until the silence is broken, the "n" comes down, and who Alison *is* is defined irretrievably. Here we have the moment in time, the single object of the key invested with the power to speak, the utterance of "lesbian," and the *drawing* of this very instant. But we also have the repetition of crisis, played out again and again in an attempt to interpret, to make meaning. The bringing together of each element in the panel, the page, and the whole of the memoir suggests how essential the defining of the subject, the development of the artist, and the cycles of troubles and traumas generated by epistemological crisis are to Bechdel's work.

It is the trouble and trauma of *not knowing* that lies at the heart of *Fun Home*. The knowledge that she is a lesbian comes early in the narrative, and the process of what it means to know this and live this knowledge is part of the story. However, it is the *not* knowing of her father, the *not* knowing the truth of his death, that is the challenge presented for Bechdel. It is the pretending to *not know* the thing they all know—Bruce Bechdel's queerness—that is the challenge presented for the family and is integral to how *Fun Home* unfolds (or unfolds and refolds). Bechdel's privileging of the epistemological questions raised by intimacy, by sexuality, of being "closeted" and "coming out," is what makes *Fun Home* so groundbreaking, as memoir, as comics, and as coming-out story.[11]

An earlier, more ironized version of Bechdel's coming out may be found in "Coming Out Story," first published in a special solely Bechdel-authored-and-drawn issue of *Gay Comics* (#19, 1993).[12] This issue features a few explicitly life-writing-oriented pieces, like "The Power of Prayer" and "True Confession"; it also includes installments of the comic strip *Servants to the Cause*, a short-lived serial focusing on a group of gays and lesbians working at a periodical reminiscent of the *Advocate*, which is in fact where the strip originally appeared from 1988 to 1990. "Coming Out Story" has a bit of fun with the genre of the coming-out narrative through the artist's signature self-referentiality and metaleptic storytelling practice (as evidenced by the title). This piece, in the form it takes as collected in *The Indelible Alison Bechdel*, also offers up

Bechdel's annotations on the origin of the story and the process of drawing it, generating a further metaleptic layer. In addition, however, the annotations reveal the challenges presented by the very form of the coming-out story and the constraints it places on knowing the self and inner life.

In the piece for *Gay Comics*, the cartoonist draws on touchstones we find in *Fun Home*: the devouring of books of LGBTQ interest, the shaping and making visible of the lesbian subject through reading and drawing, the discovery of campus community and the first encounter with a lover. In *Fun Home*, the "coming out" emplotment jostles against the "portrait of the artist as a young person," or *Künstlerroman*, emplotment, until these multiple selves and stories coalesce. Multiple versions of the self, and multiple commentaries on those selves, suggest that Bechdel is not entirely comfortable with the confines of the conventional coming-out narrative. In one annotation, she writes, "Sometimes I regret having written this piece ["Coming Out Story"] because it's had the effect of 'freezing' the story for me. Now when someone asks me how I came out, I feel like I'm quoting myself" (*Indelible*, 35). In a sense, in *Fun Home*, Bechdel is taking up the challenge of "quoting herself," transcending that past self, by challenging the form of the coming-out story to contain multiple selves, not just the one that is "frozen" in that moment of emerging self-knowledge.

Through the creation of metaleptic narrative layers and commentary alongside stories of self-discovery and the work of the intimate personal archive, Bechdel reimagines what autography—what memoir as and in comics—can do. In *Are You My Mother?*, once again Bechdel has composed a text that is recursive and allusive. Even more so than *Fun Home*, this second memoir is entirely resistant to emotional and narrative closure. Helen Bechdel, who died in 2013, shortly after the publication of *Are You My Mother?*, had a fraught relationship with her artist daughter. In the memoir, Bechdel represents her mother as being proud of the work while never wanting to discuss its particulars, and struggling with the ongoing acts of self-disclosure that drive Bechdel's art. While *Fun Home* concludes with an image of the child Alison leaping into the arms of her father, the final image of *Are You My Mother?* shows the child Alison crawling away from her mother. The image is presented in a single four-by-six-inch panel spanning two pages, a god's-eye-view perspective on the two, framed all around with a wide border of the deepest black.

Are You My Mother? takes self-knowledge, the journey into the self via memory and dreams, as its central concern. Embedded within the narrative of attempting to come to terms with Helen and the past via extensive therapy and psychoanalysis, lensed through the theories of D. W. Winnicott and the writings of Virginia Woolf and Adrienne Rich, is the story of trying to create *Fun Home*. Thus in one memoir does Bechdel tell the story of the creation of another memoir, which was itself the story of the creation of herself as an artist and her understanding of herself as an out lesbian. Furthermore, she uses the delving into one version of herself in one memoir to account for the telling of another version of herself in another memoir. The stories within stories, the labyrinthine recursivity of each text, and the two together reveal that any simple attempt to explain Bechdel's texts as reparative, as having the effect of healing the trauma of loss and shame through storytelling, must in fact fall a little short. The cartoonist returns again and again to the work of finding new ways to envision relationality, intimacy, interdependence, and the inner life, as well as the forces that isolate subjects from others.

As in *Fun Home*, literary allusiveness and intertextuality, and representations of textuality and reading—the hand-drawn re-creation of text as image, the portrayals of authors, the Alison character depicted in libraries and bookstores—hold a great deal of significance. Unlike the earlier book, however, what is privileged is a reading "through the mother," as Tammy Clewell has observed (63). Bechdel engages with Woolf and Rich, rather than Proust and Joyce. The family stories told in *Fun Home* and *Are You My Mother?* move away from the lesbian community and kinship of *Dykes to Watch Out For* and travel inward, focusing on going back through multiple selves to construct a sense-making story that can never fully make sense of people who can never fully be known. Yet the earlier work of *DTWOF*, of a piece with the more recent memoirs, reveals an interest in finding the people and the spaces that allow us to make sense of ourselves in relationship with others, and is itself an archive of that search.

The challenges of self-disclosure and connection continue to concern Bechdel, even to challenge the artist herself. As of this writing, Bechdel's promised new work, *The Secret to Superhuman Strength*, has been delayed several years. What was meant to be a memoir of Bechdel's involvement with fitness culture has, in the artist's words, turned into a meditation on mortality. In one interview she says, "It's about what it's like to live in an ageing body, knowing you're going to die" (Cooke). One might suggest that as her own self enters a new phase of life—older, left without the parents who had such a shaping influence on her identity and her narrative arc—Bechdel is looking for new ways to tell her story. In the same interview, she says, "I'm only able to write about myself. But it is becoming increasingly vivid to me that we must live in connection with other people" (Cooke). I think this survey of her work has shown that this has in fact perhaps been vivid to Bechdel all along.

Critical Approaches to the Comics of Alison Bechdel

The essays in *The Comics of Alison Bechdel: From the Outside In* are informed by theories of performance art, the visual arts and dance, information and network theory, rural studies, cartography, archival work and archive studies, psychoanalysis, affect studies, adaptation studies, and narrative theory. Contributors provide new insights on major themes in Bechdel scholarship, such as gender performativity, masculinity, lesbian politics and representation, trauma, and life writing.

The essays across the collection share many points of intersection: considerations of men and masculinity, gender performativity and fluidity, memory and radical subjectivity, and the relationship between comics and queer theory / comics as queer theory. The book's three parts build on the theme of "from the outside in." Part 1, "In and/or Out: Queer Theory, Lesbian Comics, and the Mainstream," makes a claim for Bechdel's influence on comics, especially lesbian comics/comix, situating her in conversation with other comics artists and charting possible influences on her own work. It also considers Bechdel's positions in relation to lesbian and mainstream culture, attempting to take into account her shifting artistic identities as lesbian cartoonist and acclaimed memoirist.[13] Vanessa Lauber opens the collection by providing a closer look at Bechdel's relationship to queer theory via relational aesthetics and the concept of radical hospitality; the questions of how we read queerness through Bechdel's comics, and how those comics themselves intervene in queer and lesbian culture, identity, and theory recur throughout the volume. Anne N. Thalheimer details the specific shifts wrought by *Dykes to Watch Out For* regarding gender and comix, with particular attention to how the character of Lois, a poly drag king, fits into and pushes against the boundaries of lesbian comics, reflecting changes in what it means to be lesbian and to represent lesbian identity. Katherine Parker-Hay furthers the focus on *Dykes to Watch Out For* by analyzing it not in terms of identity representation but rather in terms of how the comics form functions in the transmission of theory across the spaces of everyday life. Parker-Hay shows that Bechdel reads and satirizes queer theory throughout *DTWOF*, but also that we can see moments in the comic strip where everyday life and lived experience are made legible through queer theory. Judith Kegan Gardiner discusses queer masculinity and its potential to allow for a reimagining of dominant heterosexist culture by bringing together the character of Stuart in *Dykes to Watch Out For* and the figure of Bruce Bechdel in *Fun Home*. Finally, Michelle Ann Abate extends the discussion of Bechdel's influences beyond more alternative figures like Harvey Pekar, Howard Cruse, and R. Crumb to a seemingly more mainstream and somewhat surprising source: Charles M. Schulz's *Peanuts*.

Part 2, "Interiors: Family, Subjectivity, Memory," ranges over questions of kinship, affect, and trauma while taking into account the experimental nature of Bechdel's comics. Drawing on dance studies and choreography, Alissa S. Bourbonnais persuasively suggests that Bechdel's particularly embodied texts allow us to make connections between comics studies and performance. Leah Anderst studies the musical adaptation of *Fun Home* to identify processes of narrative empathy and affect, particularly in the shift from comics form to stage production. Natalja Chestopalova reads intergenerational trauma in Bechdel's work through Freud and Lacan, delineating moments of *après-coup*, or "afterwardness," providing a valuable counterpoint to work done by Atkinson, Clewell, and Cvetkovich.[14] Yetta Howard's essay seeks to move beyond discussions of *Are You My Mother?* that emphasize psychoanalytic readings; Howard contends that these readings fail to take into account both queer subjectivity and the radically experimental nature of the text and its forms. Similarly, Tyler Bradway's work on *Are You My Mother?* grapples with queer models of kinship not made available through conventionally psychoanalytic readings.

Part 3, "Place, Space, and Community," considers the multiple places and spaces essential to Bechdel's work: interior and inward, shared and collective, and archival and affective spaces; geographical, familial, and affiliative places; and relational and identity-based communities. This part begins by returning us to Bechdel's roots in rural Beech Creek, Pennsylvania. Katie Hogan, extending work on rural queerness put forth by McIntosh and Bialer as well as Goldsmith, considers the importance of Beech Creek for Bechdel's investigation into rural queer life and identity. Reading Bechdel's use of specific elements of visual form—the map and the grid—Katherine Kelp-Stebbins uncovers the artist's processes of queering space. Next we move to the spaces of the archive. The archive is the subject of intense scrutiny in Bechdel studies by scholars such as Valerie Rohy and Ann Cvetkovich. Here Susan R. Van Dyne looks at archival material from the Bechdel papers held at Smith College to provide insight into the making of *Fun Home* and Bechdel's narrativization of self through the father. Van Dyne's contribution deepens our understanding of Bechdel's multimodal process, a source of great scholarly interest. Margaret Galvan's important archival work on LGBTQ periodicals and grassroots activism offers evidence for the profound significance of Bechdel's short-lived comic strip *Servants to the Cause* not only for Bechdel's career but also for her status as an archivist of the gay and lesbian community. That community is the focus of the final essay, by Don L. Latham and Jonathan M. Hollister. These authors analyze the workings of *Dykes to Watch Out For* from the perspective of information theory, and they show the power of shared knowledge and experience to create a community built on inclusion, intimacy, and trust—one that allows for "not just surviving but thriving amid the vicissitudes of contemporary life."

An intense desire to define and depict intimacy emerges throughout Bechdel's work; indeed, it may well be the source of its power. She concerns herself with what intimacy signifies, where its borders and boundaries lie, and how the comics artist invites the viewer and reader into a relationship of intimacy. Graphic depictions of sexuality; awkward encounters; small, intense moments of tenderness and cruelty: all speak to the entanglements of intersubjectivity and interpersonal life. Bechdel's vision of intimacy enacts in everyday life the idea that to be intimate is to accept others in recognition of both their difference and their humanness. The characters—Mo, Clarice, Ginger, Sparrow, Lois, and the others in *DTWOF*, the Bechdel family and Alison's therapists and lovers—are drawn into encounters and connections with others, as are we, and asked to acknowledge the obligations that come with intimacy and its multiple recognitions. Bechdel's work shows how these affective processes are traumatic and affirming, generative and stifling, and above all situated entirely in the real. They do make a world.

NOTES

1. *Self-Confessed! The Inappropriately Intimate Comics of Alison Bechdel* originated at the Fleming Museum at the University of Vermont in Burlington (January 30–May 20, 2018) and then moved to the Zimmerli Art Museum at Rutgers, the State University of New Jersey, in New Brunswick (September 1–December 30, 2018). Katherine Roeder asserts that, despite lingering questions about the "legitimacy" of comics art, the ever-increasing number of museum exhibitions devoted to these works and the artists who make them "suggests an institutional acknowledgment of comic art's influence on the larger culture" (2). Bechdel currently lives in rural Vermont and has been honored as the state's third cartoonist laureate.

2. A collection of interviews with Bechdel, edited by Rachel R. Martin, was published by the University Press of Mississippi in 2018.

3. See Hillary Chute's *Why Comics? From Underground to Everywhere* for a discussion of the development and impact of queer comics. Of special note is the negative force on gay and lesbian themes in comics perpetrated for many years by the Comics Code of 1954, prompted by Fredric Wertham's excoriation of such material in *Seduction of the Innocent*. These midcentury efforts to censor comics essentially put gay and lesbian comics themselves in the closet.

4. See Sam McBean for an analysis of the queer gaze in Bechdel's work. Throughout this volume, contributors follow Bechdel's use of boldface type where it appears in the comics.

5. It was not Bechdel who came up with the Bechdel test but rather her friend Liz Wallace, who is credited in the title panel, drawn like a movie theater marquee, in "The Rule."

6. For work on Bechdel specifically intervening in the study of life writing, see Julia Watson, "Autographic"; Anne Rüggemeier; and Leah Anderst.

7. This is a regularly commented-on feature of *Fun Home*. See Hillary Chute, *Graphic*; Robin Bernstein; and Anne Rüggemeier. Bechdel has also had a digital font produced based on her own handwriting, which she uses now instead of hand-lettering her text.

8. Scholarship on intertextuality in Bechdel's work has proliferated. Hillary Chute's essential chapter on Bechdel in *Graphic Women* shows the ways in which intertextuality "reanimates" Bechdel's private archive. Ariela Freedman, Jane Tolmie, and David M. Ball have considered the importance of allusions to modernist literature. Christopher Pizzino critiques the privileging by literary critics of intertextuality in Bechdel's comics, functioning as it often does in service of specious arguments for the "legitimacy" of comics; Pizzino suggests that this move misses the point of *Fun Home*'s visual art deployed in service of its "autoclastic" impulses. Just as important are considerations of reading: visual representations of reading and reading as essential for shaping the subject. See Robin Lydenberg; Heike Bauer, "Vital"; and Julia Watson, "Pleasures."

9. See Robyn Warhol for a narratological reading of *Fun Home*, especially Bechdel's use of the narrator in the spaces between word and image.

10. See Jennifer Lemberg on the significance of representations of drawing and looking and the ways in which they instantiate identity. Lemberg considers the scene, discussed earlier, between Alison and her father in the diner as well.

11. An essential work theorizing the closet is Eve Kosofsky Sedgwick's *Epistemology of the Closet*, which makes several appearances in *DTWOF* as an object of making fun. See Joanne Winning and David Bergman for arguments suggesting that both modernist fiction and post-Stonewall life writing (respectively) attempt to dismantle the binaries shaping the imaginative work of queer representation. Bergman mentions *Are You My Mother?* as an example of a post-Stonewall life-writing narrative looking to move beyond "queerness" as a simple narrative category. Paul Robinson has also studied gay life writing, particularly coming-out stories, but he focuses exclusively on texts by gay men.

12. David M. Ball also discusses the relationship between *Fun Home* and "Coming Out Story" in his analysis of Bechdel's use of intertextuality.

13. For scholarship that has informed the work of part 1, see Heike Bauer, particularly her call for readers to engage more deeply with lesbian comics in the wake of the "*Fun Home* insurgency" ("Comics," 226–27); Ann Cvetkovich; Adrienne Shaw; and David Bergman.

14. In addition to Atkinson, Clewell, and Cvetkovich, see the work of Lisa Diedrich and Monica Pearl.

WORKS CITED

Anderst, Leah. "Feeling with Real Others: Narrative Empathy in the Autobiographies of Doris Lessing and Alison Bechdel." *Narrative* 23, no. 3 (2015): 271–90.

Atkinson, Meera. *The Poetics of Transgenerational Trauma*. Bloomsbury, 2017.

Ball, David M. "Allusive Confessions: The Literary Lives of Alison Bechdel's *Fun Home*." In *Drawing from Life: Memory and Subjectivity in Comic Art*, ed. Jane Tolmie, 3–25. University Press of Mississippi, 2013.

Bauer, Heike. "Comics, Graphic Narratives, and Lesbian Lives." In *The Cambridge Companion to Lesbian Literature*, ed. Jodie Medd, 219–35. Cambridge University Press, 2016.

Bauer, Heike. "Vital Lines Drawn from Books: Difficult Feelings in Alison Bechdel's *Fun Home* and *Are You My Mother?*" *Journal of Lesbian Studies* 18 (2014): 266–81.

Bechdel, Alison, and June Thomas. "Drawing on the Lesbian Community: An Interview with Alison Bechdel." *Off Our Backs* 18, no. 8 (August–September 1988): 1, 14.

Bergman, David. "Autobiography." In *The Cambridge History of Gay and Lesbian Literature*, ed. E. L. McCallum and Mikko Tuhkanen, 643–59. Cambridge University Press, 2014.

Bernstein, Robin. "'I'm Very Happy to Be in the Reality-Based Community': Alison Bechdel's *Fun Home*, Digital Photography, and George W. Bush." *American Literature* 89, no. 1 (2017): 121–54.

Chute, Hillary. *Graphic Women: Life Narrative and Contemporary Comics*. Columbia University Press, 2010.

Chute, Hillary. *Why Comics? From Underground to Everywhere*. Harper, 2017.

Clewell, Tammy. "Beyond Psychoanalysis: Resistance and Reparative Reading in Alison Bechdel's *Are You My Mother?*" *PMLA* 132, no. 1 (2017): 51–70.

Cooke, Rachel. "*Fun Home* Creator Alison Bechdel on Turning a Tragic Childhood into a Hit Musical." *Guardian*, November 5, 2017. Accessed October 14, 2018.

Critchfield, Adam R., and Jack Pula. "On Psychotherapy, LGBT Identity, and Cultural Visibility: In Conversation with Alison Bechdel." *Journal of Gay and Lesbian Mental Health* 19, no. 4 (2015): 397–412.

Cvetkovich, Ann. "Drawing the Archive in Alison Bechdel's *Fun Home*." *WSQ: Women's Studies Quarterly* 36, nos. 1–2 (2008): 111–28.

DeCrescenzo, Teresa. "Alison Bechdel Celebrates 20 Years of Queer Comic Genius." *Lesbian News*, September 2003, 24–25.

Diedrich, Lisa. "Graphic Analysis: Transitional Phenomena in Alison Bechdel's *Are You My Mother?*" *Configurations* 22, no. 2 (2014): 183–203.

Freedman, Ariela. "Drawing on Modernism in Alison Bechdel's *Fun Home*." *Journal of Modern Literature* 32, no. 4 (2009): 125–40.

Garner, Dwight, Parul Sehgal, and Jennifer Szalai. "The New Vanguard." *New York Times*, March 5, 2018. Accessed March 17, 2018.

Goldsmith, Jenna. "Landing on the Patio: Landscape Ecology and the Architecture of Identity in Alison Bechdel's *Fun Home: A Family Tragicomic*." *disClosure: A Journal of Social Theory* 23 (2014): n.p.

Lemberg, Jennifer. "Closing the Gap in Alison Bechdel's *Fun Home*." *Women's Studies Quarterly* 36, nos. 1–2 (2008): 129–40.

"Lesbian Cartoonist Alison Bechdel Countered Dad's Secrecy by Being Out and Open." *Fresh Air*. National Public Radio. August 17, 2015. Accessed October 14, 2018.

Lydenberg, Robin. "Reading Lessons in Alison Bechdel's *Fun Home: A Family Tragicomic*." *College Literature* 44, no. 2 (2017): 133–65.

McBean, Sam. "Seeing in Alison Bechdel's *Fun Home*." *Camera Obscura* 28, no. 3 (2013): 103–23.

McIntosh, Christopher A., and Philip A. Bialer. "How Ya Gonna Keep 'Em Down on the Farm? Challenges in Rural Living for LGBT People." *Journal of Gay and Lesbian Mental Health* 19 (2005): 329–30.

Pearl, Monica. "Graphic Language: Redrawing the Family (Romance) in Alison Bechdel's *Fun Home*." *Prose Studies* 20, no. 3 (2008): 286–304.

Pizzino, Christopher. *Arresting Development: Comics at the Boundaries of Literature*. University of Texas Press, 2016.

Robinson, Paul. *Gay Lives: Homosexual Autobiography from John Addington Symonds to Paul Monette*. University of Chicago Press, 1999.

Roeder, Katherine. "Looking High and Low at Comic Art." *American Art* 22, no. 1 (2008): 2–9.

Rohy, Valerie. "In the Queer Archive: *Fun Home*." *GLQ: A Journal of Gay and Lesbian Studies* 16 (2010): 341–61.

Rubenstein, Anne. "Alison Bechdel." *Comics Journal* 179 (August 1995). Reprinted in *Alison Bechdel: Conversations*, ed. Rachel R. Martin, 17–34. University Press of Mississippi, 2018.

Rüggenmeier, Anne. "'Posing for all the characters in the book': The Multimodal Process of Production in Alison Bechdel's Relational Autobiography *Are You My Mother?*" *Journal of Graphic Novels and Comics* 7, no. 3 (2016): 254–67.

Sedgwick, Eve Kosofsky. *Epistemology of the Closet*. University of California Press, 1990.

Shaw, Adrienne. "Women on Women: Lesbian Identity, Lesbian Community, and Lesbian Comics." *Journal of Lesbian Studies* 13 (2009): 88–97.

Tolmie, Jane, ed. *Drawing from Life: Memory and Subjectivity in Comic Art*. University Press of Mississippi, 2013.

Tolmie, Jane. "Modernism, Memory and Desire: Queer Cultural Production in Alison Bechdel's *Fun Home*." *Topia: Canadian Journal of Cultural Studies* 22 (2009): 77–95.

Warhol, Robyn. "The Space Between: A Narrative Approach to Alison Bechdel's *Fun Home*." *College Literature* 38, no. 3 (2011): 1–20.

Watson, Julia. "Autographic Disclosures and Genealogies of Desire in Alison Bechdel's *Fun Home*." *Biography* 31, no. 1 (2008): 27–58.

Watson, Julia. "The Pleasures of Reading in Alison Bechdel's *Fun Home*." *Life Writing* 9, no. 3 (2012): 303–14.

Whitlock, Gillian. "Autographics: The Seeing 'I' of Comics." *Modern Fiction Studies* 52, no. 4 (2006): 965–79.

Winning, Joanne. "Lesbian Modernism: Writing in and Beyond the Closet." In *The Cambridge Companion to Gay and Lesbian Writing*, ed. Hugh Stevens, 50–64. Cambridge University Press, 2011.

Part I

IN AND/OR OUT
Queer Theory, Lesbian Comics, and the Mainstream

THE HOSPITABLE AESTHETICS OF ALISON BECHDEL

VANESSA LAUBER

Over the past three decades, Alison Bechdel's body of work has spanned from fringe, single-frame cartoons aimed at representing gay life to a critically acclaimed long-form graphic memoir that has become a referent text for understanding queer comics and the graphic memoir form. Throughout, Bechdel is a presence both in the narrative voice of her work and as the object of her own self-reflexive representation, balancing the tensions of her interests in radical politics and normativizing representation. In an early interview, she professed a goal to "show actual things" and "to reach a broader audience while staying radical politically" (Metheny). She has succeeded in reaching that broader audience: in the past decade, her graphic memoir *Fun Home* has become the darling of critics, scholars, and, in its adapted form, even theatergoers on Broadway and beyond.

It is harder to locate radical politics in the success of her work. *Fun Home*'s mainstream academic and cultural popularity can be read as a self-damning celebration of the capitulations of gay and lesbian identity politics to assimilation, against which Bechdel's comic strip dykes have wrestled through various presidential regimes. In March 2016, Samantha Power, US ambassador to the United Nations under President Barack Obama, took seventeen ambassadors on a Broadway outing to see the musical adaptation of *Fun Home*. Power celebrated the musical's ability to "humanize" LGBTQ individuals, hoping to engender greater support for LGBTQ rights internationally and emphasizing the importance of "a sense of empathy and community" (Mattila; Meyers). It is easy to imagine Bechdel's *Dykes to Watch Out For* doppelgänger, Mo, ranting about the evils of the neoliberal state in response.

Bechdel and her comic strip dykes are not alone in struggling with the tensions of identity politics and radical queerness. The persuasive power of empathy and community—goals of identity politics and rights-based movements—butts up against queer claims toward destabilizing norms and resisting assimilation. The birth of queer studies as an academic discipline is defined by its break from LGBT politics, with the goals of marriage and military service pitted against radical queer liberation. In broad strokes, LGBT studies produces sexual orientation as a category, while queer studies seeks to upend categorical thought. Bechdel's unique insight into that tension, I will argue, arises from her complex and nuanced attempts to represent marginalized identities in a form that has itself been marginalized. Her politics of the outsider cannot be cast off in a dismissive reading of her popularity in the cultural imagination, nor hewn from the longer history of her formal innovation. Taken as a whole, the paradoxical and yet coconstitutive relationship between the queerness of her forms and the mainstream popularity of her texts performs a sort of queer world-building. To the extent that her work cultivates empathy or community, it does so not only, perhaps, in the service of identity-based movements or bald market capitalism but also by modeling a more radical, relational aesthetic that illuminates the ongoing power of queer critique.

I by no means wish to fall victim to the tendency, identified by Tyler Bradway (one of the contributors to this volume), of some scholars to "prioritize a specific literary form as the ideal mode for transmuting literary affect into socially valuable force" (xxxvi). Rather, by contextualizing the construction of Bechdel's short- and long-form comics, I suggest that there is a place in the mainstream for the sort of contributory, pleasurable, and rich reading of texts that opens up space for alternative social imaginaries. I adapt Nicolas Bourriaud's concept of relational aesthetics in visual and performance arts to literary practice to suggest how the expanding mainstream audience for Bechdel's work extends the queer forms of her comics communities. Bechdel's work is an act of hospitality both collaborative and antagonistic, a practice with potential for radical transformation, even in its inherent and sometimes irresolvable tensions.

I will first lay out the theories of relational aesthetics and hospitality on which my reading of Bechdel relies, before considering how the political and representational spaces of *Dykes to Watch Out For* provide a foundation for reading *Fun Home* as a space of both hospitable aesthetics and resistant queerness.[1]

Relational Form

I invoke the performance art concept of relational aesthetics as a means to further understand the allure and imaginative possibilities of reading Alison Bechdel in various forms. The art historian Nicolas Bourriaud developed the concept of relational aesthetics in impassioned monographs on artistic practices that modestly "take as their theoretical and practical point of departure the whole of human relations and their social context" (113). His theory of this practice of visual art is particularly useful in a discussion of the discursive logic of language and image of visual narrative. Bourriaud's *Relational Aesthetics* was first published in French in 1998, announcing the death of the old avant-garde and, with it, utopian politics and teleological visions of history, echoing queer theory's critiques of normative temporalities.[2] Relational aesthetics sought to theorize art that abandoned imaginary utopias and instead enacted ways of living and models of acting collectively. To take an example from Bourriaud, the Argentinean-born Thai artist Rirkrit Tiravanija's work is perhaps the most recognized among artists associated with relational aesthetics. In his untitled solo show at 303 Gallery, New York, in 1992, Tiravanija converted the gallery space into a working kitchen, where he prepared Thai food for visitors. Rather than comprising the art itself, the food was instead the means for creating the possibility and opportunity for social interactions, with the artist as host in the social gallery space. For Bourriaud, "present-day art shows that form only exists in the encounter and in the dynamic relationship enjoyed by an artistic proposition" (21).

Some scholars, most notably Claire Bishop, have critiqued Bourriaud's notion of form as relational property, in that by understanding form itself to be the locus of meaning, he assumes that "the work is automatically political in implication and emancipatory in effect" noting that "the relations set up by relational aesthetics are not intrinsically democratic" (Bishop, 62, 67). But Bourriaud conceives of form as improvisation that motivates the relational exchange between the artist and the public and thus motivates finding meaning in a structured work that is nevertheless open. In considering Bechdel's work, I take up Bishop's critique and follow Hillary Chute's interest in "*how comics texts model a feminist methodology in their form*, in the complex visual dimension of an author narrating herself on the page as a multiple subject" ("The Space," 200). I seek to understand *Dykes to Watch Out For* and *Fun Home* together as potentially relational queer forms. To develop a notion of relational aesthetics in the reading of Alison Bechdel's work, I conceive of her authorial voice, so present in the text, as positing an invitation, in which the relational space created is one of constructive antagonism, both pleasurable and challenging, with the potential to upend hierarchies and reconstitute social possibilities: a responsive mode of relating to others that is simultaneously generous and vulnerable.

The Openness of Radical Hospitality

Jacques Derrida's theorizations of hospitality provide a useful framework for developing a notion of authorial invitation, with the author as host and reader as guest. In *Of Hospitality*, Derrida distinguishes between conditional and absolute or radical hospitality. Conditional hospitality exists within the practical stipulations that make extensions of hospitality possible, the formalized rules that define the way to receive visitors, establishing a sort of pact between host and guest, much as literary forms determine rules and expectations for a reading experience.[3] Conditional hospitality relies on normative language to solidify identity, establish responsibilities, and define boundaries and limitations. Constrained by these terms, this conditional hospitality is never fully open, according to Derrida, but rather always contains the potential for violence in the violation of its complex terms. Radical hospitality, on the other hand, gives without restriction. The host offers up everything, and paradoxically the guest becomes the host. The host must be master of the domain to extend hospitality, but hospitality also requires the willingness to give everything for the benefit of the stranger: "Even if the other deprives you of your mastery or your home, you have to accept this. It is terrible to accept this, but that is the conditional of unconditional hospitality" (70). In this study, then, I recast the hospitable relationship as that enacted between an author and reader, as an invitation. That Derrida's characterization of absolute hospitality contains the possibility of the impossible, even the compulsion or necessity to upend the dynamics of the host-guest relationship, wherein the "guest becomes the host's host," suggests its potential for envisioning a radical redetermination of reading relationships.

As theorized here, hospitable aesthetics provide a space for public feeling, for volatility, for creating new alternatives—a queer culture that Lauren Berlant and Michael Warner identified as a world-building project. In *Bodies That Matter*, Judith Butler wrote of the challenge of "politicizing disidentification," in the process of deconstructing the constraints of identity forms, using misrecognition to create and recover other new modes of being. José Esteban Muñoz likewise worked through the act of disidentification as a "step further than cracking open the code of the majority; it proceeds to use this code as raw material" for as-yet unimagined futures (*Disidentifications*, 31). Hospitable aesthetics work in a similar way, neither relying on a mainstream or normative voice to issue the invitation to act, create, or inhabit; nor relying on an indivisible subjectivity as the prerequisite for action and inhabitation—but rather providing the raw material for world-building and re-creation.

Bechdel's work, taken as a whole, provides an opportunity for this hospitality, characterized by both confrontation and cooperation, wherein origins of change and difference might be humanized and localized through the literary imagination. *Dykes to Watch Out For* lays the groundwork for potential radical hospitality in the openness of its form. The reflexivity and ironic stance of Bechdel's work help to craft an invitation to the reader. As developed in *Fun Home*, the multimodality of Bechdel's form, so often remarked on in critical studies of her art and born of her long history of alternative comics artistry, ultimately models radical aesthetics that include and extend beyond the constraints of normativizing identity politics. By offering an invitation to the reader, Bechdel as artist and author offers up the control that she has as host, presenting her work—and, in the case of *Fun Home*, her family home—and the recollection and interpretation of her life therein, as a site of relational exchange that engages both mainstream LGBT and radical queer politics.

The Space of Self-Narrative

Bechdel's work functions as such a productive site of hospitable aesthetics, in part, because of its self-reflexivity and self-narrativizing, which simultaneously engage with questions of identity and deconstruct identity's normativizing values. Bechdel has frequently discussed the tension between her desire to represent the complexity of lesbian life as a site of difference as well as representation's role in processes of normativization, as I will discuss further. Since the 1980s, identity categories have gradually been narrowed and unified in the name of social change and political representation, in turn resulting in the alienation from and rejection of the use of those identity categories as a site of political and social organizing. It was in opposition to these limitations and the production of norms that queer theory sought to distinguish itself from LGBT studies in the academy.

In the lead-up to that split, the practice and critical study of autobiographical life writing played a significant role in instituting norms, particularly around sex and gender. Critical feminist theory of the '80s and '90s further highlighted the complex generic and formal constraints of staking temporal and spatial claims for women's life writing, the sort of conditions that undermine radical change. But feminist reinterpretations of autobiography, which emerged in the early 1980s, attempted to distinguish men's and women's autobiography, organizing generic and formal claims around the desirability of locating difference in essentialized lived experience, as evinced in the work of Estelle Jelinek. Those readings risked erasing the intersectional effects of class, race, and sexual orientation and drew generalized conclusions about textual effects recast as experiential cause. This essentializing effect is a starting point for Leigh Gilmore's critique of feminist interpretations of autobiography, in which she interrogated the generic and truth-telling claims of feminist autobiographical practice. Sidonie Smith and Julia Watson, following Susan Stanford Friedman, have suggested "spatiality, rather than temporality, as a focus of critical reading practices" ("Introduction," 39). By recasting self-narrative as a function of space rather than time, we can further consider how a literary text, especially one such as Bechdel's, might provide the space necessary for a hospitable literary practice.

Indeed, Bechdel's entry into self-reflexive writing came alongside the development of both LGBT autobiographical practice and the culture of alternative comics. In the wake of Stonewall, the prototypical gay autobiography had been the coming-out narrative, an act claiming to make invisible subjects visible (extensively problematized by Judith Butler and others). The coming-out narrative of victimization gradually gave way to "stories of living in community and refusing a minoritized and stigmatized identity position" (Smith and Watson, *Reading*, 152), which marks the starting point for *Dykes to Watch Out For*.

The Hospitable Aesthetics of Comics Counterpublics

If self-narrative provides a space for hospitable aesthetics, so too do comics. Comics studies scholars have argued that the reader of comics is an active, interpretive partner in the creation of meaning from the page. Drawing on foundational work by Scott McCloud, Gillian Whitlock has described reading comics as an experience of interpretation, "not a mere hybrid of graphic arts and prose fiction, but a unique interpretation that transcends both, and emerges through the imaginative work of closure that readers are required to make between the panels on the page" (968–69). Hillary Chute characterizes comics as a form that is "*internally*, conspicuously dialogic, or cross-discursive, across its words and images" ("The Space," 199). Those words and images do not repeat each other but rather "move the narrative through a constant, active, uneasy back-and-forth," working "in relation to each other but necessarily never blend[ing]" (199). Critically for Chute, and for my interpretation here, the tension between word and image is an external dialogic that draws "its readers *in* to construct meaning in the spaces of the gutters between the panels" (199). The reader becomes a critical, relational, contributory participant not only, necessarily, in interpreting the narrative grammar of the comics but also in making meaning in the forum of public consumption. Julia Watson's study of *Fun Home* takes up the effects of Bechdel's "self-reflexive autographic," distinguishing the form of graphic memoir from traditional autobiography for the way its "recursive autographic structures" invite readers to put themselves "empathetically into its intimate picture" and thus "question the social privileging of normative heterosexuality" (53). I build on Watson's notion of *Fun Home*'s invitation to the reader but suggest more radical effects of that reading than the normativizing of homosexuality.

While Chute characterizes the participatory work of the comics reader as a "drawing in," Seymour Chatman suggests that it is, rather, a kind of "reading out." I prefer this notion of reading out, suggestive of an outward-facing, world-building impulse toward queer relationality, in which reading comics and graphic narratives is not only a practice of self-reflection and growth but also one of radical exchange. Ramzi Fawaz has adapted Michael Warner's concept of a counterpublic to the realm of comic book fandom, arguing that fan letters and correspondence created a new counterpublic in the 1960s and 1970s in which readers expressed "politically unfashionable or radical ideals through the discursive apparatus of a culturally denigrated medium" (95). By encouraging readers to take pleasure in comic book fandom, comic book "writers and artists encouraged readers to see comic book aesthetics as a vehicle for producing alternative social and political imaginaries" (96). Bechdel's own comics practice was born in the space of this counterpublic. Although her comics did not appear in published form alongside direct reader responses, she did respond to reader letters (she in fact moved to Vermont in 1991 after starting a relationship via correspondence with one of her fans [Thurman]). Bechdel accounted for reader input in shaping the narratives of *Dykes to Watch Out For*, acknowledged in the gutters of the strips with a "tip of the nib" to individual contributors (Resmer). Although the scale and demographic diversity of superhero comic fandom diverge from the more particular audience of gay comix and, even more so, Bechdel's readership, what they do share is the pleasure and possibility of the participatory and coconstitutive affective reader experience.

Hospitable Dykes

Bechdel marks the ongoing invitation to her readers by inserting a narrator's voice into the narrative of the comic strip and deploying a mock-heroic tone; she emphasizes both the seriality of the comics form and the normalizing of lesbian leads in the ongoing narrative. Implicitly hearkening back to the genre of (analog, pre-bingeing) television serials, Bechdel inserts the language of viewership: "Don't touch that dial!" (*Essential*, 31). Although anthologizing the comic strip as *The Essential Dykes to Watch For* more actively encourages a linear reading, Bechdel offers readers the ability to drop in and out of narratives, an open invitation of sorts. At the start of each strip, she thrusts the reader into the immediate narrative with a purely textual introduction that adopts the tone of "when we last left our heroes." But in *Dykes to Watch Out For*, the characters are not superhuman heroes or even bumbling cartoons (see, e.g., Rocky and Bullwinkle) but rather heroines, a community of lesbians and queers. While she might be invoking, through the text, a tradition or practice of normative viewership, the images highlight Bechdel's referential irony and in turn her self-representational impulses. She says:

> Mo is me. In fact, all the characters in "Dykes" are more or less me. All I've ever written about is myself, and this book, if I finish it [here referring to *Are You My Mother?*], may be the most solipsistic piece of insanity ever published.... But aesthetic neutrality appeals to me. I'm always striving to be a generic person. (Thurman)

Bechdel writes about herself, about lesbians like those she knows, creating "generic" people who are identifiable and to whom readers will relate. In so doing, she extends an invitation, not only to queer women to see themselves represented on the page, but to everyone to see lesbians as people.

Bechdel further addresses this outcome of normalization in her introduction to *The Essential Dykes to Watch Out For*, published in 2008, two years after the publication of *Fun Home*. That introduction is its own sort of memoir, in which Bechdel, as the character of the cartoonist, retells the history of her comic strip career in its larger historical context. She articulates her intention to derive a universal lesbian essence from particular examples. But she also notes the personal gratification she took in representation: "To be honest, it was so comforting to see my queer life reflected back at me, I would have kept drawing these dykes to watch out for just for myself" (xiv). But she notes her flawed thinking in a belief in lesbian exceptionalism. As in the comic strips themselves, so objects in frame provide the point and counterpoint of the written narrative and include a lesson in gender essentialism versus constructivism provided by Judith Butler's *Gender Trouble* (landing the "essential" gender studies joke of the collection's title) (fig. 1.1).

Bechdel's cartoonist self thus acknowledges the paradox of her efforts to catalog lesbian life as a site of difference, only to find that she has participated in a process of normalization. This is the paradox into which she invites the reader. Ultimately, tossing the illustrated representation of *The Essential Dykes to Watch Out For* into closer perspective, she invites the reader to decide and walks away. It is an invitation that is a confrontation as well as an opening. The reader takes possession of the text, along with its complicated politics, now abandoned by the author, thus upending the narrative authority.

Fig. 1.1. "Cartoonist's Introduction" and "essentialism" (*Essential*, xviii).

Figs. 1.2, 1.3. "The Baby Question" (*Essential*, 215).

Resolving the paradox of radical and mainstream politics must happen in a space in which the authorial voice has been destabilized as the site of control.

But the cartoonist as narrator—along with her conflicted politics—remains present throughout the text, and the reader is invited to dwell in the contradictions and even humor of her efforts to resolve those tensions. While following the lives of a recurring cast of characters, Bechdel places them within current events. Her characters are politically active, highly critical of big corporations, privatization, and neoliberalism. With varying degrees of success, they attempt to fight the pull of homonormative life. Bechdel heightens the humor of her characters' responses to current events by inviting the reader into parodic visual jokes, thus doubling down on her self-awareness regarding the tensions between representational, normalizing politics and the queer politics of antinormativity. Mo, Bechdel's *Dykes* alter ego, also struggles to reconcile her radical leftist politics with the lived realities of the radical queers inhabiting their lives around her. Other characters call Mo out on the hypocrisies of her staunch beliefs. In "The Baby Question," a strip first published in 1999 (figs. 1.2, 1.3), Mo waxes nostalgic about the good old days: "Smash the family! Same the state!" Her girlfriend Sydney questions whether she wants to smash Clarice and Toni and Raffi's family.

Clarice and Toni, by this point in the strip, are in a domestic partnership, living an apparently more settled, (homo)normative life. Mo responds, "Please, Sydney, I'm expressing an ideological conviction, I'm not talking about real people" (*Essential*, 215). Invoking "real people" highlights the tensions between the radical queer communities that drove the LGBT rights movement in its more radical forms and the mainstream LGBT movement for equal legal recognition. Questions that had defined the previous decade of queer political movements are discussed casually while characters brush their teeth in a scene of domestic (if unmarried) intimacy. As Mo spouts her radical nostalgia, Sydney stares directly at the reader via the mirror, visually implying that we are reflected in the mirror with herself and Mo as they converse. Readers are thus invited to reflect themselves into the midst of the conversation and to engage both the humorous hypocrisy and the question of how to reconcile radical politics with real life.

Bechdel's commentaries on the impositions of real-life politics also stage more formal interjections. She frequently inserts contemporary political commentary—such as a newspaper whose changing headlines throughout a strip satirize the tragic absurdity of real headlines (*Essential*, 223), or corporate-sponsored NPR broadcasts that provide background text to the narrative arc (194)—taking the form of textual jokes within or adjacent to images (often with startling resonance to contemporary politics for today's readers; neoliberalism hasn't changed much). In a unique strip, published immediately

Fig. 1.4. "Leadership Vacuum" (*Essential*, 214).

before "The Baby Question," Bechdel appears as her character the cartoonist, with Mo, for once, as the voice of calm reason. First published in the midst of the Clinton impeachment proceedings in early 1999, "Leadership Vacuum" captures, in its jarring departure from form, political exasperation, even as it addresses itself directly to the reader (fig. 1.4).

Bechdel here departs from the standard panel and gutter, materializing rough-sketched, crumbled, failed drafts, tossed away in one frame, unwrapped by Mo in the next, and appearing for the reader to view, with cross-hatched shading giving its crinkled edges depth on the page. The extrapanel text boxes typically reserved for Bechdel's narrative voice are given over to Mo, a small talking head, narrating the cartoonist's breakdown in a direct-address apology to the reader. Whereas Bechdel typically acts as the intermediary between reader and character narrative, this strip flips that relation, with the character mediating between reader and cartoonist. This is an even more intimate invitation, in which Bechdel foreshortens the distance between the reader and comics artist, even as the reader is forced to confront the insanity-inducing state of contemporary American politics. Per a crazed portrait in the ninth panel, the crisis of contemporary politics has shorted her "irony fuse" and her "satire chip." She can no longer maintain an aesthetic, mediated distance. As in the introduction, readers are left on their own, narrative authority performatively abandoned. Bechdel is inviting the reader into her studio, making visible the labor of her political commentary alongside the characters, who would, from their apologetic tone, prefer to just get on with the story. In experiencing the startling interruption to the serial reading experience, readers must not only confront the formal deviation of the strip itself and the interjection of political realities into the fictional lives of the comics' characters, but also think outward to the disruption that real political events cause in their own lives.

This more dramatic juxtaposition of political satire with the personal dramas of the characters in *Dykes to Watch Out For* demonstrates the mode of hospitable aesthetics in which Bechdel engages, wherein the space of the comics form enables a self-reflexive irony that is itself a complex invitation. The ironic mode, which Lee Edelman has called the queerest of all rhetorical devices, is one relative to audience, assuming a level of knowledge or common understanding for the reader to be in on the joke (23). By relying on the ironic structure of contrast inherent in stitching together the text and image of the strip, Bechdel made her audience of lesbian readers—who wished to see themselves represented on the page—the knowing reader, the ones in on the joke, rather than the butt of the joke (or worse) in mainstream media. It is the pleasure of being addressed, of the sort that Fawaz highlights as the strength of the comics counterpublic. It is a model of queer hospitality, in the mode of early LGBT political movements, built on principles of representation, community, and identification, that begins to suggest the site of a promising method whereby some of the critical force of queer theory can be redirected toward the imaginative world-building it first sought to undertake.

The Queer Hospitality of *Fun Home*

Radical hospitality relies on the guest being welcome even as her identity remains in question. Rather than a call to forswear claims to identity, it is a liberating invitation to dwell in uncertainty, to take as a starting point an openness that carries within it the possibility of a relational existence and world-upending change. The productive tensions within the aporia of radical hospitality would seem to speak to similar goals as the antinormativity strains of queer theory, the both/and that pushes to encompass multiplicities and resists set meaning, particularly in the defining of individual subjectivities within a larger social collective. It is within that potentiality that I wish to consider *Fun Home* as a text of queer hospitable aesthetics. Taken in light of Bechdel's self-conscious ironizing in *Dykes to Watch Out For*, as well as its wider mainstream success, *Fun Home* captures the growing pains of queer history as a personal and relational experience and hopefully suggests the ways in which a hospitable practice of reading can provide the means to reconcile the tensions of radical political hope.

Bechdel does extend an invitation into her family home, but it is a home fraught with memory and withholding. *Fun Home* scholarship has discussed at length Bechdel's intricate drawing process, her meticulous cataloging of personal ephemera, and her excavating of what Ann Cvetkovich and Valerie Rohy have characterized as a "queer archive" and an "archive of feelings" in service of a recursive process of confronting the past.[4] This extensive work on Bechdel's creative practice enables my own consideration of reading as hospitality in the context of the longer arc of Bechdel's comics work. That such a rich body of scholarship has emerged on *Fun Home* suggests the power of its invitation and the ways in which its carefully constituted text remains a site of openness, confronting both the richness of its own self-realization and the traumas and tragedies of the past. To some extent, Bechdel would seem to be setting aside "the personal is political" impulses of *Dykes to Watch Out For* in favor of "the personal is personal" studies of her own family. But just as political satire serves as an ironic referent in *Dykes to Watch Out For*, so literature likewise serves a similar purpose: as the referent for establishing the complex process of reading hospitably.

Fun Home's self-reflexivity is arguably what has generated such a rich vein of scholarship on subjectivity, history, genealogies, and the nature of truth and memory. Bechdel renders transparent her own deep-rooted anxiety about the truthfulness of her own account and her ability to translate her memory to the page.[5] Her conflicted feelings about the process of self-representation build trust with the reader. By self-reflexively acknowledging her own doubts about her writing as she writes, she establishes credibility, even as she is up front about handing over to the reader the act of interpretation. The making of the self and the writing of history are the problem, and in both the textual and the extratextual world, reading and interpretation do the work of confronting the irresolvable tension between lived experience and representation. By asserting the experience of the impossibility of fully knowing or representing the self, Bechdel communicates the nonfictionality of the text. It is the complex, and what I call hospitable, work of simultaneously establishing narrative authority and relinquishing it as an act of good faith.

Even as Bechdel as narrator asserts the nonfictionality of the text, literary fiction becomes the "vocabulary in which the story can be told" (Rohy, 350). Bechdel and her father share a love of literature and the language it provides, which is simultaneously a means of avoidance and deferral within the structure of their relationship. They speak to each through Joyce; she interprets his death through his reading of Camus. He critiques her reading choices and slyly gives her a copy of Colette. Bechdel's sexual identity develops through a stack of gay books checked out from the library, and her sexual practice is fused with reading aloud (including from both Adrienne Rich and Roald Dahl). Alison's father, Bruce, also uses literature as a tool of seduction, offering texts to promising students, an act that Bechdel chooses to read ambiguously: "Whatever else might have been going on, books were being read" (*FH*, 61). Bechdel represents each member of her family as experiencing their own peculiar isolation, most notably in an innovative panel that invites the reader into the Bechdel home via circular cutouts, like peepholes, and into the isolation of their creative endeavors (fig. 1.5).

But reading, by contrast, has the potential to be a site of sociality, of conversation, and of reference, both confrontational and joyful. Much as Tiravanija served Thai food in the gallery, Bechdel serves her reader books, thus creating the possibility and opportunity for social interactions. It is into that space that Bechdel invites the reader. The visual space of the page provides the means by which Bechdel chooses to process her own complex relationships to her sexuality and to her father and his death. Readers inhabit that space with her, producing, via the complex intricacies of the recursive narrative, their own read. While *Dykes to Watch Out For* provides a space in which privileging a certain reader was a political and personal goal, the personalized

Fig. 1.5. The Bechdel home (*FH*, 134).

work of reading in *Fun Home* produces a text in which the privileged audience is one who reads, inherently, already, the reader in whose hands the book rests. By accepting the invitation to even open to the first page, Bechdel has constituted a relational space in which the reader is rendered a collaborator from the start. This does not impose or presume normative values, nor does it assume identity, fixed or unfixed, but rather opens up the possibility that the reader might accept an invitation and be transformed in acceptance. In the final panel of *Fun Home*, Bechdel executes the extended image of herself and her father as coconstituted Icaruses, plummeting into the sea (*FH*, 232). She imagines, in an act of trust and the relinquishing of control, that her father is there to catch her as she leaps from the diving board and into the pool. And facing down into the frame of the image, the reader jumps with her.

In this reading of hospitable aesthetics, Bechdel's work in developing the self-reflexive serial comics narrative enabled the development of her visual narrative in *Fun Home* as one that extends an invitation of radical queer possibility. Insofar, then, as the form is relational, Bechdel's invitation is re-extended and shifts with every reading. That reading can be performed by a UN ambassador in a Broadway theater in the service of normalizing homosexuality for legal recognition, but it can also reconstitute the creative work of collaboration, with both joy and antagonism, for a queer reader, coconstituted as a voice of collaboration. By inviting the reader into a space of interpretive play, Bechdel's work constitutes an invitation to imagine different ways of being, understanding, and creating.

NOTES

1. This essay reads Bechdel's serial comics from *The Essential Dykes to Watch Out For*, the compilation of most of the strips that Bechdel published from the early days until her hiatus in 2008. As noted in the introduction to this volume, collections were published periodically beginning in 1986, and Bechdel has revisited the strip, posting one-offs on November 23, 2016, and March 14, 2017, on her website dykestowatchoutfor.com and the website of *Seven Days: Vermont's Independent Voice*, but those are not addressed here.

2. See, e.g., Halberstam; Freeman; and Muñoz, *Cruising Utopia*.

3. As in Philippe Lejeune's notion of the "autobiographical contract" as a list of qualifications that the author of the text agrees to uphold by designating her name as the same as the "I" of the text.

4. See also McBean on the ways Bechdel represents the visual field as a source of restriction and queer pleasure and the partiality of representation; Tison on Bechdel's practices of montage, juxtaposition, and photographic re-creation as a means to recovering the self; and Lemberg on the limits of seeing and Bechdel's process of visualizing as a form of witnessing.

5. See Rohy (351–52) on childhood Alison's insertion of "I think" into her diary, indicating the breakdown of referentiality and crisis of not-knowing and self-doubt.

WORKS CITED

Berlant, Lauren, and Michael Warner. "Sex in Public." *Critical Inquiry* 24, no. 2 (Winter 1998): 547–66.

Bishop, Claire. "Antagonism and Relational Aesthetics." *October* 110 (Fall 2004): 51–79.

Bourriaud, Nicolas. *Relational Aesthetics.* Trans. Simon Pleasance and Fronza Woods. Les presses du réel, 2002.

Bradway, Tyler. *Queer Experimental Literature: The Affective Politics of Bad Reading.* Palgrave Macmillan, 2017.

Butler, Judith. *Bodies That Matter: On the Discursive Limits of Sex.* Routledge, 1993.

Chatman, Seymour. *Story and Discourse.* Cornell University Press, 1978.

Chute, Hillary. *Graphic Women: Life Narrative and Contemporary Comics.* Columbia University Press, 2010.

Chute, Hillary. "The Space of Graphic Narrative." In *Narrative Theory Unbound: Queer and Feminist Interventions*, ed. Robyn Warhol and Susan S. Lanser, 194–209. Ohio State University Press, 2015.

Cvetkovich, Ann. "Drawing the Archive in Alison Bechdel's *Fun Home*." *WSQ: Women's Studies Quarterly* 36, nos. 1–2 (2008): 111–28.

Derrida, Jacques. *Of Hospitality.* Stanford University Press, 2000.

Edelman, Lee. *No Future: Queer Theory and the Death Drive.* Duke University Press, 2004.

Fawaz, Ramzi. *The New Mutants: Superheroes and the Radical Imagination of American Comics.* New York University Press, 2016.

Freeman, Elizabeth. *Time Binds: Queer Temporalities, Queer Histories.* Duke University Press, 2010.

Gilmore, Leigh. *Autobiographics: A Feminist Theory of Women's Self-Representation.* Cornell University Press, 1994.

Halberstam, Jack. *In a Queer Time and Place: Transgender Bodies, Subcultural Lives.* New York University Press, 2005.

Jelinek, Estelle. *Women's Autobiography: Essays in Criticism.* Indiana University Press, 1980.

Lejeune, Philippe. *On Autobiography.* Trans. Katherine Leary. University of Minnesota Press, 1989.

Lemberg, Jennifer. "Closing the Gap in Alison Bechdel's *Fun Home*." *WSQ: Women's Studies Quarterly* 36, nos. 1–2 (2008): 129–40.

Mattila, Kalle Oskari. "Selling Queerness: The Curious Case of *Fun Home*." *Atlantic*, April 25, 2016. Accessed September 27, 2017.

McBean, Sam. "Seeing in Alison Bechdel's *Fun Home*." *Camera Obscura* 28, no. 3 (2013): 103–23.

McCloud, Scott. *Understanding Comics: The Invisible Art.* Harper, 2004.

Metheny, Dave. "March 1990: We Profiled 'Fun Home' Cartoonist Alison Bechdel during Her Minnesota Days." *Minneapolis Star Tribune*, December 14, 2006. Accessed January 15, 2018.

Meyers, Seth. Interview with Samantha Power. *Late Night with Seth Meyers.* NBC. Season 3, episode 90, April 4, 2016.

Muñoz, José Esteban. *Cruising Utopia: The Then and There of Queer Futurity.* New York University Press, 2009.

Muñoz, José Esteban. *Disidentifications: Queers of Color and the Performance of Politics.* University of Minnesota Press, 1999.

Resmer, Cathy. "The Essence of 'Dykes': A New Anthology Collects Alison Bechdel's Iconic Lesbian Comic." *Seven Days*, December 17, 2008. Accessed January 15, 2018.

Rohy, Valerie. "In the Queer Archive: *Fun Home*." *GLQ: A Journal of Lesbian and Gay Studies* 16, no. 3 (2010): 340–60.

Smith, Sidonie, and Julia Watson. Introduction to *Women, Autobiography, Theory*, ed. Sidonie Smith and Julia Watson, 3–52. University of Wisconsin Press, 1998.

Smith, Sidonie, and Julia Watson. *Reading Autobiography: A Guide for Interpreting Life Narratives.* 2nd ed. University of Minnesota Press, 2010.

"That Time the U.N. Ambassador Came to See *Fun Home.*" *Advocate,* March 14, 2006. Accessed September 27, 2017.

Thurman, Judith. "Drawn from Life: The World of Alison Bechdel." *New Yorker,* April 23, 2012. Accessed September 27, 2017.

Tison, Hélène. "Loss, Revision, Translation: Re-membering the Father's Fragmented Self in Alison Bechdel's Graphic Memoir *Fun Home: A Family Tragicomic.*" *Studies in the Novel* 47, no. 3 (2015): 346–64.

Warner, Michael. "Queer and Then?" *Chronicle Review,* January 1, 2012.

Watson, Julia. "Autographic Disclosures and Genealogies of Desire in Alison Bechdel's *Fun Home.*" *Biography* 31, no. 1 (Winter 2008): 27–58.

Whitlock, Gillian. "Autographics: The Seeing 'I' of the Comics." *Modern Fiction Studies* 52, no. 4 (Winter 2006): 965–79.

"GIRLIE MAN, MANLY GIRL, IT'S ALL THE SAME TO ME"

How *Dykes to Watch Out For* Shifted Gender and Comix

ANNE N. THALHEIMER

By the time Alison Bechdel's groundbreaking comic strip *Dykes to Watch Out For* ended its publication run after 527 episodes, numerous book collections, and various publication formats (including online on Bechdel's own website after her publisher was forced to close), the "dykes" in question ended up less like folks to watch out for and instead became . . . more or less like everyone else in America—which may have been the goal all along. The main characters fell in and out of love, married and divorced, had and raised children, moved into and out of houses, lost and gained and quit employment, went back to school, got tenure, bought property, survived breast cancer—all events and developments that simply mark shared parts of the American experience rather than experiences limited to LGBT communities or to a particular queerness. Similarly, Bechdel's profile as a cartoonist shifted prominently after the success of *Fun Home*; ambivalent though she may have been about it, that success brought increased attention to her full body of work as an artist that reached back over twenty-five years. Judith Kegan Gardiner (a contributor to this volume) persuasively argues that Bechdel is in fact a "significant contemporary artist" (188), and disputes the idea that *DTWOF* was simply a ramp-up to *Fun Home*. But when *Time* magazine named *Fun Home* its Book of the Year in 2006—not "graphic novel" or "comic book" but simply "book"—doing so marked a similar shift to that of Bechdel coming to be identified as a cartoonist instead of as a *lesbian* cartoonist. These shifts in identification directly parallel some of the struggles that characters in *DTWOF*, specifically Sparrow and Lois, undergo throughout the series as their identifications change in relation to their relationships with other characters, their desires and interests, and how they understand and experience binary gender.

The benefits of these broader terms (memoir, book, cartoonist) sometimes erase some of the unique aspects of those defining markers of subculture (graphic memoir, comic book, lesbian cartoonist); and at the same time, that erasure also makes it easier for a wider audience to engage with the work in question. Put another way: it's difficult to engage with work you might not know exists. Roz Warren's *Dyke Strippers: Lesbian Cartoonists A to Z*, mentioned this exact point in her collection's introduction, published in 1995: "It's tough to learn about up-and-coming (or even well established) lesbian and bi cartoonists because they are, for the most part, published mostly in regional gay and lesbian papers. The good news is that with the growth of cartoon-friendly national publications . . . this is changing (7)." More than a decade later, *Fun Home* put Bechdel's name and work in front of a vastly larger readership, some of whom had never even heard of *DTWOF*, much less engaged with it.

In a wider sense, as Bechdel's work gained greater attention and praise, the identity of that body of work shifted as well. *DTWOF* was a successful syndicated comic strip, but *Fun Home* made Bechdel famous as an author. Although *Fun Home* is about queerness and identity and family, really, so is *DTWOF*; the difference, at least for mainstream and overground media, is that the first is a memoir that is in comic form whereas the other is a lesbian comic strip. Historically, comics in America, especially comic strips, have been considered disposable and lightweight entertainment; whether you read them in the Sunday funnies or in the local LGBT paper, they have not generally been considered high art. *DTWOF* shifted this categorization, winning a number of Lambda Literary Awards, but it was through *Fun Home* that Bechdel achieved critical and commercial success and, arguably, brought lesbian comix and a comic strip about queerness to mainstream America in a way that no other lesbian cartoonist had previously been able to do.

Although Bechdel herself is ambivalent about these changes and her role in them, that ambivalence does not dilute the fact that her work has become part of American culture, whether in a high-culture sense (winning a MacArthur "genius" grant, weird though it may be, carves your name into history in a very real way, as does having your work serve as the basis for a critically acclaimed Broadway musical) or in a popular culture sense (people who have never read *DTWOF* are still familiar with the Bechdel test, and Bechdel herself appeared as a cartoon character on an episode of *The Simpsons* in October 2017 spoofing the test). Although it seems unlikely that new readers will come to *DTWOF* via the Bechdel test, new readers are coming to the work through *Fun Home*, and Bechdel's influence on both comics and American culture is remarkable. Additionally, Bechdel made a number of important points about gender in her series, not only about categories of identity like "lesbian" and "bisexual," but also in taking apart some of the ways we are taught to think about them in binary terms based on gender; her work reflects and documents some of the changes within lesbian and queer communities around these topics and serves as a unique and comprehensive historical chronicle of lesbian community in America over nearly twenty-five years.

It is important here to note that Warren's definition of "dyke strippers" was intentionally broad. Although women such as Diane DiMassa, Jennifer Camper, Nicole Ferentz, Fish, Joan Hilty, Kris Kovick, and many others were publishing lesbian cartoons, comics, and comix, few of those works were serialized comic strips, which is a specific form with space and narrative pacing limitations. "Comix" is a term used originally by artists working in defiance of the Comics Code Authority, which was created by the industry in 1954 to self-regulate content from mass-market comics publishers like DC and Marvel in the face of controversy, declining sales, and a Senate subcommittee hearing; it was not dropped by the industry until 2011. The "x" in comix was often used to indicate work that wasn't for children: more mature material that was also often self-published or published by smaller presses rather than by mass-market comics publishers. "Cartoons" and "comics" are terms often used interchangeably, even though "cartoons" tend to be a single-image panel, often with a text caption beneath it, that may also integrate speech balloons; and "comics" tend to use multiple panels, sequence, speech balloons, and other forms of visual narrative signifiers. Scott McCloud has provided definitions for, and discussed the differences between, "comics" and "cartoons," though some critics have taken issue with how broad McCloud's definitions are. Others cite his inclusivity as crucial to understanding how much comics are already a part of our visual culture. Many of the cartoons appearing in *Deneuve*, the *Advocate*, the *Funny Times*, *Girljock*, and others were frequently single-panel illustrations with a text caption underneath, cartoons similar to those in mainstream publications like the *New Yorker*. One of their better-known creators is Andrea Natalie, founder of the Lesbian Cartoonists Network. Her single-panel cartoons, dealing with gay and lesbian life, collectively titled *Stonewall Riots*, were, like Bechdel's work, first published in *WomaNews*.

However, even fewer works at the time had the intense world-building that went into *DTWOF* or the range of fully realized characters representing so many facets of what queerness can entail. "Lesbian" meant a lot of varied things in *DTWOF*, the goal being to show that there were as many ways to be a lesbian as there were lesbians. Adrienne Shaw discusses this point, stating that "lesbian comic artists both represent and define lesbian identity and community" within interconnected themes (88); "In these comics, what it means to be part of an imagined lesbian community is celebrated, questioned, and debated; in this process, the artists help define a community and identity framed by flux" (93). *Hothead Paisan: Homicidal Lesbian Terrorist* came close; Diane DiMassa built a world with varied characters, but her series mainly centered on a single character making her way through the world with a heavy dose of satire. Much as we might want to chop off the leg of a manspreader on the subway, that's just not something we can do in our daily lives—but Hothead can, and does.

These two titles are likely the best-known lesbian comix titles. Robin Bernstein describes *DTWOF* and *Hothead* in 1994 as being "in the bloodstream of lesbian culture" and as having achieved "icon status" at a time when "lesbian cartoons [were] booming and lesbian cartoonists [were] enjoying hitherto unknown respectability" (20). Fast-forward ten-plus years; when *Fun Home* was published, though lesbian cartoonists weren't "booming" in the same way they once had been, queer comics had gained dramatically increased visibility owing to shifts in media and the ease of publishing online, as well as heightened academic attention. One such example is Justin Hall's acclaimed collection *No Straight Lines*, published in 2012 by Fantagraphics Books, which examines how queer comics have begun to appear in mainstream media, after detailing a comprehensive forty-year history in which they were not quite so overground.

Additionally, for a syndicated comic strip that at first deliberately included no men, *Dykes to Watch Out For* ended its run with a number of male characters—much to the dismay of many readers, many of whom wanted to read a comic strip about *women*, specifically lesbians. However, including men in the strip afforded Bechdel the narrative possibility to explore the multivalent meanings of identification and gender not only through drag king culture, nonbinary and genderqueer characters, and characters who identify as transgender, but also by upending reader expectations about what maleness and masculinity entail while also representing a vast range of lived lesbian experiences (see Gardiner in this volume). The initial set of male characters in the series who most resemble traditional conceptions of straight masculinity are, in fact, gay and shift expectations of what men do. Later, Stuart appears as an extreme crunchy-granola lesbian stereotype: militant about boycotting ethically suspect companies, refusing to eat meat, going to Pride when nobody else in the friend group does, and so forth. Similarly, as the strip goes on, characters like Lois begin to play more and experiment with masculinity and mannerisms via drag king culture and butchness, even as a growing interest in gender on the part of Lois, particularly beyond a binary, begins to tug at her own understanding of identity.

Bechdel consciously included characters that complicated and shifted readers' understandings of binary gender and categories of identity as a way to give voice to these issues. Three instances show how *DTWOF* offers fascinating complications to binary identification that also reflect Bechdel's interest in expanding the work lesbian comics can do: Sparrow's shift to "bi-dyke" via her relationship with Stuart along with her own fluidity in identification through the series; Lois's interest in drag and her interactions with Jerry when in character as Max Axle; and, briefly, Lois's relationship with Jasmine, which leads to a fundamental redefinition of herself as genderqueer. Part of what makes *DTWOF*'s critiques of community, identity definition, and gender unique is that the artist uses the comics form to great effect in the strip's storytelling, through pacing and visual sequencing, expressions on character's faces, and so forth. In doing so, Bechdel expanded and enriched our cultural understanding of what comix can do. The low cultural expectations imposed on comic strips and comix actually provide their creators a unique opportunity to inform, educate, and document while also entertaining readers and critiquing dominant aspects of that culture, such as the binary logic underpinning notions of gender.

Bechdel once stated, "It seemed like there were already enough male characters in the world. I wanted men to read my strip and be forced to identify with the women characters, the way women and people of color are expected to identify with the zillions of 'universal' white male protagonists in comics, books, TV, movies, and everywhere else" (*Indelible*, 69). By the end of the series in 2008, Lois, who functioned as the uniting thread among all the characters' explorations of identity, gender, and the myriad shifting forms thereof, says about identification: "Girlie man, manly girl; it's all the same to me." This statement is particularly telling, because it had been most prominently through Lois's eyes and experience that the reader learned what shifts in identity and gender look like in the *DTWOF* world.

It wasn't always "all the same" to Lois, the Lothario of the strip, whose character arc took her from an initially radical, polyamorous butch lesbian identification to more or less settling down into a fairly committed and monogamous relationship with Jasmine; as this relationship evolves, she ends up coparenting Jasmine's trans-identified child, Jonas, who is transitioning to a girl named Janis. Lois was Sparrow's first female lover and helped Sparrow come out as a lesbian, an identification that Sparrow feels is deeply tested throughout her own character's arc. (There are, of course, intersectional identity considerations to do with race and ethnicity, as many of these characters are also women of color in interracial relationships, and though these issues are both important and fascinating, they are outside of the focus of this essay; see Galvan in this volume for development of these considerations.) Readers learn about Sparrow's past only through the long end narrative called "Sentimental Education" that closes the collection *Unnatural Dykes to Watch Out For,* when Ginger decides to document her friendship network for the

Lesbian Herstory Archives. These longer end narratives were only published in the book collections, rather than being serially published through syndication, and largely existed to help resolve narrative threads that appeared in the strips that might have been too long or slow paced for publication (such as "Sentimental Education") or too graphic or included nudity (such as when Toni gives birth to her and Clarice's child Rafael).

One could read the strips without seeing these end narratives and still understand what was happening with the story and characters, but the end pieces provide a richness of character development and world-building, as well as the artwork itself: Bechdel was able to use full-page panels rather than being forced to compress the narrative into smaller panels with a lot of expository dialogue or conversation. Even though work by Bechdel, Jennifer Camper, and Andrea Natalie, among others, started appearing in publications as mainstream as the *Funny Times*, this increased visibility came with publication limitations in terms of both the length of the narrative (comic strips are generally fairly short, even if part of a longer serialized narrative, and are expected to end with a punch line or witty resolution) and some of the content. Bechdel's end narratives were a way to resolve some of those narrative issues for readers without being forced to further serialize them or limit their scope. Ostensibly, the larger narrative purpose of Sparrow's past provides Bechdel a way to write about how identity and self-definition can shift, and how certain categories—like gay and straight, and even bisexual—can be limiting, reductive, and ultimately nondescriptive. Lesbian comics before this point, such as work by Mary Wings and Jennifer Camper, among others, often focused more on lesbian identity as a uniting, unifying category, whereas Ariel Schrag's body of work, which first appeared in the late 1990s, took a more inward look as she documented autobiographically her own coming-out process and her shifts in identity, rather than her place within lesbian culture or community.

But when Sparrow begins a romantic relationship with Stuart, who has a history of becoming involved with women who "turn out to be lesbians" (*Split-Level*, 149), she complicates what "lesbian" means. We know—as Adrienne Shaw has pointed out—that there are as many ways to be a lesbian as there are lesbians; the category is not monolithic or unifying. Sparrow's announcement of this shift gives rise to a pointed discussion about the fluidity of identity and the seeming limits of such frames where (to Sparrow, anyway) verbally reframing your identity is understandable, but physically reframing your identity through changing your sex is not. By having Sparrow come out as a "bi-dyke" who is in a relationship that looks heterosexual under our learned cultural assumptions (seeming man plus seeming woman equals seeming heterosexual relationship), even though all those terms are just as open for interpretation, Bechdel critically reframes the ways we are taught to think about gender identity and sexual orientation both by complicating the terms themselves and by her panel composition in the narrative of the strip.

We learn in "Sentimental Education" that Sparrow's housing collective in Washington, DC, had opened their house to lesbians who were in town for a protest march. Lois asks Sparrow: "So, what do you D.C. dykes do for fun?" Sparrow carefully replies, "Um . . . I dunno. You'd have to ask Marge. I'm not a . . . a lesbian." But lesbianism is not a wholly alien concept to Sparrow, thanks to her housing cooperative, which is made up of out and politically active lesbians. Text positioned above the panel, Sparrow narrating to Ginger for the Lesbian Herstory Archives, reads, "I didn't think I was a lesbian, but Ralph was sure starting to get on my nerves." The action within the panel shows Sparrow and Ralph having sex, and Ralph saying, "Have you stopped shaving under your arms? You're not turning **les-bee-yun** on me, are you?" The irony, of course, is that Sparrow, after sleeping with Lois, does exactly that. In an especially apt juxtaposition on Bechdel's part, Lois, in the midst of having sex with Sparrow, tells her, "You have the sweetest armpits" (fig. 2.1). Sparrow's "voice-over" (which is located above the panel to indicate speech related to but chronologically displaced from the time within the panel) says, "Lois begged to differ, and by the next morning I was inclined to agree with her" (*Unnatural*, 131).

The text-image combination offers a unique advantage for the tricky business of reframing gender identities; it is able to provide yet another comment on the scene while maintaining a critical distance from it. For example, we see Sparrow and Lois having sex in one panel. The scene is reframed by the text above it, which marks Sparrow as retelling a story. We know Sparrow is telling this story, and her retrospective position, because of visual clues; we have seen her speaking with Ginger, and we know that she, in her flashback, has the same facial features but a different hairstyle. The recollection of the past is contained within the panel, and Sparrow's present-day comments are marked as separate from it temporally because they are not physically positioned within the panel. In short, we are able to see the past and present almost simultaneously. When Sparrow offers a comment like "Lois begged to differ," she is able to highlight a particular section of the story. She didn't think she was a lesbian, but Lois changed her mind; where Ralph thought Sparrow's unshaven armpits were a negative sign indicating that she was "turning lesbian," Lois "begged to differ" with the negative assessment, stating instead, "You have the sweetest armpits" (*Unnatural*, 131). Lois reframes as attractive what Ralph finds repulsive. Later, Lois bluntly asks Sparrow, "What's it feel like to be straight?" (*Split-Level*, 48), in a reversal of her years-earlier question to Sparrow: "What do you D.C. dykes do for fun?" Sparrow's earlier answer, "I'm

Fig. 2.1. Sparrow's origin story (*Unnatural*, 131).

not a . . . lesbian" is reversed as well, as she replies, "**Lois!** I . . . I'm not straight!" (*Split-Level*, 48).

Sparrow's arc shows that identity is not fixed and static. Nothing about frames of identity precludes a lesbian from having sex with a man, much the same way that nothing keeps a heterosexual woman from being involved with another woman; scores of people have same-sex sex because they like the person in question, are curious, wish to gain experience, or earn money for doing so, all without a shift in their identity. In fact, the redefinition as "bi-dyke" causes an ideological dissonance; Sparrow, in a strip called "I.D. Fixe?," says, in response to Ginger needling her about receiving an unexpected copy of *Bride's Magazine* in the mail, "I bet my mom did this! Ever since I came out to her about Stuart, she thinks it means I'm straight. She can't understand that I'm a **bisexual lesbian!**" Ginger replies, somewhat ironically, "Well, it's a nuance that can elude the best of us," to which Sparrow retorts, "Look, in a perfect world I wouldn't have to call myself anything. But for now, bi-dyke works for me" (*Post*, 58) (fig. 2.2).

Sparrow's "perfect world" might be one where people do not have to frame (or be framed by) their identities, but without these points of reference, empty as they may be, how might people—or comic strip characters—relate to one another or to themselves? Also key in this example is Sparrow's use of the phrase "for now" to describe how she is choosing to describe her identity. "For now" implies that there may be a shift in terminology, that she in time may decide that another term (or terms) frames her identity more fully.

Fig. 2.2. Identity is complicated (*Post*, 58).

What happens to Sparrow's identity is that she deliberately chooses to reframe herself as a bisexual lesbian even though she would just as easily have continued to identify as a lesbian and been in a relationship with a man. This situation also poses a question that Sparrow's housemates Lois and Ginger struggle with: if Sparrow is a lesbian, what's she doing in a relationship—one that becomes explicitly sexual later in the series—with a (heterosexual) man? What does it mean for Sparrow to identify as a bisexual lesbian throughout this heterosexual-seeming relationship with Stuart? Having heard the tail end of the conversation between Ginger and Sparrow, Stuart chimes in and utters the first thing to complicate his seeming heterosexuality: "I think I'm a butch lesbian in a straight man's body" (*Post*, 58). If Stuart were to identify himself as "a butch lesbian" (it is unclear whether he is speaking seriously or simply trying to make a joke), Sparrow might no longer have a need, per se, to reframe herself as a bisexual lesbian; Stuart's self-framing as "butch lesbian" also could be one way to explain his continued pattern of dating women who "turn out to be lesbians," though there is no accounting for why the relationships subsequently failed (i.e., if Stuart is a butch lesbian in a straight man's body, the soon-to-become lesbian woman he is dating might want a butch— or a femme—lesbian in a lesbian woman's body). But Stuart's "straight man's body" complicates matters: while he may be a butch lesbian in his mind, his body at least is male, causing Sparrow to reframe herself as a bisexual lesbian.

Lois will deal with some of the same issues in her growing attraction to Jerry, her involvement in drag kinging, and her ability to pass as male (even as she retains her lesbian identity). The episode "I.D. Fixe?" also introduces Jerry, who arrives at the household shortly after Stuart's statement. "Who was that? Don't tell me you're seeing a man too?" Ginger asks, in exasperation, and Lois replies, "No, just lending him a tie. Though he is kind of hot" (*Post*, 59). In subsequent strips, Lois briefly wonders as her desire grows if she should redefine (or reframe) herself as "a fag" because of her attraction to "a trans man" who is also gay. "Anyhow," Ginger tells her, "Jerry likes guys. It's not like anything's gonna happen" (*Post*, 113). This is a very different and far more accepting and nuanced response from how both Ginger and Lois reacted when they first found out that Sparrow was dating Stuart, which points toward how much these characters over time evolve how they think about gender and identity. For Lois to think and speak about Jerry as "kind of hot" presents another interesting twist. Lois, who identifies as lesbian, states her attraction to Jerry, who is trans; in other words, Jerry identifies as a gay man to whom Lois is attracted, though Lois was not at all attracted to Jerry when Jerry was Geraldine, stating, "You were way too butch for me then, dude" (*Post*, 132). The implication is that Jerry, in becoming male, has become *less* butch and therefore *more* attractive to Lois (who self-identifies as butch and is not averse to butch-butch relationships), while Stuart becomes *more* butch in his "straight man's body" as a "butch lesbian" than he is ordinarily—he is often visually paired with Lois when she is dressed as Max Axle, and she is cast as far more masculine than he is.

Stuart, over the next four panels, is shown first thinking (eyes rolled upward, finger to mouth), recognizing (shown by lines radiating from his head and wide-open, surprised eyes), and then realizing (smacking his hand to his head), who Jerry is and was. "Oh my God! Geraldine from Rainbow Automotive?!" he exclaims. "I used to have such a thing for her! I mean him! I mean . . . wow!" Stuart's past attraction to a butch lesbian who is now a gay FTM trans man complicates his "butch lesbian" announcement at the same time as it reinforces it, even though Ginger (re)frames him by stating, "**Soft** butch. May**be**" (*Post*, 58). Or as Ginger articulates the issue of identity being fluid: "Skip fluid. Press 'liquefy'" (59).

Much later in the series, Lois's housemate Ginger has a brief fling with a minor character in the strip, Jasmine, who has a ten-year-old child. This child is a deal breaker for Ginger, who is characterized throughout most of the strip as a commitmentphobe, but not for Lois. Ginger at one point yells at Lois, "Are you pursuing Jasmine just to torture me? Last I heard you were into butch daddies and trans men. She's not your type at all" (*Sundry*, 124). We already know a great deal about Lois's type, having seen her throughout the series in a number of different relationships: part of a poly relationship with a much older woman; then a number of other, different women in the series; and then when she develops an attraction to Jerry, Lois is only able to act on her desire for Jerry while dressed in her drag king persona of Max Axle. For Lois, this sequence of episodes with Jerry—to whom she was not attracted when Jerry was Geraldine, making a joke about how Geraldine was way too butch for her then—is a defining moment about how limiting binary gender has become for her. It also, not incidentally, gives Bechdel the chance to talk about gender theory. She pointedly introduces gender and cultural theory in a way that integrates high academic concepts into what is still often considered a lowbrow medium in America, while also recognizing the value of lived experience (see Parker-Hay in this volume).

Jerry becoming Lois's lover only when Lois is dressed as Max Axle raises a number of points about gender and sex. If Lois, who is lesbian, dresses in drag and receives oral sex while packing a dildo from Jerry, who currently identifies as a FTM gay man who used to identify as a butch lesbian, how can that sex be deemed heterosexual (fig. 2.3)?

Defining it as so simply based on the current sex of each partner fails to recognize all the frames that factor into their respective identities. It ultimately makes little difference for these characters what sex or gender other characters in question may be if an attraction exists, despite what they have been taught to think about who they are and what they do. Interestingly, as academia and queer culture both began to develop their own shifting understandings of gender, Bechdel was documenting the same shifts in *DTWOF*. Later in the series, Sydney is introduced and begins dating Mo (widely considered the main character in the series and often seen as a sort-of representation of Bechdel herself), in part as a way for Bechdel to create a conduit into the world of the comic for the explosive proliferation of academic work on gender. Sydney's apartment and office are scattered with books possessing titles that reference theorists like Judith Roof, Judith Butler, and Eve Kosofsky Sedgwick. Clever readers know to look at those book titles: Sedgwick's 1990 landmark work *Epistemology of the Closet* becomes *Epistemology of the Living Room Floor*, for example. As academics and artists like Jack Halberstam, Diane Torr, and Del LaGrace Volcano began exploring, writing about, documenting, and participating in drag king culture and performance, these aspects of lesbian culture began appearing in the strip through Lois's growing interest in and development of her drag king character of Max Axle. Sydney, like Ginger, is a professor. Through these characters, readers are exposed to more high-theoretical concepts of gender and queerness via Sydney while at the same time encountering what that theory means for lived experience

Fig. 2.3. Lois, as Max Axle, surprised by Jerry (*Post*, 120).

through Lois's engagement with gender and drag and desire in her own relationships and life. Theory and praxis, indeed.

Lived experience is crucial for showing the many varied facets of what "lesbian" identification can entail. For example, in a 2000 strip called "Cognitive Dissonance," the extended friend group gathers in the backyard for a barbecue. The event brings together a wide range of characters with multiple different connections to one another, showing the range and depth of queer community. Someone asks about Lois's new girlfriend, an ambiguously gendered figure drawn in the background playing croquet: "As I understand it, she's not a girl . . . but a . . . wait, I had it a minute ago . . . oh, yeah. A genderqueer boydyke geek with an Oxford cloth fetish" (*Sundry*, 26). How far these folks have come; when Sparrow started dating Stuart, Lois in particular struggled with Sparrow's self-identification as a bisexual lesbian, perceived to be an identity shift wholly prompted by her relationship. Lois, as we have seen, has been the character whom readers perceive most often as challenging binary gender, upending expectations of behavior and desire, and generally being the most forward-thinking character when it comes to shifting identity. But, as we know, practice does not dictate identity. That inclusion also extends to characters whose politics (at least to Mo) lie beyond the pale: Ginger's student Cynthia, who is ultraconservative and a hawk—and also a lesbian. When told she has to reach out to other people and make friends, she replies, "Yeah right. The gay kids here hate me and the other conservatives think I'm a perv"

(*Invasion*, 121). Interestingly enough, it is Lois who first reads Cynthia as a lesbian and outs her to the rest of the group; while at the movies with Ginger and her girlfriend Samia, the three of them run into Cynthia leaving the earlier showing of the same movie they are about to see, and after one quick meeting, Lois has sussed out Cynthia's queerness by figuring out that she is attracted to both Ginger and Samia.

When Sparrow becomes pregnant late in the series, she again struggles deeply with a shift in her identity. When she gets home from work, Stuart greets her at the door with milk and urges her to put her feet up and eat the protein-and-iron rich dinner he is cooking, much to Sparrow's consternation. "God, Ginger! He's so completely into this baby, there's no room for **me**! . . . I used to be a radical lesbian feminist, goddamn it! I haven't felt this lonely and confused since I **came out**" (*Sundry*, 128). Of course, what "radical lesbian" really entails is up for debate; Diane DiMassa's Hothead Paisan, mid-rant with her friend Roz, complains about how another lesbian took her to task for eating meat and wonders about what "radical lesbian" really means: "Wouldn't a **truly** radical lesbian sleep with men? Wouldn't that be the most radical thing a lesbian could do?? Is it radical **comma** lesbian or what??" (DiMassa, 43).

Stuart, by comparison, quits his job to be a full-time stay-at-home dad. His history of dating women who turn out to be lesbians, pitched in the series as a running joke, comes full circle in the final collection of the series when the whole friend cluster goes down to City Hall upon the legalization of same-sex marriage. Some of them are going there to be married, while some are going to support the couples and to soak up the atmosphere of celebration and defiance. While there, Stuart runs into two women both dressed in bridal gowns: "Well. Look at you two! Sparrow, this is my ex, Sigrid, and my ex, Lilith" (*Invasion*, 83). The dissonance of having a straight-identified male character in the strip is addressed through the use of stereotype and running jokes; Stuart becomes a punch line, but Sparrow is the one who really struggles. Nothing about their relationship changed Stuart's identification, but Sparrow's entire identity is thrown into turmoil. Similarly, for as much as Lois quipped at Sparrow for becoming a parent, she herself essentially becomes one. When Jasmine and Lois are preparing to send Janis to a summer camp for LGBTQ youth, and are talking about the changes they see in the young person, Jasmine says, with a wistful look on her face, "I dunno. I miss my angelic little boy who played with dolls. Now I'm living with this . . . this **valley girl** who steals my clothes and ignores me" (*Invasion*, 102). When Jasmine and Lois go to pick Janis up from camp, Janis introduces a friend: "This is my boyfriend Alex. He started transitioning when he was nine!" (105).

Clearly, as we have seen, marking these texts (and people) *only* as gay, lesbian, bisexual, trans, and queer is insufficient, not only because to do so fails to consider that all texts (and people) are multiply framed, but also because these words just don't carry the same meaning they used to. Language shifts even though print is static, and if "lesbian" is a frame that is culturally determined, it must change as culture does: it is not the same word it was thirty years ago. Lesbian comix are also inevitably altered as they enter mainstream culture. As Bechdel became known as an author, as *Fun Home* in all its forms gained attention and acclaim, her comprehensive body of work gained more readers and more attention—particularly among new queer readers who were too young to have read *DTWOF* as it was being serially published. Anxieties at the time of the emergence of *DTWOF* seemed to be that if these comix are absorbed into mainstream culture, the absorption would bring an end to their discursive power because with a wider readership comes a greater amount of reader feedback and engagement; alternatively, we will lose something that is unique and specific to the LGBTQ community. Yet time has shown this not to be the case. In the end, Bechdel published two brand-new strips, the first since May 2008, showing her primary characters gathering around a dinner table. These characters were generally wiser and grayer, but as familiar and recognizable as ever, so much so that when the news came out that there were new *DTWOF* strips, Bechdel's website crashed because it couldn't handle all the traffic. What a fitting return for a tiny strip that started simply as a way for a lesbian cartoonist to document her day-to-day life and experiences because she didn't see herself or her friends represented in comics.

WORKS CITED

Bechdel, Alison. *Dykes and Sundry Other Carbon-Based Life-Forms to Watch Out For*. Firebrand Books, 2003.
Bechdel, Alison. *Invasion of the Dykes to Watch Out For*. Firebrand Books, 2005.
Bechdel, Alison. *Post-dykes to Watch Out For*. Firebrand Books, 2000.
Bechdel, Alison. *Split-Level Dykes to Watch Out For*. Firebrand Books, 1998.
Bechdel, Alison. *Unnatural Dykes to Watch Out For*. Firebrand Books, 1995.
Bernstein, Robin. "Where Women Rule: The World of Lesbian Cartoons." *Harvard Gay and Lesbian Review*, Summer 1994, 20–23.
DiMassa, Diane. *The Complete Hothead Paisan: Homicidal Lesbian Terrorist*. Cleis Press, 1999.
Gardiner, Judith Kegan. "Queering Genre: Alison Bechdel's Fun Home: A Family Tragicomic and The Essential Dykes to Watch Out For." *Contemporary Women's Writing* 5, no. 3 (2011): 188–207.
Shaw, Adrienne. "Women on Women: Lesbian Identity, Lesbian Community, and Lesbian Comics." *Journal of Lesbian Studies* 13 (2009): 88–97.
Warren, Roz, ed. *Dyke Strippers: Lesbian Cartoonists A to Z*. Cleis Press, 1995.

DISSEMINATING QUEER THEORY

Dykes to Watch Out For and the Transmission of Theoretical Thought

KATHERINE PARKER-HAY

Over the past decade, feminist and queer work has become increasingly interested in its own periodization, concerned to develop self-reflexivity regarding assumptions about time; for more than one critic of this ilk, Alison Bechdel's memoir *Fun Home* has offered a model of such reflexivity (see Cvetkovich; Hesford; McBean).[1] It is not hard to understand why *Fun Home* has been so amenable to academic analysis: with its high-cultural references, literary juxtapositions, intertextuality, and references to the archive, it is ripe for literary decoding. As Jane Tolmie comments, "Its integration into the critical worlds of literary and cultural studies has been quick, in part because of its own high degree of academic referentiality: like calls to like" (79). Valerie Rohy likewise concludes her article on Bechdel's memoir with the comment that "*Fun Home* engages some of queer theory's most timely issues: teleology, historicism, fantasy and the retroactivity of identity" (357). However, while there has been evident interest along these lines in Bechdel's memoir(s), there has been somewhat less consideration, particularly in terms of its relationship to "theory," of Bechdel's long-running syndicated comic strip *Dykes to Watch Out For*, collected over its life span in several anthologies and compiled in 2008 as *The Essential Dykes to Watch Out For*. Where the strip has been referenced in much of the previous literature on Bechdel, it is often used to support assertions on, or provide contextual background for, arguments primarily about *Fun Home*; Bechdel worked on both projects simultaneously (see Gardiner; Bernstein). If we consider *Dykes to Watch Out For* on its own terms—specifically in its collected form as *The Essential Dykes to Watch Out For*, complete with scaffolding provided by the cartoonist herself—a far more ambivalent relationship to theory emerges, of a kind quite unlike that found in Bechdel's other works. I contend that owing to its mode of production—as a serialized narrative, explicitly composed at regular increments as part of a work routine—the text is unusually positioned

Fig. 3.1. Alison's encounter with Gender Trouble (*Essential*, xvi).

to capture everyday time and thus the at times compromised ways in which theoretical ideas move through public cultures.

If Bechdel's relationship to queer studies has been understood by some critics as that of a "neat fit" (Tolmie; Rohy), then it is startling to witness the ambivalence with which she narrates her encounter with the high theory of the 1990s in the "Cartoonist's Introduction" that begins her 2008 compilation of *Dykes to Watch Out For*. In self-deprecating confessions to "camera," the cartoonist recalls the process of creating the serial. The strip is depicted as a product of daily work life, characterized by labor at regular and routine increments. She remembers how, midway through the project, she was interrupted by the success of critical theory of the 1990s that, with its characteristic scrutiny of habits and repetition, intuitively felt incompatible with the compositional foundation of her work. For instance, Bechdel establishes an exaggerated, self-deprecating, binary contrast between her serial and the conceptual elegance of Judith Butler's *Gender Trouble*.

With exasperation and disbelief, "Alison," thrusting a copy of the book against the pane of the panel, exclaims, "Oh, and apparently no one was essentially anything!" (fig. 3.1). *Gender Trouble* is shown surrounded by movement lines that radiate outward: the cartoonist is emphatically shaking the book at us with the effect that it is physicalized, so as to make plain its singularity, impact, and unique insight. This representation is iconic rather than literal;

the cover artwork is stripped away, and with these details absent, the significance of the title and author is heightened.[2] The result is that, in excess of the book as a physical object, the wide-scale shift in collective feeling that the book brings about is evoked: the book is seen to create a gigantic shudder, unsettling the feminist culture of which the serial was a part.

The introduction gives clues about the nature of the text's relationship to this feminist counterpublic. It is referenced both in "Alison's" recounting of how her readers' insatiable desire to have their community reflected back to them "egged" her on (*Essential*, xiv), and in her affectionate address to her present readers, whom at multiple points she addresses in the plural form "my friends" (x, xv). These evidence the serial's role in shaping its own public sphere, or counterpublic, acting as a social site from which readers could imagine themselves as part of a community of like individuals with common interests and desires. As Habermas writes, "The public sphere requires specific means for transmitting information and influencing those who receive it," media such as "newspapers and magazines," along with television and radio (136).[3] However, while the cartoonist may have begun her project with this public of intimates in mind, even as early as 1998 she details how her audience grew beyond these confines; and furthermore, her "peculiar reciprocity" with this growing public meant that she had the "dubious privilege" of receiving constant feedback about how to progress the narrative (*Indelible*, 207). This, coupled with her commitment to rejuvenate the strip by responding to current events and trends, meant that by the 1990s the premise and conceptual coherence of the strip had seemed to have run away from her (62). If Bechdel's serial was produced out of routine, then *Gender Trouble* is the antidote that blasts apart daily life and catapults "Alison" into a different experiential frame: in the introduction to *Essential*, she clutches the book and leans forward, her one magnified eye lending her a somewhat crazed appearance; her eyebrows are raised, as if she cannot get up to speed with what she has read and what it will mean for the strip that she has "churned out episodes of . . . every two weeks for decades" (*Essential*, xviii). The cartoonist remarks, in a knowing tone, that "this was the point at which a more sensible person would have indeed gotten a job" (xvi).

However—as the collection that the reader is about to embark on so obviously testifies to—"Alison" did not cease cartooning in favor of other employment but, on the contrary, continued to publish regular strips throughout the 1990s and into the twenty-first century. Despite initial concerns and ongoing, low-level anxiety, the daily work of the strip could continue simultaneously with, perhaps working itself out beneath, the comparatively rapid, nervous vibrations of high theory. Here I am thinking of Lefebvre's distinction between the temporality of critical thought and that of the everyday. Lefebvre writes that the everyday "could represent a lower sphere of meaning, a place where energy is stored in readiness for new creations" (12). He continues, by way of topographical metaphor:

> Behind us, as we stand at their point of intersection, are the way of philosophy and the road of everyday life. They are divided by a mountain range, but the path of philosophy keeps to the heights, thus overlooking that of everyday life; ahead the track winds, barely visible, through thickets, thornbushes and swamps. (14)

This image conceptualizes time as layered into successive levels. For Lefebvre, the everyday pertains to a partial perspective, unfolding slowly—often repeating itself or working itself out in cycles. This can be contrasted to his temporality of philosophy, which pertains to the history of events and forms a kind of surface disturbance atop comparatively slow-moving swaths of time.[4] What I find compelling about this conceptualization is the suggestion, underdeveloped by Lefebvre but taken up by others, that each of us necessarily has a foot in both the realm of habitual perception and that of more critical thought. For instance, Rita Felski argues that to gain critical focus on any one aspect is only possible when there is a network of other elements that can be relied on and taken for granted; "After all," writes Felski, "everyday life simply is, indisputably: the essential taken for granted continuum of mundane activities that frames our forays into more esoteric or exotic worlds" (77). Any complete division between the everyday and high theory is surely a fabrication; however, I find the idea of their simultaneity instructive for understanding the way in which "Alison" is unexpectedly disturbed, in both senses, by an encounter with theory, but also how it is that she is able to compartmentalize this disturbance and carry on with production relatively unabated. It provides a way of understanding the strip's capacity to register theoretical developments while remaining at enough of a distance so as not to be formally or conceptually ruptured by them—at least never beyond repair.

In the "Cartoonist's Introduction" to *Essential*, such interruption is remembered in retrospect, encapsulated as one moment of crisis: an encounter with *Gender Trouble* that jolts "Alison" out of her routine enough to reflect on the assumptions underpinning her strip. This encounter, humorously exaggerated by the retroactive nature of memory, lends precision to the otherwise abstract capacity of critical theory to shake up habitual perception; however, this dramatic, one-off bolt-from-the-blue encounter is not actually borne out within the main body of the collection itself. First, there is no single devastating encounter; on the contrary, theoretical developments are registered and their potential to destabilize habitual perception are played with and approached with interest but do not lead to permanent rupture or crisis. Indeed, the collection, all the more obvious in its compiled format, bridges a continuous stretch of time that is shown to unfold steadily and episodically, binding together almost three decades. Second, in the introduction, "Alison" is presented as nonconscious in her decisions and lacking in critical awareness; but in the collection, I find evidence that Bechdel uses the comic form in deliberate ways to explore, with characteristic deprecation, the transmission of fragile minority knowledge in terms of both its successes and its limitations. Writing about *Fun Home*, with a brief and suggestive remark about *Dykes to Watch Out For*, Ann Cvetkovich comments:

> In fact, one of *Fun Home*'s charms is that it claims a relatively unapologetic relation to lesbian feminist culture within which Alison came out, although it maintains the sense of self-deprecating humour that is the hallmark of *Dykes to Watch Out For* (and gives lie to the idea that the culture of lesbian political correctness is unremittingly sincere or serious). (124)

I want to develop this insight, to explore how the collection establishes this playful and deprecating relationship with theory that is simultaneously a hallmark of Bechdel's individual craft and something made possible by the unique formal properties of comics. Specifically, I consider instances where Bechdel uses the gutters of the comic to represent how knowledge can be lost or obfuscated as it moves through (everyday, public) time that is teeming with distractions. As a result, the collection is stirring, even instructive, for anyone invested in critical theory's capacity to effect meaningful and sustained change. The method I develop in the following section draws on the significance of the gutter as identified in comics criticism; it advocates placing one's attention on the gutters and focusing on how information is shown to be successfully, or unsuccessfully, transmitted across them.

Method: Transmission across the Gutter

By "transmission," I refer to the way an idea or concept moves through public culture and persists across time in ways that may be coherent or incoherent with itself. Deborah Withers's *Feminism, Digital Culture and the Politics of Transmission: Theory, Practice and Cultural Heritage* clarifies why knowledge transmission is imperative in certain contexts. Withers is concerned with the cultural output of social movements grounded in leftist and anticapitalist traditions, and she "examines the processes through which ideas, knowledge and cultural practices are transmitted across generations," focusing on how institutions propagate resources and how individuals find and take up these ideas (1). Withers understands such knowledge as intangible and fragile by definition. Such heritages, she explains, are connected though fragmented networks, and because such networks are not always recognized as valuable, their upkeep depends on the labor of interested individuals. Practitioners are often geographically dispersed, and so networks are prone to being "overstretched" (113). Moreover, when dealing with topics that are difficult to confront, such as desire and violence, circuits of knowledge are liable to break as individuals remove themselves from networks because of damage or exhaustion (113–15). Withers argues that when it comes to countercultural knowledge, there is often simply "not enough technical infrastructure to secure consistent transmission across time" (10, 22). This reality calls for close scrutiny of transmission processes, including inspection of where knowledge is "fragmented, blocked, obfuscated and directed in particular ways due to the technical transmissive system they are embedded in" (11).

Drawing on these ideas, I am interested in what the formal composition of the comics medium in particular can tell us about how, where, and why ideas become blocked, dispersed, and carried forward in ways that render knowledge accessible or otherwise. I suggest that comics, with their panels and gutters, have the capacity to represent some of these abstract processes in visual, material, and therefore pedagogical ways. In her study on the material form of comics, Barbara Postema writes that by definition the form "relies on the force of absences, of the gap" (50). Postema further explains that written narrative also relies on absences to build suspense for the reader, but "one of the differences between comics and textual literature is that in comics these gaps are visible in a literal way, putting the narrative process of comics on display. . . . With the gutter, the gap becomes literally visible on the comics page" (50). With strips, much can be gained by attending to what is absent in a literal sense: the reader moves back and forth between panels, scrutinizing what is present and what has not been transmitted between panels. In technical terms, the comics page is made up of individual moments, represented by the panels and the gutters that separate them. Readers are encouraged to project causality as they move forward and create closure between panels; for narrative to build, content must be projected across this infrastructure of panel and gutter, but crucially, in each transition between panels, there lies the possibility that information will be blocked, obfuscated, or left behind.

The precariousness of transmission represented by the gutter is signaled by choice metaphors in the work of two of the most eminent semioticians of comics. In Scott McCloud's *Understanding Comics*, a reader's journey across panels is conceptualized as the leap of a "trapeze artist" hurtling through the air with the hope of safe landing (fig. 3.2).

Fig. 3.2. Trapeze artist (McCloud, 90).

McCloud draws the trapeze artist/reader suspended in a gutter wider than the spaces seen throughout the book, while the commentary reports that the reader has been released "into the open air of *imagination . . .* then *caught* by the outstretched arms of the *ever-present next panel! caught* **quickly** so as not to let the reader *fall* into *confusion* and *boredom*." The figure's arms are extended wide, displaying a faith that looks ill-advised, considering the gutter's width and the angle at which the figure is inclined to fall. McCloud's widening of the gutter has the effect of elongating the duration of the figure's suspension, which lends tension to the scene; moreover, the boldface "quickly" provides a sense of anxiety: the reader may not be caught. Although Thierry Groensteen comments in his *System of Comics* that the gutter "does not merit fetishization," Groensteen nevertheless uses comparable imagery to describe the reader's journey across it (112). In his terms, to read across the page is to "jump from one panel to the next (an optical and mental leap) [which] is the equivalent of an electron changing orbit" (113). Here too the transition is presented as a "leap": not only a physical exertion but also a leap of faith because the outcome is, for a moment at least, unknown.

In this essay, I bring Withers's call for more careful scrutiny of transmission processes into dialogue with Postema's, McCloud's, and Groensteen's insights about the formal workings of comics, to develop a method that could do justice to Bechdel's handling of the transmission of theory and minority knowledge. This method foregrounds tracking if and how content is shown to change as it passes across the gutters; it promotes a sensitivity to where this process is shown to be a precarious one. In a sense, what I am suggesting is a practice of "spot the difference" between panels, the results of which I believe are a significant source of meaning and humor in *Dykes to Watch Out For*. This method is also inspired by a number of ideas developed in new work in literary methods in the humanities. This includes an interest in tracking change across the surface of a text (Best and Marcus; Love, "Close"); an interest in sliding scales of analysis, particularly those that desire to come "close" to account for the micro and the minor (see Love, "Close," "Small"); and, finally, an interest in absence *as* absence, rather than symbolic of something concealed or yet to be articulated. In this I follow Benjamin Kahan, who writes of reading the blockages of a text as "an elegant formation in and of itself" (5). It seems to me that the blockages indicated by movement across the gutter offer a good example of this kind of "elegant formation." I begin by conducting a number of "close" examinations of a series of panels, what I call micro-instances of (failed) transmission. In the conclusion, I consider the possibility of shifting the scale in the other direction, to consider the larger scale of transmission in the whole collection, as it unfolds across multiple decades.

Transmission: Micro-Instances

One example of difficult transmission can be seen in the 1989 strip "The Option" (fig. 3.3). Local lesbian-run establishment Café Topaz is a central backdrop to the action of the early strips in *DTWOF*; it is evocative of the feminist institutions that played such an important part in cultural feminism in the 1980s and with which this comic shares heritage.[5] In this scene, however, the café is catering to Lois and Emma, characters who express frustration with lesbian feminist politics and, with their sex-positive and experimental attitude toward gender and relationships, are perhaps at this point in the narrative best described as proto-queer. Lois and Emma are meeting to discuss their newly forming, nonmonogamous relationship; the scene marks a shift in the collection, as it is the first time Lois is shown in proximity to a character who shares her political stance. In the first and second panels, the specials board behind their table advertises "wheat-free dairy-free pizza w/no tomatoes." This is an affectionate jibe at the strictures of 1980s lesbian feminist culture and its notorious scrutiny of issues of lifestyle, diet, and personal style (Echols, 240). This parody of cultural feminism, which strips back the pizza ingredients to a point where no dish is imaginable, is further heightened because it seems to belong to a different historical moment from the "progressive" exchange happening beneath it. In the middle panels, the reader is absorbed by the drama of their quarrel, and the "camera" rotates 360 degrees, as if driven by the reader's desire not to miss any detail of the emerging relationship between these two fully contemporary subjects. By the third panel, the specials board

Fig. 3.3. "The Option" (*Essential*, 46).

disappears from view. The conversation could have lasted only a minute or so in real time, but by the seventh panel the board has reappeared, and its message has shifted to "vegetarian meatloaf w/steamed fries."

This scene depends on the reader's expectation that as they follow the building narrative of the foreground, most of the background details will be carried forward—"caught" by the next panel. The comics form, writes Groensteen, is characterized by a high level of redundancy and repetition; to maintain narrative continuity, "each image needs to be linked to the previous by partial repetition of its contents" (115). Humor results from the surprise realization that this did not happen here: with each panel representing a moment in time, the specials board, along with the culture it represents, is evidently not cogent enough to secure consistent transmission. In addition to its function of tickling the reader, this failure in transmission seems to signal that this kind of feminism has lost its original clarity and force: now that other ideas have come to the fore, the message is muffled, and there is only the hazy recognition that there might once have been something worth registering there. Pizza could just as easily be meatloaf; both are reducible to the genre of "bossy interference that leads to a punishingly inedible meal." This scene, lighthearted as it is, communicates the challenges of communicating ideas in a public realm that is dense with competing messages. For instance, perhaps the message signaled by the specials board is not inherently weak, but the characters (and the readers?) are distracted by newness and so fail to register and absorb its content and the intent behind it accurately.

On the other hand, it does not seem correct to suggest that Bechdel is here promoting lesbian feminist positions over "queerer" ones. I would argue that the strip is less interested in any one political identity per se and more interested in conveying the difficulties of self-fashioning coherent identities when operating from a partial perspective of the present. Explicitly anchored to the date 1989 of its title panel, the strip documents the contingencies of personal development amid social change from a perspective of the present tense, where none of the participants can be sure what they are doing or where their decisions will lead. The strip is a documentary of the present tense.[6] Lois is thrown into a situation, where she is confronted with competing ways of being and knowing; her strategy for navigating this flux is to try to get the most personal gain she can out of it. Therefore the board's near proximity to the conversation beneath it seems to signal a threat to Lois's personal development from nonmonogamous in theory to nonmonogamous in practice: when Lois realizes that nonmonogamy is likely to entail Emma sleeping with multiple partners too, and perhaps at a greater rate than herself, she grows flustered and less certain about the benefits of change. With no guarantee that affirming this new opportunity will be to her personal advantage, it becomes harder for Lois to disentangle from the culture that made her to fully inhabit something new. The specials board, then, could be seen as lending ironic distance to Lois's position and the coherence of a queer moment that is here to support it, acting as an invitation back to a kind of culture that is overfamiliar for sure, but one that could be comforting for this reason.

Another example of thwarted transmission can be seen in "Unminced Words," a segment of a strip dating from 1994 (fig. 3.4). Featured are academic Ginger and her partner Malika, two African American lesbians who are in a long-distance relationship. Malika is visiting Ginger, but Ginger, recently having had and admitted to an affair at a black gay and lesbian leadership forum, is struggling to keep up the illusion of normalcy. In the first panel, Ginger leans back on the bed and reads out a newspaper report with new findings

Fig. 3.4. "Unminced Words" (*Essential*, 124).

that "African American gay men and women have substantially higher levels of chronic stress than heterosexual blacks and whites. And lesbian African Americans suffer from more stress than their gay counterparts." Malika, seated upright with hand on hips and eyes narrowed, is only half listening. In the second panel, Ginger makes a witty retort, which Bechdel attributes to Barbara Smith: "I guess people can grasp the concept better if you call it 'stress' instead of 'oppression.'" This comment has the potential to carry weight: it exposes an ideological shortcoming, is theoretically astute, and is sharp enough to capture political imaginations. However, the moment it is articulated—in the second panel—is shared with Malika's exasperated response: Ginger must stop her evasion tactics and admit whether or not she is committed to the relationship. As the reader moves across the gutter and into the third panel, Ginger's insight is left behind; she pushes the report aside and becomes defensive. Across the final fourth and fifth panels, we see the characters' domestic dispute overwhelm the narrative as Ginger grasps at excuses for needing to live apart: she is too busy with her dissertation, she has school commitments, the apartment is too small for two.

Ginger's theoretically astute insight was transmitted successfully between the first and second panels; the panels show the transition from having successfully digested the report to having formulated a critically engaged counterresponse (it is notable that as Ginger reads the report, her expression is disgruntled, but at the point of articulating her response, she looks markedly pleased with herself). Ginger has the intellectual capability and access to queer/feminist/black cultural heritage to make insightful connections and translate them to the surrounding world. However, between the second and third panels, the results of this accomplishment are superseded by another desire: to defend herself and save face. Indeed, her motive for conjecturing in the first place was for just such reasons; Kathleen Stewart has recognized this as a hallmark of ordinary time, writing that "just about everyone is part of the secret conspiracy of everyday life to get what you can out of it" (41). However, in the context of the whole, it proves not quite as simple. In the final panel, the reader learns that it is not exactly the case that Malika has failed to absorb Ginger's comment. She gathers her belongings and inquires with an innocent air: "Will driving me to the airport be too much stress for you or should I take the bus?" Malika, then, has absorbed the content of Ginger's comment but is fully aware of the intention driving its articulation, so there is little room for her to reflect on it in earnest.

In this scene, both Malika and Ginger are able to cognitively absorb content while their attentions are focused elsewhere. What is registered in the gap between panels is less a failure of information transmitted, and more a failure of taking up and realizing information in smooth and anticipated ways. Bechdel attends to the ordinariness of these distortions, in the sense that this does not appear to be a failure of intelligence or a moral shortcoming on the part of the characters. It is significant that Ginger is employed as an academic, and her ability to cognitively absorb information is not in question; her professional aptitude for conceptual thinking, however, has little effect on the readiness with which she discards her insight when more everyday concerns press on her. I see some similarity here with Eve Sedgwick's late work, in which Sedgwick shifts, in her terms, from an interest in generating critical thought to an interest in how knowledge moves and what it *does* (*Touching Feeling*, 124). I am particularly interested in a moment where Sedgwick reflects on the way that knowing does not automatically necessitate a change in action or the sustained possession of that knowledge. There can often be, she notices, a "gap between knowing and realizing" ("Reality and Realization," 208). Sedgwick discusses how many in her circle would pride themselves on being able to absorb information quickly, so that it comes as a surprise to be confronted with the "statelier pace of realization and change" (209–10). Significantly, these gaps between knowing and realizing are not readily visible if one gains an image of critical theory through the relatively closed networks of academic papers and conferences. I suggest that, with its attunement to the everyday, *Dykes to Watch Out For* begins to answer Sedgwick's call for "the sense of how normal it is for realization to lag behind knowledge," so that the realization of ideas is "likely to be a hit-or-miss matter haplessly dependent on the contingencies of the individual" (209). I would also add that while *The Essential Dykes to Watch Out For* is perhaps not best understood through the kinds of high theory that so effectively illuminate Bechdel's memoirs, on the other hand, it is highly instructive with regard to the kind of labor and reaffirmation required to keep such minority networks of knowledge going.

Conclusion

If we take its mode of production into account, *The Essential Dykes to Watch Out For* benefits from being understood through everyday life studies. Doing so highlights the unique quality of the text: its capacity to bring us closer to the public cultures through which ideas must be transmitted if they are to be meaningfully realized. Bechdel's strips, as I have shown, can be considered as quasi case studies that present the kind of difficulties associated with transmitting ideas through public cultures that are teeming with distractions; in which people are consumed by the everyday activities, including all the quotidian acts of getting by and making the most out of what is available to them. In this way, the collection allows for a sobering estimation of the transformative powers of theory, showing how the realization of ideas depends on the desires and contingencies of individuals as they attempt to navigate ordinary life. This leads to one of my key arguments here: if certain forms or cultural products are particularly attuned to the everyday and its associated opacity, then it may be productive to consider schools of thought, queer theory being only one example, in light of how they surface in genres and forms other than the theoretical—especially those that are highly attuned to such snags and complications. It would be interesting to investigate whether such experiments could be as rewardingly conducted in other long-running strips; or whether *Dykes to Watch Out For* is unique in its self-conscious interest in the transmission of the ideas, however fragile, of particular cultures.

This chapter has stayed at the micro-level of close reading. However, a macro-scale investigation might be conducted to determine the place of queer theory—or other schools of theory for that matter—as it surfaces and develops throughout the collection as a whole. To conduct such an experiment, the compilation would need be taken as one large network to track, not only the relationship between panels directly next to one another, but also how individual panels fit within a wider whole. The aim would be to ask what the results are when it is acknowledged that, as Groensteen describes it, "every panel exists, potentially if not actually, in relation with each of the others" (146). Such an investigation risks being misunderstood as merely describing the "narrative flow" of the collection. This would fail to take into account the conditions of production: the lengthy and incremental temporality of the document. Bechdel has explained that, on commencing with the strip, she had no plan for where the narrative would end or what kind of shape it would ultimately take. She writes that keeping the strip relevant to her reading public was her major task: "People have a certain expectation, and they want what they've had before, but if you keep doing that, it dies. You have to find a way to change it just enough, but not too much to startle people" (quoted in Zuarino). As with any successful serial production, creators are attuned to what happens in public culture and try to shift to stay relevant to it, making compromises between necessary continuity and the need to function in the present (Geraghty, 18). Therefore such a wide-scale investigation, which would trace transmission across the collection as a whole, might have the advantage of gleaning shifts in lesbian public cultures, the speed and vivacity of such shifts—at least, that is, from the perspective of one particular creator and her attempts to stay relevant to her readership.

Some of the implications of these experiments seem academic in nature: reading queer theory through mediums other than the theoretical would allow interested scholars to discern a different, if not more accurate, picture of the life of theory. While I do not refute the merit of this approach in and of itself, I would argue that the implications are not abstract in nature. Meg-John Barker and Julia Schelle's 2016 *Queer: A Graphic History* is a comics history of queer studies. They begin by outlining the conceptual problems they face in trying to define queer theory and map its development, when so many queer theorists themselves refuse to say what queer theory is; but the authors nevertheless see their work as necessary, as a translation of the work of intellectual thinkers into "accessible language, and into everyday life and politics" (166). As their history nears its conclusion, they note emerging post-queer positions and comment on the sad irony that "one major problem with the idea that we're post-queer theory is that so few of its key ideas and questions have filtered into everyday life," which is shown by the fact that "around eighty percent of people have some kind of nonnormative sexuality, gender or relationship but around five percent identity as LGBT" (166). With this glaring disparity, they are drawn to conclude that "queer theory still has a major task: of communicating its ideas to the people and places that matter" (166). If *Queer: A Graphic History* aims to answer this pressing call by using the comics medium to render these ideas accessible, *The Essential Dykes to Watch Out For* offers different but related opportunities. Partly through individual disposition and style and partly through coincidence of its dates of production, the collection amasses an array of quasi case studies of the kinds of distortions that can occur as ideas move through public cultures. Itself part of the everyday, the collection draws the decades associated with queer theory together, contains them, and in doing so provides rare insight into where knowledge travels to "the people and places that matter," and the kinds of scenarios that prevent it from doing so.

NOTES

1. For notable studies of temporality in the field more broadly, see Grosz; Hemmings; Hesford; Browne; Love, *Feeling*.
2. On economy of style to heighten emphasis in comics, see Postema, 2.
3. Additionally, for women's counterpublics, see Berlant, 5–13; and for queer counterpublics, see Warner, vii–xxxi.
4. See also Braudel, 3.
5. For a study of the importance of public space for the women's movement, including independently run coffeehouses, see Enke.
6. Hesford makes a similar point about Kate Millet's autobiography *Flying*, which she sees as a "documentary of the present tense of the women's liberation" (158).

WORKS CITED

Barker, Meg-John, and Julia Scheele. *Queer: A Graphic History*. Icon, 2016.
Berlant, Lauren. *The Female Complaint: The Unfinished Business of Sentimentality in American Culture*. Duke University Press, 2008.
Bernstein, Robin. "'I'm Very Happy to Be in the Reality-Based Community': Alison Bechdel's *Fun Home*, Digital Photography, and George W. Bush." *American Literature* 89, no. 1 (2017): 121–54.
Best, Stephen, and Sharon Marcus. "Surface Reading: An Introduction." *Representations* 108, no. 1 (2009): 1–21.
Braudel, Fernand. *On History*. Trans. Sarah Matthews. University of Chicago Press, 1980.
Browne, Victoria. *Feminism, Time, and Nonlinear History*. Palgrave Macmillan, 2014.
Cvetkovich, Ann. "Drawing the Archive in Alison Bechdel's *Fun Home*." *WSQ: Women's Studies Quarterly* 36, nos. 1–2 (2008): 111–28.
Echols, Alice. *Daring to Be Bad: Radical Feminism in America, 1967–1975*. University of Minnesota Press, 1989.
English, James F., and Ted Underwood. "Shifting Scales: Between Literature and Social Science." *Modern Language Quarterly* 77, no. 3_(2016): 277–95.
Enke, Anne. *Finding the Movement: Sexuality, Contested Space, and Feminist Activism*. Duke University Press, 2007.
Felski, Rita. *Doing Time: Feminist Theory and Postmodern Culture*. New York University Press, 2000.
Gardiner, Judith. "Queering Genre: Alison Bechdel's *Fun Home: A Family Tragicomic* and *The Essential Dykes to Watch Out For*." *Contemporary Women's Writing* 5, no. 3 (2011): 188–207.
Geraghty, C. "Continuous Serial—a Definition." In *Coronation Street*, ed. Richard Dyer, 9–26. BFI, 1981.
Groensteen, Thierry. *The System of Comics*. Trans. Bart Beaty and Nick Nguyen. University Press of Mississippi, 2007.
Grosz, Elizabeth. *Time Travels: Feminism, Nature, Power*. Duke University Press, 2005.

Habermas, Jürgen. "The Public Sphere: An Encyclopedia Article." In *Critical Theory and Society: A Reader*, ed. Stephen E. Bronner and Douglas Kellner, 136–42. Routledge, 1989.

Hemmings, Clare. *Why Stories Matter: The Political Grammar of Feminist Theory*. Duke University Press, 2011.

Hesford, Victoria. *Feeling Women's Liberation*. Duke University Press, 2013.

Kahan, Benjamin. *Celibacies: American Modernism and Sexual Life*. Duke University Press, 2013.

Lefebvre, Henri. *Everyday Life in the Modern World*. Bloomsbury Academic, 2016.

Love, Heather. "Close but Not Deep." *New Literary History* 41, no. 2 (2010): 371–91.

Love, Heather. *Feeling Backward: Loss and the Politics of Queer History*. Harvard University Press, 2007.

Love, Heather. "Small Change: Realism, Immanence, and the Politics of the Micro." *Modern Language Quarterly* 77, no. 3 (2016): 419–45.

McBean, Sam. *Feminism's Queer Temporalities*. Routledge, 2015.

McCloud, Scott. *Understanding Comics*. HarperPerennial, 1994.

Postema, Barbara. *Narrative Structure in Comics: Making Sense of Fragments*. RIT Press, 2013.

Rohy, Valerie. "In the Queer Archive of *Fun Home*." *GLQ: A Journal of Lesbian and Gay Studies* 16, no. 3 (2010): 341–61.

Sedgwick, Eve Kosofsky. "Reality and Realization." In *The Weather in Proust*, ed. Jonathan Goldberg and Michael Moon, 206–15. Duke University Press, 2011.

Sedgwick, Eve Kosofsky, and Adam Frank. *Touching Feeling: Affect, Pedagogy, Performativity*. Duke University Press, 2003.

Stewart, Kathleen. *Ordinary Affects*. Duke University Press, 2007.

Tolmie, Jane. "Modernism, Memory and Desire: Queer Cultural Production in Alison Bechdel's *Fun Home*." *TOPIA: Canadian Journal of Cultural Studies* 22, no. 77 (2009): 77–95.

Warner, Michael. Introduction to *Fear of a Queer Planet*, ed. M. Warner, vii–xxxi. University of Minnesota Press, 1993.

Withers, Deborah. *Feminism, Digital Culture and the Politics of Transmission: Theory, Practice and Cultural Heritage*. Rowman & Littlefield, 2015.

Zuarino, John. "An Interview with Alison Bechdel." *Bookslut*, March 2007. Accessed October 13, 2017.

BECHDEL'S MEN AND MASCULINITY

Gay Pedant and Lesbian Man

JUDITH KEGAN GARDINER

With the portrayal of her father, Bruce Bechdel, in *Fun Home: A Family Tragicomic*, Alison Bechdel creates a haunting, complex, and ultimately tragic character who represents the vicissitudes of homosexual male life in the period of the "closet." This autobiographical memoir centers on the ambivalent relationship between her childhood avatar Alison and her father. During the same period in which she was writing the memoir, Bechdel invented another unique character who can be seen as Bruce's comic opposite. The countercultural Stuart Goodman appears in the final years of her long-running comics strip series, *Dykes to Watch Out For*, as the partner and ally of a lesbian woman and as the devoted father of a little girl.[1] These men represent the contradictions of American masculinity in the late twentieth century and the early twenty-first, contradictions also described in current scholarship in masculinity studies. Through these two unconventional and personal portraits, Bechdel demonstrates sad past and optimistic future visions of the masculinity of American men while also portraying a third possibility—that of lesbian women's masculinity. In the "Cartoonist's Introduction" to *The Indelible Alison Bechdel*, the artist explains that her early "propensity for an all-male cast" cannot be entirely explained by the "tidy feminist analysis" that culturally men are shown as closer to "neutral, generic people" than conventional representations of women. Instead she admits to a childhood "fascinated by masculinity" and to identifying in fantasy with an "imaginary world of tough men" (*Indelible*, 16, 28).

Similarly, years later in *The Essential Dykes to Watch Out For*, Bechdel describes how as a child she had "a curious fixation with the iconography of masculinity" and drew only male figures for years until she asked herself, "What if I stopped drawing guys and started drawing Dykes?" (*Essential*, viii, xiii). That she could draw lesbians came as a welcome revelation when she began her commercial cartooning career in 1983 (xiv). Twenty years of drawing mostly women followed. But she did continue drawing men, centering

Fun Home on her father's dilemma as a closeted gay man trying to live up to mid-twentieth-century American ideals of manhood. In both *Fun Home* and *Dykes to Watch Out For*, Bechdel draws herself as a butch lesbian who displays a masculine self-presentation while preferring the company of women (*Essential*, viii). Then, when she wrote her autobiographical memoir, the relationship between her father and herself became the central theme—and the question of whether his death had been a suicide, its central enigma.

The memoir's narrator Alison grows up and comes out as a butch lesbian, while her father Bruce, a married funeral home director and high school English teacher, secretly has sexual affairs with his male students and other men. Bruce is sometimes attentive and caring with his three children, but more often he is an authoritarian father who makes his children perform household tasks and strikes them in fits of rage. "In theory," Bechdel says, "his arrangement with my mother was more cooperative. In practice, it was not" (*FH*, 13). When he dies after being hit by a truck, college student Alison describes him as having "**killed himself** because he was a manic-depressive, closeted **fag** and he couldn't face living in this small-minded small town one more **second**" (*FH*, 125). However, her description in the memoir is more complex than this summary, showing him as a man of artistic talent who is filled with shame and self-loathing internalized from the homophobic culture around him. Moreover, while Bruce embodies the tortured male homosexuality of the period, he also demonstrates the broader contradictions of a mid-twentieth-century American masculinity divided between egalitarian aspirations and assumptions of male entitlement.

Bruce first appears in *Fun Home* as a father depicted in a panel playing "airplane" with young Alison, balancing her outstretched body on his raised legs while he lies next to a copy of *Anna Karenina* (*FH*, 3), forecasting his death as a suicide and reminding us that whereas "all happy families are alike, each unhappy family is unhappy in its own way." *Fun Home*'s opening words are "like many fathers," as Bechdel casts Bruce as sometimes typical of other men and fathers, and sometimes as different. In text placed in the gutter above the panel, narrator Bechdel judges the "discomfort" of the game of airplane "well worth the rare physical contact" and "certainly worth the moment of perfect balance when I soared above him" (*FH*, 3). This "perfect balance" between father and child is rare, however, for Bruce is dictatorial about his daughter's behavior, appearance, and domestic environment. Despite her insistence that she "**hate**[s] pink" and "**hate**[s] flowers," he discounts her decorating preferences by saying "tough titty," thus taking on the role of a rejecting mother who will not breast-feed her child, a role Bechdel ascribes to her own distant mother in an autobiographical interview with two psychoanalysts years later (*FH*, 7; Critchfield and Pula). A scene of the three Bechdel children sitting around the

Fig. 4.1. Bruce, in a rage (*FH*, 21).

Christmas tree is offered with the comment "Sometimes, when things were going well, I think my father actually enjoyed having a family. Or at least the air of authenticity we lent to his exhibit. A sort of still life with children" (*FH*, 13). This tableau is ironically juxtaposed with Jimmy Stewart's happy family in the Christmas movie *It's a Wonderful Life* playing on the Bechdels' television set (13). In Bechdel's illustration of the scene, Bruce's dark silhouette, glass in hand, stands bisected by the borderline of the comic panel. In her use of black and white with green wash, Bechdel shows her father's contrasting moods as they colored her childhood, sometimes conventionally paternal, but often unpredictably angry and menacing. On one page, for example, Bruce, in a rage at his family, smashes a glass on the floor, but in another panel at the bottom of the same page, he calmly reads to Alison from Kipling's *Just So* stories and sings to her, "Won't you be my pony girl? Marry me," as she lies tucked up in bed (*FH*, 21; fig. 4.1).

Many scenes of her childhood emphasize Bruce's efforts, against Alison's resistance, to reinforce her feminine gender and the imperative social conformity. She insists on her ingenuous straightforwardness in contrast to his moral deceptiveness and "artifice" (*FH*, 16). She is "Spartan" to his "Athenian," "butch to his nelly" (15). He enlists his children in housework to maintain their house as a shrine to his aesthetic values, values so strict that he takes over her *Wind in the Willows* coloring book because she puts blue where he thinks yellow belongs (130). Although one might consider Bruce's aesthetic interests as feminine, he enforces them on his children with masculine authority. Thus, though Bechdel draws a photograph of her father as a young man in drag as "lissome" and "elegant," she represents her experience of him as a father as commanding and masculine (120). At home and at church, he acts as a traditional patriarch. However, as she does not discover until she is in college, his facade of social conformity has cracks: "He appeared to be an ideal husband and father . . . but would an ideal husband and father have sex with teenage boys?" (17).

The sociologist and masculinity theorist Michael Kimmel states that the "unifying emotional subtext" for "the guy code" of young American men "involves never showing emotions or admitting to weakness," presenting a surface that shows "everything is under control. . . . Winning is crucial. Kindness is not an option, nor is compassion." This is "what it means to be a man," Kimmel reports, describing masculinity norms in the United States for much of the twentieth century (*Guyland*, 45). Appearing to follow these codes, Bruce presents a conventional masculine demeanor. What we see of his gay sexual life is covert and predatory. He plies a handsome adolescent with beer, is arrested on a tip from the boy's brother, and is sent to a male psychiatrist—with whom he flirts. But despite his wife's anxiety, the incident passes without dire consequences. Bruce maintains his aesthetic confidence and the disdainful mastery of his pedagogy, where he is shown reading *Architectural Digest* magazine while conducting a high school English class. Bechdel notes her father's "awesome capacity for cognitive dissonance" in this case, at the same time that she grows closer to him when she takes his English class in high school (*FH*, 199).

In contrast to these displays of masculine competence and assurance is Bruce's "shame" and "fully developed self-loathing," which Bechdel says fills their house like the smell of antique furniture (*FH*, 20). Bruce's homosexual behavior, which his wife Helen describes to teenaged Alison—night cruising in Manhattan and catching a lice infestation—comprises actions that are crude and masculine, not sissy-like (216). Thus what we see in the ways Bechdel draws Bruce's behavior occasionally verges on the homoerotic but is mostly normatively masculine, including his domestic reign over his family and his violent rages (21). This tension is never resolved, as Bechdel represents Bruce's contradictory performance of normatively masculine behavior and what she later perceives as his suppressed longings to embody femininity.

Current theories of masculinity include simple role theory relying on dominance, which Bruce enforces on his family, and psychological approaches to masculine gender as defensive differentiation from women. His impassioned courtship letters to Helen, as his future wife, show him deftly playing the role of heterosexual lover, while his later domestic behavior enforces his dominance over his wife and children. Moreover, though homosexual himself, Bruce is homophobic. He sneers at the butch lesbian truck driver whom child Alison recognizes "with a surge of joy" (*FH*, 118), and he directs his students to criticize the homosexual teacher in *The Catcher in the Rye* (199). Bruce met Helen in a college performance of *The Taming of the Shrew*, about which Bechdel comments that it is a "troubling play" in which the "willful Katherine's spirit is broken by the mercenary, domineering Petrucchio" (69). Bruce shares with hegemonic masculinity this masculine desire for dominance, an impatience with any kind of weakness, and internalized homophobia.

When a judge sentences Bruce to see a psychiatrist after he is arrested for buying beer for a thirteen-year-old, Alison at first finds the incident an "exhilarating" "approximation" of her "dull, provincial life to a *New Yorker* cartoon," but she is soon deflated by her "father's abject and shameful mien," as he tells her, "I'm bad, not good like you" (*FH*, 153). In this illustration, he faces her across the cartoon panel, tight-lipped, eyes cast downward as the steam from his coffee cup shapes a question mark in the air (153; fig. 4.2).

Kimmel claims that homophobia is almost universal in men: the "homophobic flight from intimacy with other men," he says, "is the repudiation of the homosexual within—never completely successful and hence constantly reenacted in every homosocial relationship" ("Masculinity," 63). He argues that "homophobia, men's fear of other men, is the animating condition of the dominant definition of masculinity in America," and this masculinity is at its core "a defensive effort to prevent being emasculated" (50, 67). It is in congruence with such theories that Bechdel describes Alison's unspoken verdict at her father's funeral that Bruce "was a manic-depressive, closeted **fag**" who "couldn't face living in this small-minded small town" (*FH*, 125). That is, Alison solves the mystery of her father's death, which animates all of *Fun Home*, by appealing to a diagnosis of individual mental illness, the contradictions of closeted homosexual life in rural America, and the pervasive hostility of hegemonic masculine ideology to Bruce's character and interests. On the same page as Bechdel depicts Alison's rebellious unspoken thoughts at her father's funeral, her next mirroring panel shows Alison, like her mother and brothers, outwardly conforming to social conventions for funerals while inwardly identifying with her father's suicidal impulses, thinking, "I'd kill myself too if I had to live here" (125).

Fig. 4.2. "I'm bad, not good like you" (*FH*, 153).

Whereas Bruce's early death seems tragically overdetermined by social and psychological factors, Bechdel creates Bruce's comic opposite in the allegorically named Stuart Goodman, one of the central characters in the later years of her long-running serialized comic strip, *Dykes to Watch Out For*. Until Stuart's arrival, males are peripheral in *Dykes*. They include the conventional father and brother of Mo, Bechdel's version of herself in the series; her girlfriend Sydney's snobbish professor father; and Clarice and Toni's son Raffi, who is traditionally masculine in behavior, though he gets in fights with his schoolmates when he once decides to wear nail polish. Bechdel explains that "for a long time" she "didn't have men in the strip except as background characters" because "there were already enough male characters in the world." Instead she wanted her male readers to be "forced to identify with the women characters, the way women and people of color are expected to identify with the zillions of 'universal' white male protagonists" in popular culture. However, because she didn't want Raffi "to be all alone," she introduced Carlos as his attentive, unemployed gay Hispanic babysitter (*Indelible*, 69).

In contrast to these minor and often stereotypical characters, Stuart models a new kind of man. A late addition to the central characters of the series,

Stuart is an original creation whom we might consider Bechdel's comically utopian alternative to the self-loathing Bruce. Stuart enters the series in 1997, about the time when the cartoonist begins shaping her memoir about her father. Bruce is an angry, neglectful husband and the father of three children. He is also handsome, vain, a closeted homosexual, a churchgoing Catholic, a small business owner, a social conformist, domestic tyrant, and high school teacher who has sexual relations with some of his male students. Stuart is opposite to Bruce in nearly every respect. He is a scruffy, chubby, bearded and balding agnostic Jew, a social activist, environmentalist, and LGBTQ ally, who comes to live communally and counterculturally with his partner Sparrow and her lesbian household. Later he becomes the devoted father of a daughter. He is unafraid of contradictions and apparently free of homophobia.

Bechdel introduces us to Bruce in *Fun Home* by showing him playing with Alison as a child before describing his harsh behavior to his children. The book's opening game of airplane is a rare exception to his general lack of physical affection or contact with them. Bruce's death in a highway accident is foreshadowed early in *Fun Home*, while his past as a "stuck in the mud" child, a soldier taunted for his bookish ways, a writer of romantic letters to his future wife, and an active homosexual is treated thematically rather than in chronological order, as we are shown over the course of the memoir's non-linear presentation the tightening constrictions on his life leading to his early death (*FH*, 40). In the cartoon serial *DTWOF*, in contrast, events are chronological, with incidents in the lives of the characters unrolling in relation to, parallel with, and temporally bound by the political and popular history that Bechdel includes via headlines and gutter-level commentary in her comic illustrations. The options for her characters expand as they grow older, even as their lesbian community loses its distinctiveness and blends into the American mainstream.

Stuart is first introduced as the surprise date—surprise because male—of Asian American Sparrow, a lesbian feminist activist who lives communally with sister lesbians African American college teacher Ginger and white bookstore employee Lois. When Stuart's car runs off the road on winter ice, Lois rifles through his wallet to find his AAA card, deciding "maybe he **is** a lesbian" when she discovers his little amount of cash and low bank account, his "groovy p.c. credit card, co-op membership, and therapist's card": "If that's straight white male privilege, we're not missing much," she concludes (*Essential*, 198). Stuart is briefly shown at his job as a progressive fund-raiser, wearing a jacket and tie as he argues to a male bureaucrat from the Goliath Health Plan that the plan should help provide food for old people: "Consider your bottom line, Mr. Flack!" Stuart argues. "Did you know every dollar spent on nutrition saves $3.25 in hospital costs?" (*Essential*, 203). Sparrow has strong radical feminist views that often indict men, though she is ambivalently dating Stuart and finally decides to have sex with him. She criticizes Lois, who likes to appear in drag performances, by saying, "Men are destroying the planet! Why compete to see who can mimic them most convincingly?" (232). However, Sparrow seems to make an exception for Stuart in her antimale views, and they are soon a steady couple, while she adjusts her self-description to identify as a "bisexual lesbian" (230).

In contrast to Bruce's shame and self-loathing, Stuart's shame is largely political, although he does regret that he could not afford to support a family financially as his father did. He moves in with Sparrow, Ginger, and Lois "in a quasi-marriage of convenience," the cash-strapped lesbian housemates welcoming him as a paying renter (*Essential*, 210). He goes to Pride celebrations in 2000 when his women housemates stay home, but avoids the 2004 Gay Pride events, instead joining Mo, Bechdel's avatar, at the "Gay Shame" counterdemonstration—which Mo suggests should be "**American** shame," to "make it more inclusive"—so as "to protest how Pride has gotten so corporate" (311). His politics are not just symbolic but active and economic. For example, he suggests that Lois give her tax rebate "to the homeless alliance . . . thanks to the matching grant program" he set up (264). He proves eager but not very competent at home improvement projects, in another contrast to *Fun Home*'s Bruce. When Sparrow announces she's a "bi-dyke," Stuart declares he thinks he "is a butch lesbian in a straight man's body" and is countered by his housemates' reply: "**Soft** butch. **May**-be" (230). He sometimes wears a T-shirt that says, "I'm not a lesbian but my girlfriend is," and he's fine with Lois dating "a genderqueer boy dyke geek with an oxford cloth fetish" who followed her home "from the [2000] Democratic convention protests" (245, 248). He plays Powerpuff Girls with a lesbian friend's son, Jonas, who wants to become a girl (262). He remains political in an idealistic way throughout the series: after 9/11 he and Sparrow fast to extend their "energy to heal and transform the tragedy," with Sparrow saying they can make their ideal real and "change the world by living as if" (268).

Sparrow wants Stuart to get a vasectomy to avoid birth control worries, but he replies, "You know I want to have a baby eventually" (*Essential*, 274). The couple is affectionate with each other, kissing as "baby bear" and "baby bunny" (275). When accidentally pregnant Sparrow says she may have an abortion, Stuart cries from disappointment. Lois tells Stuart he would "make a great father," and Ginger responds, "People say that about any half-sentient male as long as he's not actually a convicted pedophile," a glancing allusion to *FH*'s Bruce. In reply, Stuart says that may not be a disqualification for many men, but he "**would** be a good father" (279). Stuart is enthusiastic when he sees his baby's ultrasounds, saying, "Believe me, in this house, we have very few preconceived ideas about what a girl is" (286). Shortly after the baby arrives, Stuart quits his job. The next thing the members of the usually chaotic household know, "the walk is shoveled, the house is warm and clean, dinner's cooking," baby Jiao Raizel has had her bath, and Stuart exclaims, "Quitting my job was the best thing I ever did" (303). Proud of his new role, Stuart starts a blog called *Subversive Parenting: Notes from a Stay-at-Home-Dad*, and he insists that his daughter is "never setting foot inside one of those conforming mills," as he deems regular schools (313, 316).

Stuart opposes (and is opposite to) hegemonic masculinity in many respects, though he also embodies some of the traditional positive masculine values that Kimmel describes as aspects of "democratic manhood," like responsible fatherhood and engaged citizenship (*Manhood*, 293). Stuart is poor and frugal and makes some foolish decisions, like selling the car his partner needs for work. Although often self-righteously "politically correct," he can generously waive his doctrinaire ideas. For example, though a vegetarian, he buys meat for a conservative young lesbian when his housemates invite her to move in. "Straight," but attracted only to lesbians, he keeps his baby daughter strapped to his body, in yet another contrast to the physically distant Bruce. During the 2008 presidential election, Stuart argues that even though Hillary Clinton is a "hawk, we need a woman president because it'll empower girls to be leaders, and that's our only hope for ever dismantling the patriarchy" (*Essential*, 389). Like Voltaire's Candide, the innocent Stuart ends the series in 2008 planting his own garden, with his young daughter by his side, so that his household can be food self-sufficient (390; fig. 4.3). Stuart may thus be seen as Bechdel's harbinger of a new, twenty-first-century model of heterosexuality, fatherhood, and masculinity.

Stuart's biggest differences from the repressed and conventional Bruce are his emotional openness and vulnerability, his willingness to admit his errors, and his loyalty to his lesbian-centered countercultural community. Bruce belongs to the conventional institutions of middle-class America but is alienated and unhappy in all of them as soldier, husband, church-attending Roman Catholic, and disengaged high school teacher. In contrast, Stuart is one comic but hopeful model of masculinity centered on caring fatherhood and egalitarian gender relations. The sociologist Barbara Risman reinforces this view when she makes fathering a central point in her campaign for a less sexist future: "When males take full responsibility for child care," she says, "they develop intimate and affectionate relationships with their children," and "nurturing their children is good for men's health" as well (quoted in Kimmel, *Manhood*, 296).

Kimmel positions the experience of humiliation as central to the development of heterosexual masculinity; anxiety about humiliation and ridicule is

Fig. 4.3. Stuart planting his garden (*Essential*, 390).

a common theme in popular culture as well, and numerous digital platforms have emerged where men express this shared anxiety. For example, the Good Men Project, a site begun by Tom Matlack, features content created by a community of users that "explore[s] the world of men and manhood in a way that no company ever has ("About Us"). It claims most American men fear "rejection, irrelevance, and disappointment," which together "add up to the fear of failure—of failing to be . . . a man" ("About Us"). Similarly, a user on the social platform for readers Goodreads claims that while most women fear rape and death, "most men fear getting laughed at or humiliated by a romantic prospect" (de Becker). Bechdel's portrait of Stuart Goodman conversely shows the strength of the man who is not afraid of looking ridiculous to others. In a congruent theme, the feminist theorist Jack Halberstam outlines a queer theory of failure as socially progressive because it counters the capitalist values of accumulation and material success with failure and therefore with the ability to bring fresh perspectives forward (*Queer Art of Failure*).

Stuart's deviation from hegemonic masculinity doesn't make him feminine. He wears a kind of kilt that his housemate Lois refers to as a skirt, but

Fig. 4.4. Mailing anti-Trump postcards ("New 'Dykes'").

his bushy-bearded, balding appearance remains masculine, as do his assertiveness and sense that he knows what is best for his family and community, though he usually does consult with his household. Bechdel has said she decided to expand beyond a solely lesbian cast because she wanted to include in her comics more "people who share" her "worldview," not just those who are "queer like me," and Stuart is often shown as a parallel figure to Bechdel's cartoon alter ego Mo (Levine, 57).

Unlike the long-running television cartoon series *The Simpsons*, in which over thirty years the characters stay the same age, Bechdel's imagination has her characters changing in response to the changing history and circumstances of the postmillennial United States. After Donald Trump was elected president in 2016, Bechdel drew a few additional *DTWOF* strips. In "Postcards from the Edge," Stuart wears a T-shirt that says "Make America Think Again" and a pro-feminist "pussy" hat to protest Trump's sexual harassment boasts; Stuart sits at a table with his partner, daughter, and friends, collecting anti-Trump postcards to mail to the president ("New 'Dykes'"; fig. 4.4).[2] That is, Stuart remains still partnered with Sparrow and caring for his daughter Jiao Raizel, still counterculturally overzealous, and still a political dissident. In this update long after Bechdel stopped regularly drawing and publishing *DTWOF*, he is still a leftist, progressive, at times ridiculous counterculture figure and a close and loving father to his daughter.

Bechdel's contrasted portraits of Bruce and Stuart indicate some issues and idiosyncrasies of contemporary American male masculinities. She also treats masculinities as they appear in women, especially in butch lesbians like herself. *Fun Home* traces many of Alison's conflicts with her father to her rejection of femininity, and her efforts at more masculine self-presentation as a response to counter his efforts to coerce her into gender conformity. She gives many examples of her preference for masculine gender and self-representation both in her autobiographical memoir and in her life. *Fun Home* shows Alison visiting Europe as a youngster and being elated when she gets permission to go topless at the beach like the local boys (*FH*, 73). She revolts against her father's desire to decorate her bedroom with flowered wallpaper and adorn her with accessories like hair barrettes and a pearl necklace (99). Bechdel draws the child Alison as consistently resisting everything feminine and often as explicitly preferring a masculine self-presentation. For example, she describes getting a sensual, almost forbidden feeling of pleasure in putting on her father's formal clothes, although the game of dress-up fizzles when her visiting female buddy loses interest (182).

The connection between the flight from the feminine and its connotations of an unwelcome sexuality is made explicit in *Fun Home* when the three Bechdel children visit an earthmoving machine engaged in mountaintop removal. A neighborhood man gives Bruce a nude pinup calendar, and Bruce warns Alison that the picture is "dirty." Although she says that the calendar looks "clean enough" to her, she absorbs the message that such provocatively sexual images are dangerous, and so she tries to persuade her brothers to call her Albert rather than Alison (*FH*, 111, 113). Similarly, she enjoys being nicknamed "butch" by some local boys when playing ball (96), and she identifies herself as "butch" in opposition to her father's "nelly" (96, 15). Throughout *Fun Home* Alison repeatedly enjoys passing as a boy and shrinks from feminine identification.[3]

In *DTWOF*, Bechdel's lesbians display a variety of gender appearances and behavior, but most of the main characters are 1990s-style fit and fairly androgynous lesbians with short hair and no clear-cut role differentiations between members of the couples, even when they decide to have children. Mo, Bechdel's version of herself in the series, is distinguished by her eternal striped polo shirt and grumpy, politically correct attitude, while one of her girlfriends, the feminist theorist Sydney, models "femme aggressiveness" and goes into debt from her susceptibility to consumer goods (*Essential*, 178). One of the longest-established couples in the series is Toni, a Hispanic accountant, and her African American lawyer partner, Clarice. Both have curly hair, wear trousers, and don't fall into obvious gender roles, even though Toni is their son's biological mother.

The major character who might most consistently be characterized through the concept of female masculinity in appearance and behavior is Lois, the cheerfully promiscuous housemate of Sparrow and Ginger (and later Stuart), who looks like the Belgian boy cartoon hero Tintin and delights in engaging in drag performances (see Thalheimer in this volume for readings of Stuart, Sparrow, and Lois). Lois teases Mo by pretending to take hormones and transitioning to becoming a man, but finally admits, "I enjoy being a girl. In a perverse kind of way" (*Essential*, 262). On the other hand, the boy Jonas, son of Lois's girlfriend Jasmine, who is transitioning to being a girl named

Janis, is shown as selfish and petty, not wanting to help with chores lest her arms get "all muscley" and her fingernails mussed (372). Janis is perhaps the most stereotypically feminine character in *DTWOF*, and the most negatively portrayed.

Jack Halberstam argues that "masculinity must not and cannot and should not reduce down to the male body and its effects," and that lesbian masculinity is not an imitation of male masculinity but rather a powerful and independent gender formation (*Female Masculinity*, 1). Halberstam argues that female masculinity disrupts the conventional connection between cultural privilege, misogyny, and male embodiment and so negates current masculinity theory, which Halberstam says "always boils down to the social, cultural and political effects of male embodiment and male privilege"; instead, strength and physical dominance should be considered not male attributes or even human potentials but specifically aspects of female masculinity (Halberstam, "Good," 345).

Bechdel in *DTWOF* adopts a broader, more flexible approach to the potentials of gender; thus the lesbians over the course of the serial vary in their gender presentations and attitudes. In both *Fun Home* and *DTWOF*, Bechdel portrays and sometimes celebrates her sense of herself as a masculine person and the claims of lesbians in general to be "more highly evolved" than other people (*Essential*, xv). In the "Cartoonist's Introduction" to *DTWOF*, she makes this claim with tongue in cheek as she explains the origin of her career as a cartoonist: "I saw my cartoons as an antidote to the prevailing image of lesbians as warped, sick, humorless, and undesirable" or, in the other popular extreme stereotype, as gorgeous supermodels. She continues, "But by drawing the everyday lives of women like me, I hoped to make lesbians more visible not just to ourselves but to everyone. . . . If people could only see us, how could they help but love us," since "lesbians were so awesome! . . . At the forefront of every social justice movement" (*Essential*, xv).

In speaking about herself, Bechdel is agnostic about her masculine self-representation. She says that her gender performance grew by imitating men's masculinity because in her family, where both her mother and father disparaged women and preferred men, "it was safer to be a boy" (Critchfield and Pula). She explains:

> Therapy helped me to access my grief and understand the structure of my family . . . where my own neuroses come from. . . . And I do not actually give a lot of thought to "why I'm gay," but obviously it could be both genetic and environmental in my case, but it does not really explain my butchness, my masculinity, and my decision to present myself in a more masculine way. (Critchfield and Pula)

But whereas Halberstam's theory of female masculinity may be too restrictive, Halberstam's exposition of the advantages of queer "failure" does suggest alternatives to masculine and capitalist mainstream goals, possibilities to express "a basic desire to live life otherwise" that Bechdel also explores, not only through her dykes but also through her character Stuart (Halberstam, *Queer*, 2). This glimpse of an alternative and nonsexist masculinity is congruent, as well, with Judith Newton's analysis of countercultural progressive men for whom political opposition to the capitalist mainstream provides ego strength and self-esteem. Newton describes her "project" as "not just to reenchant the category 'men'" but the invention of "specific subjectivities for men that are more responsive than before to at least some female feminist demands." Newton goes on: "One new ideal, for example, is that of the 'generative father,' a man who takes on housework and physical and emotional care of children ... as an essential part of his own personal growth" and as congruent with a "model of manhood based primarily on the struggle for social justice" (Newton, 180–81). Such a reconfiguration of sexist norms could lead "to the massive reconstruction of dominant masculine behaviors and ideals—economic individualism, the obsessive pursuit of winning and success, the suppression of tenderness and nurturing" and "that time-consuming and lowly labor of doing for others" (190).

Masculinity theorists like Kimmel and Raewyn Connell stress the toxic and unjust aspects of hegemonic or dominant masculinity. Connell regrets that "the pattern of difference/dominance is so deeply embedded in culture, institutions, and body-reflexive practices that it functions as a limit to the rights-based politics of reform" (Connell, 232). People now tend to reject a critique of male dominance as an attack on difference, he claims, leading to "gender vertigo and violence," an insistence on trying to retain the gender status quo ante rather than being willing to try more egalitarian practices (233).

Kimmel, too, emphasizes the negative aspects of most historical masculinity formations as homophobic, racist, heterosexist, and sexist. Many American men, he says, react to contemporary movements for women's equality with hostility and a failure to adapt to new conditions. He argues that masculinities have historically been antifeminine, homosocial, homophobic, racist, heterosexist, and sexist, and now they are characterized by an aggrieved "entitlement" (Kimmel, *Manhood*, 244). American men, he claims, feel powerless, fearful of emasculation and humiliation by other men and by women. However, he does hold out a positive possibility for the future of male masculinity, which he calls "democratic manhood"—"a manhood of responsibility, tested, and finally proved, in the daily acts that give our lives meaning ... egalitarian, accepting and even embracing the equality of the women in our lives, and preparing our children for the lives they will surely live of greater gender and sexual equality." A crucial part of democratic positive masculinity is nurturing fatherhood (Kimmel, *Manhood* 293, 297). In the context of such positive theories, we can see Bechdel's Stuart as similarly proleptic, as an original portrait of a progressive, countercultural man, one willing to seem ridiculous to the mainstream—and sometimes to his partner and commune—to consciously live and promote his own values of gender equality, ecological awareness, and sexual liberation for all people.

In her preface to *Dykes to Watch Out For*, Bechdel asks her readers whether lesbians are "more highly evolved" than everyone else. Are they "essentially the same," "or essentially different"? (*Essential*, xviii). One charm of her comics series is surely that she has captured both, portraying a rich lesbian community that is positive, celebratory, and depathologizing. Now that the normality of the LGBTQA community is less in doubt to the American mainstream than when Bechdel began cartooning, however, we may be more appreciative of her particular accomplishment in the creations of her two most striking and evocative male figures: on the one hand, her father Bruce Bechdel as a version of the tragic era of the closet that also demonstrates the tragedy of hegemonic—and hence heterosexual—masculinity, which placed such harsh and restrictive pressures on men; and on the other, the idealistic, optimistic, if at times ludicrous portrait of Stuart Goodman, who avoids toxic masculinity by fully investing in countercultural values, even as the counterculture itself has disappeared, and in being an ally to sexual and gender nonconformists.

Both books end with hints of alternative futures, even for the doomed Bruce. *Fun Home* ends with Bruce reversing the myth of Icarus and the "Icarian games" with which the book begins by "being there" to "catch" child Alison when she "leapt" into a swimming pool. In contrast, the kilted, bearded, and still politically correct Stuart, disappointed that his partner doesn't agree to having a second child, ends the strip *Dykes to Watch Out For* by explaining to his daughter that she can't have an inflatable pool in her backyard because "we need that space" to be "completely food self-sufficient" in future winters.

NOTES

1. I contrast the genres of tragic *Fun Home* and comic *Dykes* in Gardiner, "Queering Genre."
2. Bechdel, channeling Stuart, asks her readers to do the same.
3. As Bechdel herself describes her pleasure in being hailed as a young man and asked to carry a piece of furniture up the stairs (Bechdel, "Alison"). This story appeared as a comic in a 1995 *Dykes to Watch Out For* calendar (image for the month of May) under the title "My Life as a Boy" and is reprinted with other autobiographical writing in *Indelible* (56).

WORKS CITED

"About Us." The Good Men Project. 2018. Accessed March 14, 2018.

Bechdel, Alison. "Alison Bechdel's Shortest-Ever Job." *New Yorker Radio Hour*, August 25, 2017. Accessed March 14, 2018.

Bechdel, Alison. "New 'Dykes to Watch Out For' Tackles the Ides of Trump." *Seven Days*, March 14, 2017. Accessed July 17, 2019.

Connell, Raewyn. *Gender in World Perspective*. 2nd ed. Polity, 2009.

Connell, R. W. *Masculinities*. 2nd ed. University of California Press, 2005.

Critchfield, Adam R., and Jack Pula. "On Psychotherapy, LGBT Identity, and Cultural Visibility: In Conversation with Alison Bechdel." *Journal of Gay and Lesbian Mental Health* 19, no. 4 (2015): 397–412.

de Becker, Gavin. *The Gift of Fear and Other Survival Signals That Protect Us from Violence*. Dell, 1999. Quoted on Goodreads.com. Accessed March 14, 2018.

Gardiner, Judith. "Queering Genre: Alison Bechdel's *Fun Home: A Family Tragicomic* and *The Essential Dykes to Watch Out For*." *Contemporary Women's Writing* 5, no. 3 (2011): 188–207.

Gardiner, Judith Kegan. "Female Masculinity and Phallic Women—Unruly Concepts." *Feminist Studies* 38, no. 3 (2012): 584–611.

Halberstam, Judith. *Female Masculinity*. Duke University Press, 1998.

Halberstam, Judith. "The Good, the Bad, and the Ugly: Men, Women, and Masculinity." In *Masculinity Studies and Feminist Theory: New Directions*, ed. Judith Kegan Gardiner, 344–67. Columbia University Press, 2002.

Halberstam, Judith. *The Queer Art of Failure*. Duke University Press, 2011.

Kimmel, Michael S. *Guyland: The Perilous World Where Boys Become Men*. Harper, 2008.

Kimmel, Michael S. *Manhood in America: A Cultural History*. 3rd ed. Oxford University Press, 2012.

Kimmel, Michael S. "Masculinity as Homophobia: Fear, Shame, and Silence in the Construction of Gender Identity." In *Sex, Gender, and Sexuality: The New Basics; An Anthology*, ed. Abby L. Ferber, Kimberly Holcomb, and Tre Wentling, 58–70. Oxford University Press, 2009.

Levine, Judith. "The Dykes Next Door." *Ms.* 11, no. 6 (October–November 2001): 52–58.

Newton, Judith. "Masculinity Studies: The Longed For Profeminist Movement for Academic Men." In *Masculinity Studies and Feminist Theory: New Directions*, ed. Judith Kegan Gardiner, 176–92. Columbia University Press, 2002.

MO VAN PELT

Dykes to Watch Out For and Peanuts

MICHELLE ANN ABATE

Mo Testa, the beloved protagonist of Alison Bechdel's comic strip *Dykes to Watch Out For*, has been seen as an autobiographically inflected representation of the cartoonist. The two figures share a strong physical resemblance: both Mo and Bechdel sport short black hair, wear glasses, and have a lanky physique. In addition, they possess a variety of similar personality traits: as the cartoonist has commented, Mo reflects her tendency to be insecure, neurotic, and obsessive (Critchfield and Pula, 399). While Mo has long been viewed autobiographically, I offer an alternative way of approaching and understanding her character. Mo Testa certainly functions as Bechdel's alter ego, but I make a case that she may also have her roots or origins in a well-known character from US comics: Linus van Pelt, from Charles Schulz's *Peanuts*. Slightly younger than the other characters in the comic, Linus is the best friend of main character, Charlie Brown. Linus is also the most contemplative, introspective, and—with his beloved blue blanket—insecure character in the comic: the traits that typify Bechdel's Mo.

Alison Bechdel was born in 1960, the year Christopher Caldwell identifies as the beginning of the golden age of *Peanuts*. While Schulz's newspaper strip debuted in 1950, its heyday occurred during the following decade. Throughout the 1960s and early 1970s, the period of Bechdel's youth, *Peanuts* permeated American print, popular, and material culture, a phenomenon that coincided with Bechdel's childhood. The future cartoonist grew up at a time when *Peanuts* wielded massive cultural presence and powerful creative influence. Given the ubiquity of Schulz's strip during the 1960s and 1970s, it seems certain that Bechdel was not merely exposed to, but would have been familiar with, Schulz's characters—including Linus—while she was growing up. This essay recuperates the popularity of *Peanuts* during Bechdel's formative years. I contend that Schulz's strip exerted an influence on *Dykes to Watch Out For*.

Accordingly, I do so by examining a variety of compelling and heretofore overlooked areas of overlap that exist between *DTWOF* and *Peanuts*. More specifically, Mo recalls key facets of Linus's personality. Exploring the similarities between Mo and Linus reveals a compelling kinship between Bechdel's work and one of the best-known strips in the history of American comics, while it also sheds new light on the relationship that *DTWOF* has to history, popular culture, and life writing. The way Bechdel may have consciously or unconsciously incorporated facets of Schulz's comic adds a new dimension to how we understand her life informing her work. Much has been written about how happenings in *DTWOF* were influenced by events that were taking place during Bechdel's adulthood as she composed the strips. The elements of *Peanuts* suggest that *DTWOF* may have been just as significantly shaped by cultural experiences from the cartoonist's childhood.

"A Profound Influence on Society and Culture of Its Own Time": Going Nuts for *Peanuts*

When *Peanuts* debuted on October 2, 1950, no one could have predicted its mass popularity. Charles M. Schulz's strip about a group of elementary-aged children reflecting on the simple joys and recurring sorrows of life would become "the most successful comic strip in newspaper history" (DeLuca, 308). By the time of Schulz's death on February 12, 2000, his comic had become part of the fabric of American society. Characters like Charlie Brown, Snoopy, and Lucy were more than merely household names. In the words of Fred Hunt, they were "universal icons," readily recognized even by individuals who had never read Schulz's strip. Given this situation, Jared Gardner and Ian Gordon rightly characterized *Peanuts* as nothing less than "a hallmark of the second half of the twentieth century" (3).

Although *Peanuts* has been a fixture in American popular culture for generations, it reached the apex of popularity during the 1960s. David Michaelis, in *Schulz and Peanuts: A Biography*, in fact, gives the section of his book that documents this era the telling title "Zenith" (401). During the 1960s, *Peanuts* experienced unprecedented levels of success not merely in the history of Schulz's creation but for any comic strip in American history.

First and foremost, *Peanuts* enjoyed tremendous circulation. Chip Kidd writes, "At its peak, the comic strip ran in over 2,600 newspapers, with a readership of 355 million in seventy-five countries, translated into twenty-one languages" (n.p.). These figures are astounding enough on their own, but they represent just one facet of the comic strip's presence in American print culture. Beginning in 1952, *Peanuts* strips were collected and reprinted in paperback editions. By 1966, in fact, no fewer than twenty different titles had been released, collectively "selling four and a half million copies—or one [book] every thirty seconds" (Michaelis, 339). The success of the paperback volumes inspired the release of new material, including Robert L. Short's *The Gospel According to Peanuts* (1964) and Schulz's *Happiness Is a Warm Puppy* (1962). The former title became a "national best seller in hardback, snapped up at the rate of four thousand copies a week, with more than ten million of its paperback edition eventually scattered throughout the world" (Michaelis, 352). Meanwhile, by 1967, *Happiness Is a Warm Puppy* "would sell 1,350,000 copies in three languages" (339). Additionally, it spawned a series of spin-off volumes, each with "hefty seven-figure sales, and unprecedented stints on the bestseller lists" (Kidd, n.p.).

The success of *Peanuts* in American print culture facilitated its migration to other cultural platforms and media venues. On December 9, 1965, the animated television special *A Charlie Brown Christmas* premiered on CBS. As Michaelis has relayed, "Almost half the people watching television in the United States tuned in—some fifteen and a half million households" (359). The program would go on to win an Emmy Award for Outstanding Individual Achievement.

The *Peanuts* gang also appeared onstage. On March 7, 1967 the off-Broadway musical *You're a Good Man, Charlie Brown* debuted in New York City. Like the animated Christmas special, the show was an immediate hit, enjoying a four-year run in New York alone. Moreover, as Schulz reflected in an interview in 1992, *You're a Good Man, Charlie Brown* became "the most performed musical in the history of American theatre. . . . Every school and church and high school and grade school and kindergarten you can think of has put this thing on" (Timeline).

Schulz's creation likewise found its way to the radio airwaves. In November 1966, a pop singing group called The Royal Guardsman released the song "Snoopy vs. the Red Baron." The song would eventually reach number 2 on the Hot 100 list. Moreover, its success would inspire the Royal Guardsman—with Schulz's approval—to release the full-length album, *Snoopy and His Friends* (1967). The record launched several additional radio hits, including "The Return of the Red Baron" and "Snoopy's Christmas."

By 1970, in fact, it seemed that no facet of US print, visual, or material culture was untouched by *Peanuts*. The characters appeared in the feature-length film *A Boy Named Charlie Brown* (1969), as balloons in the annual Macy's Thanksgiving Day parade, and as the official mascot for NASA's Apollo 10 mission (Kidd). Arguably overshadowing all these elements, however, was the veritable bonanza of *Peanuts* merchandise. Spearheaded by Connie Boucher at Determined Productions, Schulz's characters were licensed to appear on seemingly every consumer product imaginable during the 1960s: toys, clothes, home decor, jewelry, school supplies, sporting goods, stationery, health and beauty products, bedding, cookbooks, and games (Michaelis, 337–39).

As even this brief overview indicates, Charles M. Schulz's *Peanuts* "had a profound influence on society and culture of its own time" (Inge, 104). M. Thomas Inge makes the following observation about the cultural force that the strip had attained by 1969: "No other American artist or writer in any other field of creative endeavor has ever been known to reach and earn the admiration of so many people simultaneously as Charles Schulz has done at such magic moments in his career" (106). When historians discuss influential happenings in American popular culture during the 1960s, they commonly mention events like the hippies, the miniskirt, and the British Invasion. Schulz's strip needs to be included in this list. In the same way that the decade was known for Beatlemania, it was also filled with *Peanuts*-mania.

Good Grief:
The Shared Emotional Registers of Peanuts and *DTWOF*

Not surprisingly, given the ubiquity of *Peanuts* both during her childhood and during the period when she was drawing *DTWOF*, Bechdel was familiar with Schulz's strip. In an interview published in *Off Our Backs* in 1988, the cartoonist mentioned Schulz's comic. Discussing her early attempts at cartooning, for instance, she reflected: "I was also intimidated by trying to create real characters like Charlie Brown, Lucy, or Linus. It seems really scary to create genuine characters and then have to develop them in a believable way" (14). Then, a few questions later, when asked if *DTWOF* is sufficiently "universal" to be enjoyed by heterosexual readers, she asserts: "*We* do it every day. Any woman, any gay person, any person of any color whatsoever other than white picks up the daily paper and makes these incredible leaps of identity to understand Peanuts, Garfield, The Phantom and all that garbage" (14).

Bechdel also briefly mentioned Schulz in a blog post titled "On Suffering," from October 16, 2007. "I've been thinking about Charles Schulz ('Peanuts') and how this new biography portrays him as a depressed, ambitious, driven, bitter person who devoted himself to his cartoon children and neglected his real ones," she writes. This observation leads Bechdel to contemplate the relationship between suffering and art, musing, "When I read the bit about how Schulz's wife (the first one or the second?) had an item on her mental to-do list, '9–9:15, Comfort Sparky,' I flinched with rueful recognition."

These few references aside, however, Bechdel has said little else about Schulz or *Peanuts*. In various articles and interviews, she has discussed a number of cartoonists whose style has influenced her own or whose work she admires. In a 2006 discussion with Hillary Chute, for example, Bechdel named R. Crumb, Harvey Pekar, Harvey Kurtzman, Howard Cruse, and Art Spiegelman as important sources of inspiration ("An Interview," 1012). Charles Schulz, however, was not among them. Likewise, Bechdel has also occasionally identified the comics that she enjoyed as a young person. To that end, she has referenced her love for *Mad* magazine as an adolescent, along with her enjoyment of Little Lulu and Disney comics as a young child (1012). Once again, however, *Peanuts* has not been among them.

Although Bechdel has never directly mentioned Schulz's work as influencing her own, she was surely aware of it. Born on September 10, 1960, Bechdel came of age during an era that was saturated with *Peanuts* images, products, and paraphernalia. Her childhood took place amid what *Life* magazine rightly called "The Great Peanuts Craze." Indeed, as the *Off Our Backs* interview reveals, even if Bechdel herself was not a daily reader of the strip, she was familiar with it. Charlie Brown and company were everywhere when she was growing up and first began cartooning. Schulz's comic strip and characters appeared not just in the newspaper, but on the stage, screen, television, radio, clothing, toys, stationery, books, home decor, school supplies, and even the moon.

The ubiquity of *Peanuts* during Bechdel's coming of age calls for a consideration of the possible influence on, and a noting of the clear affinities with, *DTWOF*. Indeed, in features ranging from the plot and characters to the tone and themes, a number of similarities exist between the two comics. These points of correspondence between *Dykes to Watch Out For* and *Peanuts* are strong enough and numerous enough to suggest that Bechdel's early exposure to *Peanuts* shaped *DTWOF*.

On the surface, *Dykes to Watch Out For* seems to have little in common with *Peanuts*. After all, Bechdel's "strip features a cast of recurring characters in a lesbian community in an unnamed mid-sized American city, and it often comments explicitly on current events" (Bernstein, 127). This focus ostensibly places it far outside the realm of Schulz's comic about a group of elementary-aged, suburban, and seemingly (mostly) all heterosexual children. Indeed, Bechdel herself has called *DTWOF* "half op-ed column and half endless, serialized Victorian novel" (quoted in Bernstein, 129). Over the course of its run from 1983 to 2008, the comic engaged with a myriad of social, political, and economic issues that are far outside the realm of the *Peanuts* universe: from attacks on women's reproductive rights and the inequities inherent in laissez-faire capitalism to the brutality of the nation's military-industrial complex and the rise of social consciousness around gender fluidity and trans identities.

When we read *DTWOF* in the context of *Peanuts*, a number of striking parallels arise between the comics. Even in just a few of Schulz's strips, the general message or overall philosophy becomes clear: the comic explores how "we are flawed souls who occasionally have a redemptive experience, a moment of release, of joy, but then we revert to our old patterns and we suffer again" (DeLuca, 301). Charlie Brown never kicks the football. Snoopy never receives an acceptance letter for his latest Bulwer-Lyttonesque novel. Linus never meets the Great Pumpkin. Instead, all the characters remain hobbled by the same problems, flaws, and disappointments. Even when they try to change their attitudes or their actions, they cannot. Eventually they revert to their old ways. Charlie Brown may vow that he will never again believe Lucy's promise to refrain from pulling the football away at the last moment; however, time after time, he capitulates, demonstrating that we can never really change.

This observation also accurately describes the world of *DTWOF*. All of Bechdel's characters follow this pattern. Mo remains the same high-strung, neurotic, and panicky individual in the final episode of the series that she was in the first strip. Likewise, Clarice is the same idealistic workaholic that she was when we first met her in law school. Finally, and perhaps most vividly of all, even a bout with breast cancer doesn't change many facets of Sydney's personality. As the "Cast Biographies" page on Bechdel's *Dykes to Watch Out For* website indicates, Sydney's personality can still be accurately described as the "credit card debtor with a penchant for the theoretical and disdain for knee-jerk liberalism" (Bechdel, "Cast Biographies").

One of the features that made *Peanuts* not only so popular but even so hip and edgy during its heyday in the 1950s and 1960s was that it incorporated the growing postwar interest in psychoanalysis. In the strip that appeared on March 27, 1959, Lucy opens a booth whose sign advertises its function: "Psychiatric Help 5¢." While Charlie Brown is her most frequent client, all the characters sit on the stool and talk with her at one point or another. As Geraldine DeLuca points out, however, "Therapy is not the route to salvation in *Peanuts*. Schulz's characters do not get over great losses. They do not change" (301). Indeed, even after numerous sessions over many decades, Charlie Brown remains the same depressive, luckless person he was before. In a feature that is difficult not to view as Schulz's commentary about the efficacy of psychoanalysis, Charlie Brown's therapy sessions with Lucy are repeatedly presented as fruitless at worst and absurd at best.

The strip that appeared on May 30, 1969, forms an excellent case in point (fig. 5.1). It shows Charlie Brown talking to Lucy at her psychiatric booth. "I don't know what to do," he says in the opening panel. "Sometimes I get so lonely I can hardly stand it. . . . Other times, I actually long to be completely alone" (*1969 to 1970*, 65). Lucy's suggestion for how to solve his problem is thoroughly unhelpful. "Try to live in-between . . . Five cents, please!" she tells Charlie Brown in the final panel, making an abrupt end to the session (65).

Fig. 5.1. Final panel from *Peanuts* strip of May 30, 1969 (*1969 to 1970*, 65).

Therapy forms a recurring feature of Bechdel's strip as well. Numerous comics take place in the office of Mo's therapist as Mo discusses her worries and struggles. From the personal troubles that she is experiencing in her private life to the geopolitical problems plaguing the world at large, the topics of her sessions change, but this feature of the strip remains the same: Mo goes to therapy. Akin to Charlie Brown's interactions with Lucy, Mo's time talking with a therapist is not presented as psychologically productive, emotionally enlightening, or personally transformative. Although she frequently discusses problems such as anxiety and insecurity, she never makes much progress on these issues. Instead her experiences in therapy are often shown as unsatisfying. The comic titled "The Soliloquy" from 1990 offers a great example. Mo has ostensibly come to her therapist's office to discuss difficulties in her relationship with Harriet (fig. 5.2). But, as both the thought bubbles and speech balloons reveal, she spends the bulk of the session wondering if her therapist actually likes her. After multiple panels engaging in private ruminations such as "I wonder if she **likes** me? After all, it's not her job to **like** me. . . . Still, **does** she?" Mo finally asks her therapist this question directly (*Sequel*, 20). Her response is just as anticlimactic as the advice that Charlie Brown received from Lucy two decades before; moreover, it likewise signals the abrupt end of their session. "Of course I do!" Mo's therapist tells her in the final panel of "The Soliloquy," "But I see our time is up now. Let's explore this further next week, shall we?" (*Sequel*, 21).

In addition to mirroring general events from Schulz's comic, *DTWOF* contains a variety of elements that form even more specific instances of overlap. A frequent occurrence in *Peanuts* is when one character is experiencing a rare moment of happiness, pleasure, or joy, and another is quick to point out how the sentiment is fleeting, hollow, or foolish. For instance, in a strip that first appeared in the late 1950s and was reprinted in the 1970 paperback *Go Fly a Kite, Charlie Brown,* Snoopy is depicted in the opening panel doing his famous happy dance: his back feet are moving rapidly, his front paws are opened wide, his head is thrown back, and there is a big smile on his upturned face (n.p.). An angry Lucy watches him approaching and glowers at him. "The

Fig. 5.2. "The Soliloquy" (Sequel 20-21).

whole world could get blown up at any minute and all **you** think of is **dancing**!!" she exclaims (n.p.).

Similar sentiments occur repeatedly in *DTWOF*. In the strip "High Anxiety" from 1987, Clarice and Toni encourage Mo to have more fun. Their pal is currently unemployed, and they urge her to "just take time out to do something you really enjoy" (*More*, 36). Mo's response recalls that of Lucy upon seeing Snoopy gleefully dancing. In a series of panels, she wonders how anyone could possibly enjoy themselves when "out in the **real** world they're **bombing abortion** clinics . . . holding **Nazi** and **KKK** rallies . . . trying to **quarantine** people who might have **AIDS**" (37). Mo makes strikingly similar remarks a few years later, in the 1992 strip "Mo Zone." The sequence opens with Clarice, Harriet, Toni, and the protagonist dining at their favorite local boîte, Café Topaz. As Toni comments in the first panel, however, Mo is not enjoying her entrée. "How can I **eat**? An ozone hole could open up over our heads any minute now!" (*Spawn*, 20).

While the core cast of *Peanuts* remained the same, Schulz would also introduce new characters to the strip. From the birth of Charlie Brown's sister Sally in the late 1950s to the arrival of Rerun in the early 1970s, the cartoonist kept the strip fresh and interesting in part by adding fresh and interesting new characters. On August 22, 1966, a figure who would quickly become a beloved member of the *Peanuts* gang made her debut: Patricia Reichardt, better known as Peppermint Patty. Schulz said that he added her to reflect the changing times, as well as the new types of young people who were emerging from them (Timeline). With Patty's "distinct personality, athleticism, and trademark sandals" (Timeline), she reflected key facets of the 1960s: the changing nature of girlhood, the shifting style of national fashions, and the increasingly individualistic and even outspoken nature of American youth. Although Peppermint Patty is depicted as having a crush on Charlie Brown, readers have commonly seen her as a lesbian character. As Vicki Reich, Heather Hogan, and Ben Saunders have all discussed, Patty embodied a variety of personal, behavioral, and sartorial traits that had long been associated with lesbians, from wearing Birkenstocks to playing softball (Reich, para. 4–7; Hogan, para. 3–12; Saunders, 13–21). This association only strengthened when the character Marcie debuted on July 20, 1971. A shy, nerdy intellectual, Marcie follows Peppermint Patty around, calling her "Sir"—a trait that places their interactions in dialogue with butch/femme role play that emerged in lesbian bar culture during the twentieth century (Faderman, 159–87). Peppermint Patty and Marcie quickly became icons of lesbian culture during the 1970s and 1980s (Reich, para. 3). Many queer women read them as a same-sex couple or, at the least, as occupying a place on Adrienne Rich's "lesbian continuum" (Hogan).

This development has obvious resonance for *DTWOF*. While Peppermint Patty was not the first character in American comics who could read as lesbian, she was exceedingly well known.[1] Peppermint Patty quickly became one of the core *Peanuts* characters, appearing frequently in the strips, playing a role in the animated Christmas special, and being featured on a bevy of merchandise. Alison Bechdel has often said that she created *DTWOF* out of a desire for increased queer visibility. Adam R. Critchfield and Jack Pula echo this point, writing, "Syndicated in numerous gay and lesbian, feminist, or other alternative newspapers across the United States, the comic strip held up a rare mirror in which many lesbian, gay, bisexual, and transgender (LGBT) individuals could see themselves represented" (398). Before the appearance of *DTWOF*, Peppermint Patty largely occupied this role and served this function for the lesbian community. Indeed, Hogan, Reich, and Saunders have all made substantial claims for how this comics character occupied an esteemed personal place and even important cultural function for queer women. Akin to Mo and the other lesbians of *DTWOF*, Peppermint Patty provided an important site of visibility. She was then, and remains now, an iconic figure among lesbians. Accordingly, it seems difficult to fully separate the significance of this character with that of Bechdel's comic. In many ways, in fact, Peppermint Patty was the most visible, beloved, and important comics character for lesbians in the United States before the appearance of *DTWOF*.

Even the title of several of the Peanuts Philosophers series of gift books—which were released from 1967 to 1969—are comments that could easily have been uttered by characters in *DTWOF*, especially Mo. The titles include *Everything I Do Makes Me Feel Guilty* (1969) and *We All Have Our Hangups* (1969). The same observation applies to the sentiments expressed by various *Peanuts* figures inside these books as well. In *We All Have Our Hangups*, for example, Lucy chastises Snoopy: "You wouldn't be so happy if you knew about all the troubles in this world!" (n.p.). In *Everything I Do Makes Me Feel Guilty*, Charlie Brown sits at a table, writing a letter to his pen pal. "Did you have a nice summer?" readers see that he has inquired via the scribbly cursive printed above his head. Then, in the following panel, Charlie Brown reports on his own experiences: "Mine could have been better, but it could have been worse" (n.p.) Far from seeing this situation as a disappointment, he tells his pen pal: "For me, that's good." Bechdel's Mo would likely say the same thing.

The Philosopher in the Striped Shirt: Mo and/as Linus

Of all the ways that the plot, characters, and themes of *DTWOF* recall facets from *Peanuts*, one connection seems especially striking: the affinities between

Mo and Linus. As Charles Schulz once observed about Charlie Brown's best friend, "Linus, my serious side, is the house intellectual, bright, well-informed, which, I suppose, may contribute to his feelings of insecurity" ("Linus van Pelt"). Linus is the character who offers philosophical commentary about the happenings in the lives of the *Peanuts* gang. He is thoughtful, reflective, and exceedingly intelligent. Whereas figures like Charlie Brown, Lucy, and Peppermint Patty focus on individual events or specific details, Linus identifies the connections among and between these occurrences to see the larger social, cultural, and political ramifications. His perceptive nature, however, is precisely what makes him anxious and even somber. Linus knows enough about the world to recognize its awe-inspiring possibilities, but also to see its disheartening problems. This quality forms one of the reasons Linus is almost always carrying his trusty blue security blanket: he needs the comfort that it provides. Charlie Brown's sidekick is concerned with the ontological, theological, and epistemological implications of life events: What does it all mean? Why are we here? Is there a greater purpose? Not surprisingly, such weighty contemplations routinely leave Linus unsettled or even depressed.

The same sentiments, of course, could also be used to describe Mo. Many of her signature traits and hallmark qualities are ones that she shares with Linus: from her insecurity and intellectualism to her philosophical nature and her role as the reflective commentator—along with frequent killjoy—for the group. Furthermore, even Mo's penchant for striped clothing can be seen as taking a sartorial cue from Linus, who is always clad in a T-shirt with horizontal stripes strikingly similar to Mo's. These areas of physical, psychological, and personal overlap invite us to see these seemingly disparate characters as being in dialogue. However unexpected and even unlikely, Mo Testa can be seen as Mo van Pelt in many ways.

Linus's contemplative, philosophical, and insecure nature is a recurring feature of the strip. While he is sometimes presented as playing baseball with the rest of the gang, he is more frequently depicted sagely ruminating, anxiously wondering, or wisely opining. "Lucy says that half of our heart is filled with hate and half is filled with love," Linus relays to Charlie Brown in a strip that was reprinted in a 1970 paperback, for example. He continues in the second panel: "And she says this hate and love are always fighting within us . . . always quarreling, battling, struggling" (*Go*, n.p.). At this point, Linus has become completely unnerved by this situation. The third panel shows him in a state of anxious panic: he is clutching his stomach, his eyes are open wide in anxiety, and his whole body is trembling. Consumed with worry, Linus desperately shouts in the fourth and final panel: "**PEACE!**" (*Go*, n.p.).

That said, it doesn't take weighty concerns about humanity's internal struggle with good and evil to send Linus into a panic. He is frequently driven

Fig. 5.3. Final panel from *Peanuts* strip of February 27, 1969 (1969 to 1970, 26).

there by far more quotidian events. For example, in a strip reprinted in *Good Ol' Charlie Brown* (1965), Linus strikes out at baseball. He returns to the bench, picks up his blanket, and begins sucking his thumb. The expression on his face is a mix of worry, sadness, and anxiety (n.p.). In a series of strips that appeared from late February to early March 1969, Linus becomes thoroughly outraged when his favorite teacher is dismissed at school (fig. 5.3). "Do you ever have the feeling of impending doom?" he asks Charlie Brown after he reads him the newspaper story about the teacher's strike (*1969 to 1970*, 26). In the following day's strip, when Lucy breaks the news that his beloved teacher has been fired, Linus's looming unease turns to impassioned outrage. "FIRED! THAT CAN'T BE! THEY CAN'T FIRE MISS OTHMAR!" he erupts when Lucy informs him (26). "**SHE HAS A CONTRACT! SHE HAS TENURE! SHE HAS HER OWN PARKING PLACE!**" Linus exclaims even more stridently in the next panel (26). Furthermore, Linus sustains this level of outrage for several more strips (fig. 5.4): "**I'LL WRITE A LETTER OF PROTEST! I'LL BLOW THIS THING WIDE OPEN!!**" he ardently vows in the next day's comic (26).

Bechdel's Mo, of course, is famous for her impassioned tirades, her moments of righteous outrage, and her tendency to panic. Akin to Linus, Mo's episodes are routinely sparked by everyday events in mundane settings. The strip "Angst in Right Field" from 1987 manifests an excellent case in point (fig. 5.5). As the exposition box that opens the strip relays, "It's softball season again, and Mo's having a touch of **Weltschmerz** in the last inning" (*More*, 46). The drawing that appears below these lines shows Mo standing in left field. The thought bubble above her head reveals her ruminations. "It's so peaceful

Fig. 5.4. *Peanuts* strip of March 1, 1969 (*1969 to 1970*, 26).

out here," she reflects (*More*, 46). As with Linus, this moment of peaceful tranquility quickly turns to more grandiose contemplations—and geopolitical concerns. "You'd never suspect that somewhere political prisoners are being **tortured**, people are **starving**, **chemicals** are spilling, **missiles** are piling up," Mo muses to herself in the next panel (46). Over the next eight panels, she continues along these same lines, getting increasingly agitated as the softball game unfolds on the infield in front of her. Near the end of the strip, Mo's ruminations prompt her to exclaim aloud in a manner that recalls Linus's earlier exasperated eruptions: "How can we stand here playing **softball**? I mean, what's the **point?!?**" (47).

The Peanuts Philosophers series of gift books contains not one but two volumes dedicated to Linus: *Linus on Life* (1967) and *The Meditations of Linus* (1967). "There's no heavier burden than potential!" he announces in a strip collected in the former title (n.p.). In the latter book, Linus makes observations about the absurdities of modern life, such as the following: "There's something symbolic about being run over by a portable TV while reading a book" (n.p.). As such remarks indicate, Linus is the member of the group who observes—and opines. Indeed, the official *Peanuts* character profile calls him "the most insecure but the smartest out of all the characters, with the most intellectualism; a philosopher and theologian."

This description likewise encapsulates Mo. Her character bio on Bechdel's *Dykes to Watch Out For* website, in fact, deems her a "worrier and kvetch extraordinaire" ("Character Bios"). When Mo is not philosophizing, she is panicking; when she is not fired up with righteous indignation, she is sinking into gloomy despair; when she is not fighting injustice, she is battling self-pity. In a strip that was reprinted in the paperback *Good Ol' Charlie Brown* (1965), Linus watches a leaf fall from a tree. Over the course of several panels, the leaf flutters to the ground while he observes silently. Then, after the leaf has landed on the grass, Linus lets out a sigh. In the final panel, he offers the following glum takeaway: "Nobody's happy where they are" (n.p.). One can imagine Mo making the same observation in *DTWOF*.[2]

Fig. 5.5. "Angst in Right Field" (*More*, 46–47).

Locating the Past in the Present:
Childhood, Memory, and Autobiography in *DTWOF*

Much has been written about the importance of childhood, memory, and autobiography in Bechdel's *Fun Home*. Ann Cvetkovich, for example, has explored "the role of child as witness" in the graphic memoir (111). Julia Watson has discussed "autobiographic disclosures and genealogies of desire" in the book (27). Jennifer Lemberg has detailed how memory serves as a mechanism for presenting "that which would which otherwise remain unseen," in Bechdel's telling of both her own life story and her father's (131).

Although the analyses by Cvetkovich, Watson, and Lemberg all possess a different specific focus, they are united by their shared belief that Bechdel's book is inextricably connected to the past. *Fun Home* is not simply a memoir; it is also a cultural time capsule. The text offers a rich historical archive about the cartoonist and her family. *Fun Home* contains drawings of photographs that were taken during Bechdel's youth, it reprints letters that her parents exchanged during their courtship, and it reconstructs conversations that she had with her mother or father when she was in college. Given this situation, little has been written about *Fun Home* that does not mention childhood, memory, and autobiography. These issues are regarded not merely as the memoir's recurring motifs but as its core pivot points.

A significant portion of *Fun Home* takes place during Bechdel's childhood and is filled with references to popular culture from that era. In the opening chapter, for example, a panel shows the future cartoonist and her brother watching *Sesame Street* (*FH*, 14). On the facing page, another image shows the young Bechdel playing in her bedroom, where she has a trash can that has Harvey Ball's now-iconic yellow smiley face emblazoned on it (15). A sequence that takes place in the closing pages of the chapter shows a box of Quisp cereal sitting on the family's kitchen table; meanwhile, her father is wearing a necktie adorned with peace signs (18). The references to popular culture that permeate the opening chapter of *Fun Home* continue throughout the book. Indeed, when the cartoonist discusses the many differences between herself and her father in the opening pages, she identifies her interest in contemporaneous events as a key distinguishing feature. In the panel that contains the smiley-face trash can, Bechdel says that she was "modern to his Victorian" (*FH*, 15). As a child, the future cartoonist not only paid attention to popular culture but enjoyed and even identified with it.

Awareness of this issue with regard to *Fun Home* stands in marked contrast to common critical perspectives about *DTWOF*. Whereas the cartoonist's graphic memoir is widely seen as being steeped in the past of her childhood, her serial comic strip is just as strongly associated with the contemporaneous present of her life as an adult. As Robin Bernstein and Susan Kirtley have discussed, *DTWOF* routinely incorporated current events. The backdrop to the plot for many episodes, in fact, would be a recent sociopolitical occurrence: the Iran-Contra hearings in the 1980s, the passage of the Defense of Marriage Act in the 1990s, the War on Terror in the early 2000s, and so on. The strip would detail what the characters thought about the event, how they were reacting to it, and the impact it was having on their lives. Accordingly, if *DTWOF* is seen as a form of life writing at all, then it is seen as being driven by events that were occurring during the time that Bechdel was drawing the strips.

The possible influence that *Peanuts* had on *DTWOF* changes this perception. More than simply being influenced by events that were occurring during the cartoonist's adulthood, the strip may also have been shaped by ones that transpired during her childhood. Critics have long regarded *DTWOF* as being rooted in the present, but the suggestive echoes that it possesses to Schulz's comic open up the possibility that it has equally strong ties with the past. Reading Mo Testa as Mo van Pelt reveals that Bechdel's exploration of childhood, memory, and autobiography are not limited to *Fun Home*. Instead, these issues have played an important—but overlooked—role throughout her cartooning career.

NOTES

1. Sanjak, from Milton Caniff's *Terry and the Pirates*, is commonly identified as the first lesbian character in American comics. She debuted on February 12, 1939.

2. Bechdel and Schulz share connections beyond simply their creative work. Their backgrounds and personalities also overlap in compelling ways. Both cartoonists, for example, describe themselves as shy introverts who view the world with apprehension and even anxiety (DeLuca, 301; Bechdel and Hall, 15–21). Additionally, and even more powerfully, the lives of Schulz and Bechdel were shaped by the death of one of their parents when they were young adults: Schulz's mother died of cancer when he was twenty; Bechdel's father died—likely from suicide, as she explores in *Fun Home*—when she was nineteen. The biographer David Michaelis identifies the death of Schulz's mother as the single most important event in the cartoonist's life. The first chapter of his six-hundred-plus-page biography, in fact, recounts this event. Michaelis presents it as changing Schulz irrevocably and thus being the key to understanding him and his life (Michaelis, 3–8). Similarly, Bechdel has discussed both inside and outside the pages of *Fun Home* how the death of her father—along with her discovery of his secret homosexual liaisons—was a profound turning point in her life. "Because of him," she remarked in an article that appeared in *Rolling Stone*, "I was determined to be very out and open about my queerness. My whole career has kind of spun out of that dynamic" (quoted in Yarm, para. 3).

WORKS CITED

Bechdel, Alison. "Cast Biographies." *Dykes to Watch Out For*. Accessed October 11, 2017.
Bechdel, Alison. *Dykes to Watch Out For: The Sequel*. Firebrand Books, 1992.
Bechdel, Alison. *More Dykes to Watch Out For*. Firebrand Books, 1988.
Bechdel, Alison. "On Suffering." Blog Archive. *Dykes to Watch Out For*. October 16, 2007. Accessed July 26, 2018.
Bechdel, Alison. "The Soliloquy." *Off Our Backs* 20, no. 7 (1990): 24.
Bechdel, Alison, and Marny Hall. "Ordinary Insurrections." *Journal of Lesbian Studies* 5, no. 3 (2001): 15–21.
Bernstein, Robin. "'I'm Very Happy to Be in the Reality-Based Community': Alison Bechdel's *Fun Home*, Digital Photography, and George W. Bush." *American Literature* 89, no. 1 (2017): 121–54.
Chute, Hillary. "An Interview with Alison Bechdel." *Modern Fiction Studies* 52, no. 4 (2006): 1004–13.
Critchfield, Adam R., and Jack Pula. "On Psychotherapy, LGBT Identity, and Cultural Visibility: In Conversation with Alison Bechdel." *Journal of Gay and Lesbian Mental Health* 19, no. 4 (2015): 397–412.
Cvetkovich, Ann. "Drawing the Archive in Alison Bechdel's *Fun Home*." *WSQ: Women's Studies Quarterly* 36, nos. 1–2 (2008): 111–28.
DeLuca, Geraldine. "'I Felt a Funeral in My Brain': The Fragile Comedy of Charles Schulz." *The Lion and the Unicorn* 25, no. 2 (2001): 300–309.
Faderman, Lillian. *Odd Girls and Twilight Lovers: A History of Lesbian Life in Twentieth-Century America*. Columbia University Press, 1991.
Gardner, Jared, and Ian Gordon. Introduction to *The Comics of Charles Schulz: The Good Grief of Modern Life*, ed. Jared Gardner and Ian Gordon, 3–9. University Press of Mississippi, 2017.
Hogan, Heather. "Peppermint Patty and Marcie: BFFs and GFs?" *AfterEllen*, June 24, 2009. Accessed October 11, 2017.
Hunt, Fred. "Top 10 Comic Strips from Each Decade." Top Tenz. March 26, 2014. Accessed October 11, 2017.
Inge, M. Thomas. *Comics as Culture*. University Press of Mississippi, 1990.
Kidd, Chip. *Only What's Necessary: Charles M. Schulz and the Art of Peanuts*. Abrams, 2015.
Kirtley, Susan. "The Political Is Personal: Dual Domesticity in *Dykes to Watch Out For*." *Inks: The Journal of the Comics Studies Society* 1, no. 1 (2017): 40–55.
Lemberg, Jennifer. "Closing the Gap in Alison Bechdel's *Fun Home*." *WSQ: Women's Studies Quarterly* 36, nos. 1–2 (2008): 129–40.
"Linus van Pelt." Peanuts Wiki. Accessed October 12, 2017.
Mendelson, Lee. *Charlie Brown and Charles Schulz*. Signet, 1970.
Michaelis, David. *Schulz and Peanuts: A Biography*. Harper Collins, 2007.
"Peppermint Patty." Peanuts Wiki. Accessed October 12, 2017.
Reich, Vikki. "The Case of Peppermint Patty." Blog post. *Up Popped a Fox*, November 21, 2012. Accessed February 10, 2018.
"The Return of the Red Baron." *Snoopy and His Friends*. The Royal Guardsmen. Laurie Records, 1967.
Saunders, Ben. "Peppermint Patty's Desire: Charles Schulz and the Queer Comics of Failure." In *The Comics of Charles Schulz: The Good Grief of Modern Life*, ed. Jared Gardner and Ian Gordon, 13–28. University Press of Mississippi, 2017.
Schulz, Charles M. *The Complete Peanuts: Dailies and Sundays, 1967 to 1968*. Fantagraphics, 2008.
Schulz, Charles M. *The Complete Peanuts: Dailies and Sundays, 1969 to 1970*. Fantagraphics, 2008.

Schulz, Charles M. *Everything I Do Makes Me Feel Guilty: And Other Wisdom of Charlie Brown.* Hallmark, 1969.
Schulz, Charles M. *Go Fly a Kite, Charlie Brown.* 1959. Holt, Rinehart, and Winston, 1970.
Schulz, Charles M. *Good Ol' Charlie Brown.* 1957. Holt, Rinehart, and Winston, 1965.
Schulz, Charles M. *Linus on Life.* Hallmark, [1967].
Schulz, Charles M. *The Meditations of Linus.* Hallmark, 1967.
Schulz, Charles M. *We All Have Our Hangups: And Other Thoughts of Snoopy.* Hallmark, 1969.
Smith, Briana. "Watch Out! Alison Bechdel's Comics as Cultural Commentary." *Feminist Collections* 25, no. 2 (2004): 1.
"Snoopy vs. the Red Baron." The Royal Guardsmen. Charles Fuller Productions, 1966.
Snoopy and His Friends. The Royal Guardsmen. Laurie Records, 1967.
"Snoopy's Christmas." *Snoopy and His Friends.* The Royal Guardsmen. Laurie Records, 1967.
Thomas, June. "Drawing on the Lesbian Continuum: An Interview with Alison Bechdel." *Off Our Backs* 18, no. 8 (August–September 1988): 1, 14.
Timeline. "About the Man." Charles M. Schulz Museum. Accessed October 10, 2017.
Watson, Julia. "Autobiographic Disclosures and Genealogies of Desire in Alison Bechdel's *Fun Home*." *Biography* 31, no. 1 (2008): 27–58.
Yarm, Mark. "Alison Bechdel on Her Genius Grant and Family Secrets." *Rolling Stone*, December 5, 2010. Accessed October 9, 2017.

Part II

INTERIORS
Family, Subjectivity, Memory

DANCING WITH MEMORY IN *FUN HOME*

ALISSA S. BOURBONNAIS

> To be haunted by the dead means to be beset with sound, smell, taste, image, memory, after the material body is gone. To attempt to write about dance after the performance is over is to submit to a similar haunting, but one that promises the possibility of a more orderly re-membering. There are documents to consult: reviews, photographs, scores, notes, sometimes even video. If one could place these artifacts delicately and precisely enough on an operating table one might reconstruct, if not completely resuscitate, the moving body.
> —PEGGY PHELAN

I have always found the way Bechdel uses her own body in her composition process to be one of the most compelling aspects of her work. Her method of posing for photographs to re-create specific positions, which she then sketches, is a performance itself. In a February 2017 interview with Kara Swisher on an episode of the podcast *Recode Decode*, Bechdel explained:

> The camera really transformed my work a lot. I used to make little, quick reference sketches for my drawings, or I'd look at myself in the mirror, or, if it was a really complicated scene, I'd take a Polaroid, which was really expensive.... But once you could take digital photos, it was endless. You could take as many free pictures as you wanted. And I did that. For all the scenes in *Fun Home*, I posed for all the characters.... Yeah, it's a little obsessive.

Her latest project of sketching life-sized drawings of herself in poses representing the various exercise fads of her life, *The Secret to Superhuman Strength*, further reveals her physical, intellectual, and interpretive interest in embodiment. In a November 2017 interview with Rachel Cooke in the *Guardian*, Bechdel answers questions about this new endeavor:

> It's about physical fitness and . . . *mortality*—and that's the hard part, the mortality. It's about what it's like to live in an ageing body, knowing you're going to die. The exercise part [Bechdel, who has a black belt in karate, has long been keen on fitness] is like the sugar to make the medicine go down, the medicine being all these big questions of life. . . . I have to feel whatever I'm doing is impossible, otherwise I will just not do it. That's what motivates me.

It is this obsession with the impossible and how Bechdel places the body at the crux of chronicling impossible tasks, like accurately representing memory and experience, that I find most fascinating in her memoirs.

Fun Home is a text unparalleled in its ability to simultaneously perform memory and the act of remembering. While critical attention to performance and performativity in Bechdel's body of work continues to thrive, especially since the Broadway musical adaptation of *Fun Home* (see Anderst in this volume), a glaringly overlooked facet of performance and embodiment in her work is what we stand to gain through the insight of dance and the ways in which dance scholars theorize the body. It may seem that the chasm between two art forms such as dance and graphic narrative is too great to form a basis for comparison; however, that is not the case at all. Rather, in a delicate excavation that considers the process of composition as much as the product—that is to say, *how* a graphic memoirist composes her work, and the finished work itself—there may be no greater analogue than the work done in dance studies, a field in which critics are absolutely required to build their analysis on a varied archive of materials that move far beyond the initial performance of the dance.

Specifically, taking "choreography" as a critical term has useful applications for understanding the movement of bodies through texts, and readers' empathetic connections to the text from the outside in. Susan Foster proposes that choreography can productively be conceptualized as a theorization of identity—corporeal, individual, and social. She believes that "each moment of watching a dance can be read as the product of choices, inherited, invented, or selected, about what kinds of bodies and subjects are being put forth" (Foster, 4). Thus, "choreographing empathy" entails the "construction and cultivation of a specific physicality whose kinesthetic experience guides our perception of and connection to what another is feeling" (2). *Fun Home* and perhaps other autographies are uniquely equipped to position bodies in the text that simultaneously tell a story as well as the author's experience of remembering and reordering that story. Considering the ephemeral nature of performance alongside the ephemeral nature of memory in *Fun Home* illuminates new ways of understanding both.

This essay considers the relationship between choreography and embodiment in *Fun Home* in two main ways. First, I explore how Bechdel choreographs an embodied reading experience via the organization and structure of her archive. Particularly, I highlight how Bechdel's chapter title images contribute significantly to the task of placing the body at the center of both the writing and reading experience. Nearly every page of *Fun Home* offers rich examples through which to consider embodiment and performance, but I select the chapter title images as the best way to demonstrate a reading informed by dance scholarship because they allow us to consider choreography in a literal sense of sequencing steps that progress from one movement of narrative to the next, and, more importantly, because Bechdel's deliberate choice and placement of single images for each chapter title signal the role of the body in both composition and performance.

Second, I focus on choreography in the writing process itself. The single best example of Bechdel's metacommentary on the writing process is her retelling of her "memoir origin story": her first journaling experiences as a child, which appear in "Chapter 5: The Canary-Colored Caravan of Death." I begin with a brief discussion of the chapter title image and why it might differ markedly from the title images previously discussed—instead of centering a specific body, chapter 5 offers only a general landscape scene—and proceed to read the ways in which child Alison's task of recording increasingly complex experiences with sex, death, and growing up is all but impossible. That is, until she learns to document the impossible through her own writing system of erasure. I argue that we can better understand both Bechdel's composition process and her narrative about the composition process by following methods that dance scholars use to understand a performance through choreography that shapes both the performance and viewers' reaction to that performance.

To study embodied reading is to study embodied readers. Bechdel choreographs an embodied reading experience through the deliberate ways in which she places bodies in the text. Katherine Hayles, in her landmark 1999 work *How We Became Posthuman*, defines embodiment as the unique context in which information is enacted. A reader's engagement with the storyworld is made meaningful through engagement with the material world in which she is reading. Hayles makes an enormously useful distinction between "the body" and "embodiment": "Whereas the body can disappear into information with scarcely a murmur of protest, embodiment cannot, for it is tied to the circumstances of the occasion and the person" (197). Embodiment, then, is an expression of context, an action. Hayles explains that "embodiment is akin to articulation in that it is inherently performative, subject to individual enactments, and therefore always to some extent improvisational" (196). The use of "performativity" as Hayles incorporates it into her understanding of embodiment is rooted in definitions of performativity via Judith Butler.[1] The most relevant scholarship on *Fun Home* informing this essay takes up subjectivity and personhood in relation to memory and narrative construction. Ann Cvetkovich writes about *Fun Home* as an emblematic text offering queer perspectives on traumatic memory that challenge the relation between the catastrophic and the everyday. Robyn Warhol approaches *Fun Home* through postclassical narrative theory and "autography," to emphasize that a level of awareness in self-consciously creating narrative is central to any reading of this text. In a 2006 interview with Hillary Chute, Bechdel comments on the intensity of creating a narrative based on family history: "I wanted to get a purchase on the material before I had to grapple with [my mother's] feelings about it." Part of what it means to "get a purchase on the material" concerns Bechdel's relationship with a material, bodily archive, just as much as with the feelings connected to that archive.

I am interested in the relationship between what it means to grapple with feelings wrapped up in an embodied reading of this text as it relates to the way Cvetkovich understands subjectivity, and how those feelings manifest in the bodies in the text in metacommentary on the composition process, as Warhol points out. Bechdel's metacommentary emphasizes a performance of identity, and how it relates to the subject position of the reader in *Fun Home* most starkly though the individual chapter title images. Embodiment is tied to the circumstances of a variety of factors at the beginning of each chapter, and those spatial and temporal factors dictate a reader's expectations for and attitude toward the upcoming material in each sequence.

The chapter title panels are a striking element of *Fun Home* that usually appears as an afterthought, if at all, in Bechdel scholarship. Each chapter begins with a single page that includes one illustrated panel above the text of the title, as follows:

Chapter 1: Old Father, Old Artificer (1) [close-up of Bruce]
Chapter 2: A Happy Death (26) [grave monument]
Chapter 3: That Old Catastrophe (55) [portrait of parents]
Chapter 4: In the Shadow of Young Girls in Flower (87) [photo of young Bruce sunbathing]
Chapter 5: The Canary-Colored Caravan of Death (121) [landscape]
Chapter 6: The Ideal Husband (151) [close-up of mother in dressing room mirror]
Chapter 7: The Antihero's Journey (187) [child Alison and Bruce at pool]

Bechdel has used digital technologies to sketch these images, but they are realistic reproductions of photographs, rather than the cartoon style of other narrative panels within the chapters. The title panels appear as static photographs from the past, while the narrative panels within the chapters appear as dynamic action happening in present time. Additionally, the reproductions of the title page photos have tabs drawn at each of the corners to look as if they have been secured in a traditional photo album or scrapbook. A reader who opens the book, whether reading a printed copy or on an electronic reader, has the experience of holding and paging through a personal family album starting from the first page as a result of Bechdel's deliberately crafted framing, which considers the body of the reader and how that reader will interact with her book.

If we take choreography to apply critical pressure on the relationship between embodiment in the text and processes of embodied reading, then we can draw a parallel to the idea that Bechdel forces her readers to choreograph their own reading process; however, is this not also a claim for the intensely controlled nature of Bechdel's composition process? When she poses for pictures in which she tries to re-create positions she remembers her father and other family members standing in, Bechdel enacts a kind of performance of memory that is at once embodied and narrative. Foster argues that, rather than a natural or spontaneous connection, a dancer's performance draws on and engages with prevailing senses of the body and of subjectivity in a given historical moment (4). Both Foster and Hayles tie bodily experience to an expression of context that necessarily takes into account movement through/in a given time and space.

A reader might not call what Bechdel does "dancing," but certainly the highly choreographed nature of the movement of physical bodies through this narrative text creates a dance with memory. The single image for "Chapter 1: Old Father, Old Artificer" is a photo of Bechdel's father, Bruce, from the waist up. He is shirtless, his body facing sideways, elbow out with hand on hip, while his face looks straight into the camera (1). He is perfectly centered in front of the house, a few steps in front of the porch. Is this Alison's story or Bruce's? Arguably, Alison and Bruce are the joint protagonists in Bechdel's story. The reader constantly shares Bechdel's gaze, and wrapped up in that gaze is the physicality of handling a material archive. To dance with memory in *Fun Home* is to move, to follow a sequence, and ultimately to perform. Choreographing memory entails a performative aspect of remembering, which Bechdel executes with painstaking detail. The panel for the first chapter signals key structural elements of the story: that the choreography of this narrative moves with and through artifacts, such as family photos, that capture and document subjects in specific moments in time; and that the narrative will follow a trajectory of movement that proceeds from such artifacts.

Bechdel draws attention to the process over the product in her chapter title, "Old Father, Old Artificer." The relationship between the artifacts on which the narrative is built and the artificer she sees in her father is playful yet ominous. From the Latin *arte*, "by or using art," and *factum*, "something made," the artifact that is the opening photograph is a simulacrum made by Bechdel, and it is no coincidence that the photograph chosen makes the house nearly as central as Bruce himself as a focal point. Bechdel narrates:

> His greatest achievement, arguably, was his monomaniacal restoration of our old house. (4)
>
> It was his passion. And I mean that in every sense of the word. Libidinal. Manic. Martyred. (7)
>
> He used his skillful artifice not to make things, but to make things appear to be what they were not. (16)
>
> He appeared to be an ideal husband and father, for example. But would an ideal husband and father have sex with teenage boys?
>
> It's tempting to suggest, in retrospect, that our family was a sham. That our house was not a real home at all but the simulacrum of one, a museum.
>
> Yet we really were a family, and we really did live in those period rooms. (17)

The entanglement of artifact and artifice in the beginning of *Fun Home* demonstrates Bechdel dancing between the dichotomies she believes the house symbolizes to her, in retrospect: simulacra or the real thing? The title panel spotlights Bruce as the creator of this "museum," but the chapter panels themselves turn starkly to highlight Bechdel as the creator, the artificer, the maker of her own narrative. As readers we are primed to follow the choreography set in place by the relationship between the reproduced family photographs and the cartoon action of the children running wild in previously pristine period rooms of the old house. Interestingly, the cartoon style takes on the more authentic role in the narrative: the story suggests that Bechdel's drawings of chaos (really living in those period rooms) represent reality, while the staged family photographs on holidays are inauthentic, further artifice perpetuated by Bruce to conform to societal expectations for a proper family.

The title panel for the final chapter of *Fun Home*, "The Antihero's Journey," is Bechdel's reproduction of a photograph at the pool in which child Alison is jumping into her father's open arms in the water (187). In this image, only the back of Bruce's head and his arms are visible, head and arms tilted up out of the water toward Alison. Alison is in midair, legs tucked under her, arms and head tilted down toward her father. The significance of this memory in the pool and its relationship to the final passage of the text has been extensively discussed in Bechdel scholarship, but the role of the title panel deserves further analysis. The reproduced photographs do more than recall a specific memory from which to launch into the next chapter: they perform a choreographed sequence that, taken as a whole, directs us back to the crucial role the body and embodiment play in this text. Foster explains that "choreography can stipulate both the kinds of actions performed and their sequence of progression," and writes that by

> sometimes designating minute aspects of movement, or alternatively, sketching out the broad contours of action within which variation might occur, choreography constitutes a plan or score according to which movement unfolds. Buildings choreograph space and people's movement through them; cameras choreograph cinematic action; birds perform intricate choreographies; and combat is choreographed. Multiprotein complexes choreograph DNA repair. (2)

The examples she suggests here are both illustrative and helpful in considering a number of reference points in Bechdel's work, from viewership, to architectural space, to biological actors that become points of obsession in several instances throughout *Fun Home*. We can trace Bechdel's plan for how movement unfolds on a structural level through the title images. The first and last chapters take Bruce as their object but shift the focus of Bechdel's gaze from Bruce to herself. Chapters 2 and 5 focus on things and places, rather than people: the grave monument and landscape, respectively—the latter of which I discuss at length in the second half of this essay. Chapters 3 and 6 highlight Bechdel's mother, first in the staged portrait in the house with her husband, last alone in a close-up that shows her preparing for a theater production. Right in the middle (one almost wonders if Bechdel planned an uneven number of chapters for this very purpose) is chapter 4, which begins with a title panel image of young Bruce sunbathing.

Unlike the reproduced photos for every other chapter, this middle chapter takes as its central image a photo that seems to be smaller, more worn, and not slotted into an album. The photo bears faint imprints and evidence of folding, showing that the photograph was hidden away, not displayed in any family album. It is the same photograph that appears on the chapter's final page, except in the latter instance it is clearly in Alison's hands. Earlier in the memoir, Bechdel articulates the "translation" she sees between herself and Bruce in these photos, which she speculates were taken by their respective lovers. But here I shift the focus back to the earlier photograph's actual subject matter. In the chapter's penultimate panel, Bechdel narrates:

> What's lost in translation is the complexity of loss itself. In the same box where I found the photo of Roy, there's another one of dad at about the same age. He's wearing a women's bathing suit. A fraternity prank? But the pose he strikes is not mincing or silly at all. He's lissome, elegant. (120)

The choreography of this panel simultaneously centers embodied reading and embodied performing. As readers, we see Alison the character's hands on the photo, drawing the eye to the frame and the kinesthetics of the page. We also see a conscious performance on the part of the photograph's subject: Bechdel's narration hazards a flimsy explanation ("a fraternity prank?"), which she immediately discounts, seeing her father's figure as "not silly at all" but "lissome, elegant." This line makes explicit in written language what was already implicit in the visual performance.

The grace in this photograph is entirely projected through Bruce's body. Rather than laughing or dismissing the photo as a prank, Alison has a deeply thoughtful and affective response. Let us remember again that Foster proposes that choreography can be productively conceptualized as a theorization of identity—corporeal, individual, and social; that when we watch a dance, we inherently see decisions about what bodies are put forth. These decisions, "made collectively or individually, spontaneously or in advance of dancing, constitute a kind of record of action that is durable and makes possible both the repetition of a dance and analysis of it" (Foster, 4). My earlier claim that Bechdel's unique composition process is performative dovetails with the use of dance as a metaphor for memory itself. The record of action that Foster calls "durable" comprises a combination of action, perception, reception, and reflection. Bechdel choreographs action through a deliberate structure that foregrounds image over text in the chapter titles, and the pivotal middle chapter places the one secret photograph as a powerful key at the center. The key in this instance is not meant to unlock or solve a puzzle but rather to illuminate a deeply embedded connection between Alison and her father that runs throughout the memoir. "In the Shadow of Young Girls in Flower" is filled with memories and anecdotes in which Bruce is obsessed with Alison presenting femininity, while Alison becomes more and more obsessed with men's fashion. The performance of gender in style, tone, and attitude is a complex choreography, and the image of a body in a bathing suit embodies this complexity.

The previously mentioned title panel for the final chapter returns again to bodies in bathing suits, but the image of Bruce as a young man posing elegantly in the photograph presumably taken by his lover contrasts with the image of a little girl gleefully jumping into her father's arms in the pool. As with the entire memoir, the final moments of *Fun Home* are carefully crafted simulacra of events from Bechdel's life, reinterpreted, reordered, and reproduced in narrative form. It is possible that the structure grew out of the experience she had finding the hidden bathing suit photograph, and perhaps finding that photograph gave the memory of playing at the pool new significance (see Van Dyne in this volume). The final product is likely a result of some recursive combination of influences. David Middleton and Steven D. Brown clarify the distinction between popular conceptions of memory and what memory constitutes in a social psychological sense: "We place memory at the center of lived experience—not as the storehouse of that experience, but, instead, as a relational process at the intersection of different durations of living. To approach remembering and forgetting in this way is to deliberately blur the boundaries between the individual and the collective" (1). It is precisely this blurring of boundaries between the individual and the collective that yields a demand for order, especially in Bechdel's storyworld, which allows readers to experience how it might feel for Bechdel herself to look on these personal memories.

We can consider the same panels in terms of what Scott McCloud calls closure: "Comics panels fracture both time and space, offering a jagged, staccato rhythm of unconnected moments. But closure allows us to connect these moments and mentally construct a continuous, unified reality" (67). In other words, the medium itself requires a degree of active engagement from the reader to connect the dots in the space between panels when every single action or thought is not illustrated. This, of course, speaks to the way memory works, and especially the way in which the act of remembering is often portrayed in graphic memoir. The highly choreographed structure of *Fun Home* allows us to see how events and experiences may have unfolded for Bechdel during her composition process, and why she would be drawn to, and motivated by, the very impossibility of the project.

The paradox in the project of self-representation is the expectation of being at once uniquely subjective and factually accurate while maintaining the value of the work, conventionally determined through its veracity. This is an argument that Leigh Gilmore makes, which she extends to a focus on the ways in which traumatic experience intervenes in what constitutes truthful representation of experience. Gilmore contends that autobiographical conventions

> appear to constrain self-representation through its almost legalistic definition of truth telling, its anxiety about invention, and its preference for the literal and verifiable.... As a genre, autobiography is characterized less by a set of formal elements than by a rhetorical setting in which a person places herself or himself within testimonial contexts ... in order to achieve as proximate a relation as possible to what constitutes truth in that discourse. (3)

The relevance of this rhetorical setting cannot be understated; however, I would argue that, in the last two decades especially, the formal elements characterizing contemporary American memoir have shifted enormously, such that the incorporation of mixed media in the project to tell one's life experience has created new ways of discovering and interpreting exactly what we mean by "experience."

This is another angle from which dance scholars can help us understand the varied dimensions and challenges of writing about memory. Peggy Phelan considers the problematic nature of writing about the past in terms of sensory haunting that outlives experience: "To be haunted by the dead means to be beset with sound, smell, taste, image, memory, after the material body is gone. To attempt to write about dance after the performance is over is to submit to a similar haunting, but one that promises the possibility of a more orderly remembering" (15). The process of reordering depends on what constitutes the performance archive. As Phelan explains, "There are documents to consult: reviews, photographs, scores, notes, sometimes even video. If one could place these artifacts delicately and precisely enough on an operating table one might reconstruct, if not completely resuscitate, the moving body" (16). Interestingly, Phelan describes this process of reconstructing the past as "delicate." Does this language indicate fear of breaking something perceived to be so fragile; or respect and humble admiration for the work of studying the past; or some other affective relationship to the work of cultural criticism that might include fear, admiration, and an appreciation for the difficulty of analyzing a "text" such as a body in motion mediated through multiple documents?

Being haunted by the past is a thematic concern of *Fun Home*, and getting every detail of each image right, particularly with and through photographs, is an obsession for Bechdel. Susan Sontag theorizes, "To remember is, more and more, not to recall a story but to be able to call up a picture.... Harrowing photographs do not inevitably lose their power to shock. But they are not much help if the task is to understand. Narratives can make us understand. Photographs do something else: they haunt us" (89). Bechdel has crafted her narrative around the haunting image of the secret photograph hidden away from the official family history documented in the photos preserved in the album. The affective power of photographs that Sontag suggests can highlight again why it might be that Bechdel's deliberate choreography puts forth certain bodies in this memoir, and why some of those bodies appear in seemingly static photographs rather than in dynamic present-tense narrative. It is important to consider that the dichotomy presented between image and text is one in which the photograph is popularly assumed to be a "factual" representation of reality, a carbon copy. However, every photograph, and likewise every drawing, is still shaped by perspective, tone, focus, and subject. *Fun Home* offers instances in which images contribute significantly to the "task to understand." The choreography, the sequence of events unfolding through the chapter title panels, directs our gaze to the embodied reading Bechdel herself experiences as she constructs that sequence in great detail.

Interesting exceptions to the body-centered title images in *Fun Home* appear in chapters 2 and 5. The title for "Chapter 2: A Happy Death" presents a single image of Bruce Bechdel's imposing grave monument, arguably still drawing our attention to, and even signifying a body through, the physical object of remembrance (25). It is the title image for "Chapter 5: The Canary-Colored Caravan of Death" that stands out in stark contrast to the others (121). Rather than centering a body with a photograph of either of Bechdel's parents, this image centers no single presence at all; instead Bechdel offers a general landscape photograph. A dark tree line divides the lower third of the image from the upper lighter open sky. We can infer from the contents of the chapter that this photo represents the point of view of Alison and her father watching a sunset in the woods together. Perhaps the most notable aspect of the image is that while it differs from the other title images in subject matter, it still retains the realistic photo-album tabs at the corners to indicate that this, too, was a photo selected and ordered into the official family history. If we look at the other images placed at the beginning of the chapters, we see far more narrativity within each individual photo than we do in this landscape shot. The only way to discern how the landscape shot connects to a narrative is through the closure, in McCloud's sense of the term, that we as readers draw between it and other panels throughout the text.

I would argue that this title image deliberately obscures the narrative that the other images foreground, and I believe the reason for this is that Bechdel uses it to choreograph the upcoming sequence of other erasures in her personal record keeping. To think of choreography as a theorization of identity allows for a conception of movement in which bodies are more than the object of theory; bodies become the active subject, the point of view in the world in which they move. Bechdel choreographs memory through the body of the text itself, and if we use a conception of embodiment from dance studies to read the body of the text, we can better understand the relationship between writing and performance in *Fun Home*. Another way in which this memoir embodies the act of dancing with memory is through the myriad interactions "Alison Bechdel" the narrator has with "Alison" the character through discussion of Bechdel's own journaling process. Multimodal narrative makes this type of interaction visible to the reader in several ways. In "Chapter 5: The Canary-Colored Caravan of Death," Bechdel narrates:

> Then there's my own compulsive propensity to autobiography.
>
> At some point during my obsessive-compulsive spell, I began a diary. Dad gave me a wall calendar from one of his vendors to write in, a curious memento mori.
>
> And appropriately enough, my first entry was made on that moveable feast of mortality, Ash Wednesday.
>
> Actually, the first three words are in my father's handwriting, as if he were giving me a jump start.
>
> "Just write down what's happening." (140)

The panels interspersed with this text oscillate between images of young Alison and her father looking at and writing in the date book, and close-up images of the book itself, in which handwriting and hands become the central focus. The tone of these panels offers Bechdel's characteristic dry humor in presenting thoughtful, self-aware commentary. Readers are able simultaneously to see young Alison documenting mundane details from her day, and Bechdel narrating in retrospect. This retrospective narrative follows the wider thematic arc of autobiography and what record keeping means to Bechdel in the present, while also highlighting minute details that seem unimportant to the broader arc, such as an arrow pointing to a tail tied around Alison's waist with the text box "Halloween costume remnant," but nonetheless bring specific scenes and memories to life (140). Bechdel's illustrative retelling of her autobiographical origin stories embodies the complex choreography that sets a path for writer and reader to experience the act of remembering together.

What happens next is perhaps the most striking, and telling, instance of Bechdel's relationship with her writing, documentation, and storytelling. Overlaid with panels of close-ups of her childish handwriting, she explains:

> But in April, the minutely-lettered phrase *I think* begins to crop up between my comments.

> It was a sort of epistemological crisis. How did I know that the things I was writing were absolutely, objectively true?
>
> My simple, declarative sentences began to strike me as hubristic at best, utter lies at worst.
>
> All I could speak for was my own perceptions, and perhaps not even those. (141)

Bechdel's "epistemological crisis" reaches even further extremities when she relates, "To save time I created a shorthand version of *I think*, a curvy circumflex. . . . Then I realized I could draw the symbol over an entire entry" (142–43). This escalation from the self-doubting words "I think" to a single symbol ∧ has the effect of both confusing and empowering young Alison.

The negating symbol is a way to exert some degree of control over her own record keeping, but in retrospect, Bechdel shows the startling contrast between events that had great emotional impact, and their subsequent erasure from her diary:

> Considering the profound psychic impact of that adventure, my notes on it are surprisingly cursory. No mention of the pin-up girl, the strip mine, or Bill's .22. Just the snake—and even that with an extreme economy of style.
>
> Again, the troubling gap between word and meaning. My feeble language skills could not bear the weight of such a laden experience. (143)

The panels in this passage add a third dimension beyond what we see in the previous section in which Alison receives the journal from her father for the first time. Here we see close-ups of the writing, Bechdel's commentary, and now images of the actual events she describes—or rather obscures—in her written record.

The curvy circumflex that collectively symbolizes Alison's self-doubt and obsessive-compulsive disorder is the embodiment of her continued need to write and not-write; the symbol, while an erasure of language used to describe events, is still a presence. It is a figure that takes up space on the page, and it has visual characteristics of its own that evolve over time. When she first uses the symbol, it is small and faintly drawn, appearing over specific words. Later it balloons to cover entire entries that are "almost completely obscured," and these symbols are large, dark, and written multiple times over (148). The panels with these larger symbols show the intensity with which they were drawn,

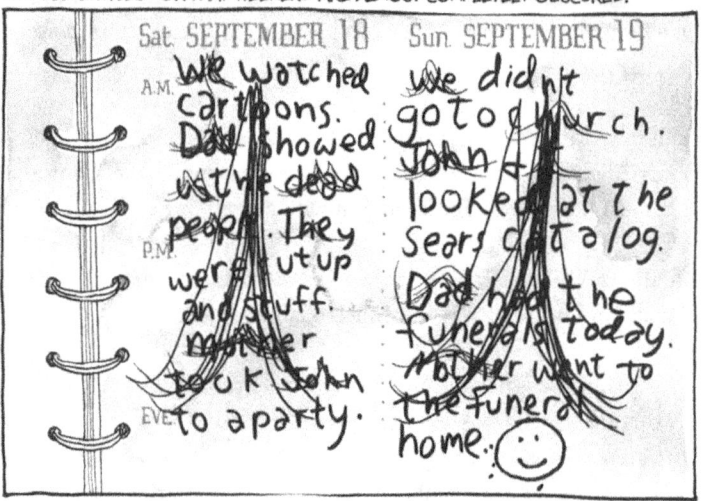

Fig. 6.1. Bechdel writing and not-writing the body (*FH*, 148).

pressed into the paper over and over again. Throughout the chapter, Bechdel contrasts the obscured journal entries with increasingly significant life events related to sex, death, and growing up (fig. 6.1).

The text of *Fun Home* does the work of retracing, rather than uncovering, the narrative obscured by the circumflex. In this way, Bechdel is dancing with memory in a more literal way: taking steps back, following a sequence of movement that her material archive has preserved, and taking steps forward along the same trajectory as she continues developing that same archive with, through, and in her memoir.

Bechdel describes her epistemological crisis with truth and memory in similar terms as the performance studies scholar André Lepecki in theorizing dance:

> This is a crisis of the visible, of how to approach the visible body as its dancing presence plunges it into the past, into history, into a representational field that is perhaps too excessive to be regimented, contained, tamed. This is the epistemological crisis of writing in motion, writing as a body moving in the interstices of visibility. (4–5)

In both instances, Lepecki and Bechdel are responding to the desire to reconcile a moving body, and the point of view attained through that body, after the present moment is gone. The intense difficulty of knowing what has happened when any record or documentation may be, in fact, unknowable is embodied in the dancing body, and the body of memory put forth especially in the form of graphic memoir. *Fun Home* centers bodies: bodies in motion, bodies in static preservation, bodies in confluence and conflict with a present body of the text. For Bechdel and Lepecki to identify this struggle as a crisis is to further emphasize the degree to which the body contains within it experience and information that may not be translatable in a verbal or written communication but are nonetheless present, active, and relevant to an ongoing process of choreographing memory.

Dancing with memory in *Fun Home* means traversing narrative lines where much of the meaningful dialogue between past and present becomes visible only through the relationship between text and image. Multimodal narrative allows for creators and audiences alike to witness more explicitly the implicit affective responses to the very act of remembering through storytelling. Some of the most potent instances of embodied reading in *Fun Home* are those in which we see Bechdel the creator in dialogue with "Alison" the character. Excavating past selves to follow the trajectory of past movement is part of the work of autobiography, of artistic expression of memory. The textual and visual choreography operates on multiple temporal levels, and through multiple modes of communication.

NOTES

1. See especially Judith Butler, "Performative Acts and Gender Constitution: An Essay in Phenomenology and Feminist Theory," and other essays, in *Performing Feminisms: Feminist Critical Theory and Theatre*, ed. Sue-Ellen Case (1990).

WORKS CITED

Butler, Judith. "Performative Acts and Gender Constitution: An Essay in Phenomenology and Feminist Theory." In *Performing Feminisms: Feminist Critical Theory and Theatre*, ed. Sue-Ellen Case, 270–82. Johns Hopkins University Press, 1990.

Chute, Hillary. "An Interview with Alison Bechdel." *Modern Fiction Studies* 52, no. 4 (2006): 1004–13.

Cooke, Rachel. "*Fun Home* Creator Alison Bechdel on Turning a Tragic Childhood into a Hit Musical." *Guardian*, November 5, 2017. Accessed March 18, 2018.

Cvetkovich, Ann. "Drawing the Archive in Alison Bechdel's *Fun Home*." *WSQ: Women's Studies Quarterly* 36, nos. 1–2 (2008): 111–28.

Foster, Susan Leigh. *Choreographing Empathy: Kinesthesia in Performance*. Routledge, 2010.

Gilmore, Leigh. *The Limits of Autobiography: Trauma and Testimony*. Cornell University Press, 2001.

Hayles, Katherine. *How We Became Posthuman: Virtual Bodies in Cybernetics, Literature, and Informatics*. University of Chicago Press, 1999.

Lepecki, André, ed. *Of the Presence of the Body: Essays on Dance and Performance Theory*. Wesleyan University Press, 2004.

McCloud, Scott. *Understanding Comics*. Kitchen Sink Press, 1993.

Middleton, David, and Stephen Brown. *The Social Psychology of Experience: Studies in Remembering and Forgetting*. Sage, 2005.

Phelan, Peggy. "Trisha Brown's *Orfeo*: Two Takes on Double Endings." In *Of the Presence of the Body: Essays on Dance and Performance Theory*, ed. André Lepecki, 13–28. Wesleyan University Press, 2004.

Sontag, Susan. *Regarding the Pain of Others*. Picador, 2004.

Swisher, Kara. "Full Transcript: Alison Bechdel, Onstage and on *Recode Decode*." Recode.net, February 13, 2017. Accessed March 22, 2018.

Warhol, Robyn. "The Space Between: A Narrative Approach to Alison Bechdel's *Fun Home*." *College Literature* 38, no. 3 (2011): 1–20.

"IT BOTH IS AND ISN'T MY LIFE"

Autobiography, Adaptation, and Emotion in *Fun Home*, the Musical

LEAH ANDERST

I don't cry often. While I do at times well up and shed a few tears at the movies, in general my state of mind is exceedingly even keeled. So I was surprised to find myself crying in the viewing room of the New York Public Library's Performing Arts Research Library one afternoon. Sitting in the quiet space with headphones over my ears, I was nearly at the end of a video recording of the Broadway production of *Fun Home*, the musical adaptation of Alison Bechdel's graphic memoir, and near the middle of "Telephone Wire," a number sung by Alison and her father Bruce, when I felt the tears coming. This wasn't uncontrollable weeping; I didn't have to leave the room for fear of bothering the other researchers there, studious and apparently unemotional note takers, all. I paused the recording, wiped my tears and blew my nose, hit the rewind button on my screen, and watched the affecting scene all over again.

What had happened? I'd read Bechdel's graphic memoir a number of times; I'd taught the book in a class focused on memoir, and I'd published an article about it in a life-writing studies journal. I'd seen the original musical production when it premiered at the Public Theater in New York City in October 2013 before its move to Broadway in April 2015, where it won a number of Tony Awards. I'd seen the traveling production in Hartford, Connecticut, during the summer of 2017, a few weeks before viewing the recording. I knew the story and the characters well. I knew what was coming. There in the library, among other researchers, and facing a small television screen, I didn't anticipate tears.

Bechdel herself describes a similar experience. In April 2015, *Vulture*, the online arts accompaniment to *New York Magazine*, published Bechdel's *Fun Home* coda, "Play Therapy." Over eight pages, Bechdel describes receiving drafts and recordings of songs as its two writers, Lisa Kron and Jeanine Tesori, worked on the adaptation; she describes attending a performance of the musical; and she shows herself responding very strongly to the work. In the

Fig. 7.1. "Play Therapy," 5.

second half of "Play Therapy," Bechdel describes her initial expectations that the musical, whose words she represents coming out of her computer screen (fig. 7.1), would be light and "artificial." Her actual reaction was quite different than those expectations would have implied.

She says of the musical, "It seemed to get to the emotional heart of things more directly than my book had" (fig. 7.2). What Bechdel expected to be "artificial," an "arm's-length take," instead brought the emotional impact of the past experiences closer to the surface. Musical, a genre that is sometimes thought of as building distance between the story and the audience—musical numbers are, after all, not representative of everyday life—here draws Bechdel closer to the characters she created, closer to their experiences, and to their emotions.

The image accompanying these words in "Play Therapy" depicts Bechdel attending a workshop reading. While all the members of the audience stand clapping, we see Bechdel at the left, blowing her nose with a few droplets spraying above her head. The reading has brought the author of the source material to tears. And this comics coda suggests that if one of the goals of her narrative is to reach an emotional core for her readers, the musical version reaches that goal more efficiently for its viewers.

Although Bechdel seems to make a case for the affective and emotional power of musical performance over the narrative in comics form, my goal here is not to compare the two narratives with an eye toward better or worse, more or fewer tears, but rather to explore how the musical form unearths new

Fig. 7.2. "Play Therapy," 6.

ways of thinking about how we experience and engage with this story. A few driving questions here will be: How does performance communicate feelings to an audience differently than does a book? How does the musical, adapted not by Bechdel herself, allow us new avenues to consider voice, presence, and authority in this story? And what are the impacts of the genre-pushing choices made by the creators of this particular musical? With its two iterations, *Fun Home* offers a unique case study for exploring affect across genres. Bechdel's own surprised experience represented in "Play Therapy" and mine at the library reveal something interesting about the ways we might engage with narratives in the different forms they take.

Scholarship surrounding the aesthetics of emotional and empathetic responses to narrative is now myriad. Narrative theorists like Suzanne Keen and Robyn Warhol have written important books that outline and analyze the many ways we may empathize or "feel with" fictional literary characters. Brian Massumi and Peggy Phelan have produced similarly field-shaping works on affect in theater and performance studies. Particularly key to my discussion of *Fun Home* the musical are Erin Hurley's *Theatre and Feeling* and Scott McMillin's *The Musical as Drama*. Hurley's book presents a succinct yet thorough discussion of theater as a "feeling-technology" that "offers 'super-stimuli'; that is, it concentrates and amplifies the world's natural sensory effects" (28, 23). Feelings, she argues, have long been at the heart of theatrical practice, consumption, and scholarship, and her study aims to "bring theatrical feeling into focus as a research object and method" (3). Scott McMillin's book explores the aesthetics of musical theater and aims to complicate a long-standing idea that musicals are inferior to other performed genres and are rather uncomplicated, "integrated" works. Instead McMillin places the disjunction between book and number, the spoken lines of dialogue and the songs, at the center of his poetics of musical theater. This disjunction, this incoherence innate to the musical form, shapes the ways we perceive and experience many elements of theatrical narrative. This disjunction has the potential to alienate its audience, in the Brechtian sense. With its "feeling-technologies" of music, lyrics, and staging, however, musical often has the opposite effect, drawing audiences closer to a character's mind, and this is especially true in *Fun Home*.

Two broad elements in both versions of *Fun Home* stand out for their potential to affect readers and audience members emotionally, and it is these two elements that guide my discussion: voice and time. Narrative voice in a memoir may encompass a number of voices. Traditionally there are two: the voice of the autobiographer at the moment of writing, called the *narrating-I*, and the sometimes multiple voices of the character(s) she creates out of her former selves at different ages in the past, the *narrated-I* (also called *experiencing-I*).[1] These distinct voices generally occupy different parts of the storyworld, with the narrating-I a controlling voice outside the story and the narrated-I inside. Within the delimited areas of a staged production, musicals and plays can create distinct physical spaces to represent the inside and the outside of a story, but they can also create opportunities for those spaces to overlap and for actors to breach barriers. And like a prose or graphic genre, a musical or a play may also feature a narrator; the Stage Manager character in Thornton Wilder's *Our Town* (1938) is perhaps the most famous example. In *Fun Home*, the musical, the narrating-I Bechdel created for her memoir becomes a character, flesh onstage treading the same boards as the two younger Alisons, forming a trio of embodied voices. And this character who yet retains some of the authority of Bechdel's narrating-I plays an important role in guiding the responses of the audience.

Like narrative voice, the different uses and depictions of time in a book versus a live performance can have important effects on the ways that audience members are invited into a narrative. Most cogent in this respect are the ways that a musical moves between pause and progression. McMillin calls these moments of pausing in a musical "lyric time": "The song inserts a lyrical moment into the cause-and-effect progress of the plot, a moment that suspends book time in favor of lyric time, time organized not by cause and effect (which is how book time works) but by principles of repetition (which is how numbers work)" (9). With its alternation between the book and the numbers, a musical creates a distinct experience where the plot pauses as characters break into song, and in these moments the audience focuses its attention on the bodies, words, and interactions of actors, so that the emotions they portray take on exaggerated proportions. In many musicals, these numbers interrupt the plot, giving the audience time to linger on a particular moment, idea, or character. In short, the affective experiences of a memoir reader and of an audience member at a musical are strongly dependent on and distinguished by the two art forms' presentations of narrative voice and of time.

With book and lyrics by Lisa Kron, music by Jeanine Tesori, and directed in its two initial productions by Sam Gold, *Fun Home* the musical was well received by critics and audiences. It won five Tony Awards in 2015 after its move to Broadway, where it was staged in the round.[2]

Shortly after the Tony Awards, Bechdel described in an interview with *Rolling Stone* her reaction to the musical and to seeing parts of her life and her work performed by others onstage. "It's overwhelming," she said. "I haven't found a way to express the super bizarre surrealness of seeing my life on the stage and watching it play out multiple times. It's a very strange ontological position to occupy. It both is and isn't my life" (Collins). As Bechdel's words attest, although this musical stages parts of her life, it is quite distinct from the book she created. While the musical takes her memoir as its primary source material, the creators reshaped the story, cutting some scenes and developing and expanding on others, and putting many parts of her life into song. And the work of the actors and crew members continued this blurring between the various Alisons on set; they would refer to Bechdel herself as "T-Rab," or "the Real Alison Bechdel" (Paulson). The musical, then, occupies a generic space somewhere between memoir and biography, between nonfiction and fiction.

In an episode of CUNY TV's *Theater Talk*, Kron, Tesori, and Bechdel share details about the ways the musical grew from the graphic memoir. Kron describes being concerned with creating character arcs for the musical that she felt were not present in the book. One such example of this is Helen, Bechdel's mother, whose emotional life is more directly addressed in the musical than in the book. Of Helen in the musical, Bechdel says, "These guys [Kron and Tesori] fleshed out the character of my mother in ways that I didn't in the book. I knew my mother would read the book, so I tried to keep her character as minimal as possible." Focusing her memoir primarily on her father and herself, Bechdel's other family members recede into supporting characters in her book, but with the outside perspective they brought to the text, Kron and Tesori found ways to portray these characters with greater detail.

That a performer and playwright like Lisa Kron would see the potential for a stage adaptation in *Fun Home* is not surprising. Kron has written similarly autobiographical works, including the one-woman show *2.5 Minute Ride*

(1996), about her father, and an ensemble play, *Well* (2006), about her and her mother's allergy-related illnesses. *2.5 Minute Ride* is particularly relevant in this discussion of *Fun Home*. In *2.5 Minute Ride*, Kron ties together two familial stories: personal accounts from her family's annual trip to Cedar Falls, Ohio, where they visit an amusement park, and a trip she took with her father to Europe to visit the sites where his immediate family members died in the Holocaust. So, like Bechdel, Kron conceives of and writes her own life story through her father's.

Without delving into an exhaustive, evaluative list of the ways Kron and Tesori's adaptation alters the graphic memoir, I will mention several of the more salient changes. A few details that are absent or minimized in the musical are Alison's period of obsessive compulsive behaviors during her childhood; Helen's graduate work and her acting; Bruce's handwritten letters sent to Helen while he served in the military, letters that Bechdel re-creates meticulously in her memoir; the extensive use of literary allusions and frames through which Alison views herself and her parents; and the author's re-creation of family photos. In removing these details from the story, the musical emphasizes the twinned stories of Alison's coming of age and her father's tumbling to death. Where these aspects were cut, however, other areas of the book were magnified in ways that, as I hope to show, allow audiences new avenues into the text and into the characters.

An important point of comparison between the two works, and one that has a vital impact on the ways that readers and viewers are invited into the story, is the voice of the adult Alison Bechdel, the cartoonist-memoirist. From the first page of *Fun Home* and throughout the entirety of the book, readers hear Bechdel's narrating-I, a voice that at once presents the story and shapes the way we understand the drawn scenes from her past. This voice dominates the book, often far exceeding any words exchanged between characters within the drawings. Its presence is unmistakably strong and at times even exerts a stronger, more overt influence than the drawings it accompanies.

On the last page of the memoir's first chapter, for instance, we see five panels depicting a very young Alison learning to drive a riding lawn mower, first with her father's help and then on her own while her father continues other yard work nearby. Within and across the five images, the two characters do not speak to each other, and we read these words from the voice of the narrating-I (slashes indicate when the words are positioned in the gutter atop a panel, and brackets indicate words printed inside a panel):

It's true that he didn't kill himself until I was nearly twenty. / But his absence resonated retroactively, echoing back through all the time I knew him. / Maybe it was the converse of the way amputees feel pain in a missing limb. / [He really was there all those years, a flesh-and-blood presence steaming off the wallpaper, digging up the dogwoods, polishing the finials . . .] / . . . smelling of sawdust and designer cologne. / But I ached as if he were already gone. (*FH*, 23)

The voice of the adult comics artist shapes our reading of this visual content. What might be taken lightly as an everyday scene—a father and daughter working in the yard together—instead becomes a series of images colored by longing, loss, and suicide. In concert with the somber, monochromatic color wash, her narrating-I in effect directs how we "read" these drawings. That voice keeps us at a distance from the characters she has drawn; they are mediated, even barred, by Bechdel's retrospective, authoritative voice, which speaks from above and with omniscience. On this page, that voice asks us to engage with her narrative perspective, looking back, rather than with the perspective of the young child, who likely feels nothing so keen in that moment of lawn mowing as the cartoonist does in the moment of drawing.

Kron and Tesori had to find a way to bring that strong textual narrating-I onto the stage. So they transformed Bechdel's narrative voice into one of the three Alisons who take the stage. In the foreword to the published musical, Kron discusses this process: "Our source for this inside information is the narrative voice in the captions that surround every frame, which points out every instance of delusion, denial, hypocrisy, and retroactive irony. The voice is erudite, wry, and aching—the voice of a truth-seeker. It's what makes *Fun Home Fun Home*. We turned that voice into a character and made it the center of our musical" (7). The voice that, in the book, exists primarily in textual, alphabetical form (in a font created based on Bechdel's own handwriting), in the musical, takes shape through an actress who occupies the stage along with the other two actresses who portray the child Alison and the young adult Alison.[3] Here we have a body, in other words, a body who speaks in ways that do echo Bechdel's narrating-I but whose physical presence—whose audible voice, facial, and bodily expressions—adds dimensions to this figure that are nearly absent in the graphic memoir and from the readers' reception of the story. Importantly, too, because this character occupies the same stage as the other, younger Alisons, the figure who sometimes forms a barrier between Bechdel's narrating-I and the interior life of her drawn characters in the graphic memoir can instead step aside here to allow direct access to those other Alisons.

This character, described as "43 years old, a cartoonist," is called simply "Alison" in the script, and the other two actresses portray "Small Alison," "around 9 years old," and "Medium Alison," "19 years old, a college freshman" (Kron and Tesori, 5). "Alison" often stands or sits at a drawing table onstage, watching and commenting on the scenes and songs playing out onstage involving the younger Alisons and her family members. Like Bechdel's narrating-I that floats in the gutters around the panels in the text, this character often stands outside of the action rather than inside of it; she more often reflects on what is happening onstage than participates in scenes herself. This stage direction from the musical's beginning shows the adult Alison as both the cartoonist who creates and also a figure who occupies the stage with her creations: "Adult ALISON enters and crosses to her drawing table. Next to the table, on the floor, is a battered cardboard box. She rummages around inside it, looking for something to draw. She finds a ring of keys. She arranges it on her table, picks up her pen, and begins to draw" (Kron and Tesori, 9). Especially very early in the musical, this "Alison" often says the word "caption," to highlight something she is writing over a drawing. In an early scene that re-creates the first pages of the memoir, "small Alison" is hoisted into the air by her father. The actress playing the cartoonist stands off to the side of the scene, commenting while her younger self enjoys the game:

> ALISON. Caption: My dad I were exactly alike.
> SMALL ALISON. I see everything!
> ALISON. Caption: My dad and I were *nothing* alike.
> SMALL ALISON. I'm Superman!
> ALISON. My dad and I . . . My dad and I . . . (Kron and Tesori, 12)

Onstage the adult Alison speaks lines and sings songs that mirror the words and the sentiments that come through to the reader of *Fun Home* via Bechdel's narrating-I, but she is also a character onstage, walking us through the difficult process of selecting memories from her past and finding objects to draw from. Thus Kron's character is a version of Bechdel's narrative voice, but she is now an embodied creation, whom Kron has given more than just words. She has given her things to do onstage.

So while this character maintains something of the controlling relationship with the past and the stories that are told by a narrating-I in an autobiographical narrative, she is also, importantly, a character existing inside a theatrical storyworld over which she does not have complete control. Where she was an omniscient narrator in Bechdel's memoir, she does not exercise the same omniscience in the musical. In a few key moments, for instance, "Alison" enters into the story and loses some of what we might call her "narrative authority" or "narrative agency." During these moments, the story seems to happen to her rather than her making the story happen through drawing and narration.

Fig. 7.3. Alison and her father in the car (*FH*, 221).

Most notable in this respect are a scene and number toward the end of the musical—the number, "Telephone Wire," in fact, that prompted the flow of my tears in the library's viewing room. This scene adapts the two pages near the end of her memoir where Bechdel draws herself and her father driving together during one of her visits home from college. She doesn't realize that it will be one of the last times she sees her father alive, and she hopes for an opportunity to connect with him about their newly discovered shared sexuality. The drawings and the words on these pages of the memoir show the two broaching a moment of connection but never quite arriving there (fig. 7.3).

Alison and her father share childhood memories of wanting to dress up as the opposite gender, and the narrating-I links their conversation to literary father-child relationships: "It was not the sobbing, joyous reunion of Odysseus and Telemachus. / It was more like fatherless Stephen and sonless Bloom . . . [of James Joyce's *Ulysses*] / . . . having their equivocal late-night cocoa at 7 Eccles street" (*FH*, 221). Bechdel conveys the figurative wall between the two, a wall that, built by shame and embarrassment, neither would scale to meet the other more fully.

This page and the one that immediately precedes it are drawn in a way that sets them apart from the other pages of the memoir. Whereas Bechdel's panels are generally inconsistent sizes, even on the same page, here she has evenly spaced twelve panels of equal size, and within each panel is a nearly identical drawing of Alison as a college freshman and Bruce in profile sitting in the front seat of the car. The visual repetition here juxtaposes time passing quickly on what could be a crucial moment with the stasis that characterizes their emotional movement toward each other. Bechdel draws the image over and over, requiring her readers to pause on each panel, to see the same image again and again; and as in the panels depicting a young Alison learning to drive the family's lawn mower, so here the narrating-I retrospectively adds her reading of the experience, inflected by a literary allusiveness.

In the book, Bechdel's narrating-I generally hovers over or atop scenes. In these pages, however, her words sit within the same field as the two characters, printed in the black spaces inside the car. In a similar move, the musical places its version of this narrating-I inside the scene, but instead of occupying a space with her younger self, the actress playing Alison replaces Medium Alison onstage and voices both perspectives. Just before moving to the car area of the stage (simply a bench placed inside a spotlight where the two will sit together, facing forward), Bruce turns to Alison (the narrating-I Alison) rather than Medium Alison, the character we see in the scene in Bechdel's book. Bruce beckons her to join him within the area of the stage that represents the car interior, and the actress playing adult comics artist Alison responds to his "Kiddo? . . . You ready?" with some confusion before joining him on the bench, inside the scene, inside the story. The "real" scene took place with the college-aged daughter, but Kron opts for placing the writer-cartoonist there instead. The two have a dialogue partly spoken, partly sung, that is quite similar to the one had by the younger Alison and her father in the book, but with some added reflections from the adult's perspective.

The title of this number, "Telephone Wire," refers to one of two phrases that Alison repeats as she sings. Sitting in the car with her father, at times in silence and waiting for the opportunity to open up to him or for him to open up to her, Alison repeats the phrases "telephone wire" and "at the light" as she gears herself up to broach the acknowledgment that she and her father are both gay. While many of the scene's lines of dialogue between the two characters are included in the song, the number is largely internal, with the refrain representing Alison's repeated and increasingly distressed thoughts: "Say something, talk to him. . . . At the light [repeated]. . . . Like, you could say, so how does it feel to know that you and I are both—" (Kron and Tesori, 67–68). So this number shifts between plot development, a scene unfolding with dialogue between characters, and a pause inside the character's mind as she reexperiences this memory. The characters exchange a few lines, but the song's principal strength is its ability to plunge the audience into the mind of Alison.

McMillin's discussion of musicals often hinges on the distinction between book and number and the different orders of time that they imply. While he does not address *Fun Home*, his remarks highlight an important feature that manifests in this particular number. During a musical number, he writes, "The plot is suspended for the time of the number, which carries the characters into new versions of themselves" (44). In this example, "Telephone Wire" operates both as a driver of plot (Alison and Bruce play out a scene) and as a pause in the plot (the lyrics plumb Alison's mind, both the emotions she experienced in the past and those she experiences in this present moment as the adult cartoonist looking back). So music here, "lyric time" and the repetitive words of the song, slows the plot and opens a window into the mind of the character, holding and extending the attention of the audience. In another important study of musical theater, Raymond Knapp explains the role played by music as it relates to time and to emotional engagement: "Music notoriously does not unfold in 'real time,' but rather imposes a kind of suspended animation so as to intensify selected emotional moments, and through this dramatic hiatus directs us all the more urgently to see behind the mask/makeup/costume of the performer" (12). This is precisely what we see happening in "Telephone Wire." The character's anticipation mixed with anxiety is placed in stark relief.

Near the number's end, Alison's lyrics reach a desperate pitch as she understands that this memory will not change now that she relives it: "Make this not the past, this car ride! This is where it has to happen. . . . This can't be our last—" (Kron and Tesori, 70). These lines, particularly "make this not the past," place the adult Alison in an unusual discursive and dramatic space. Whereas the earlier verse seems to come more from Medium Alison's perspective, here she speaks from her retrospective perspective, reliving a moment from her past that was full of potential but never reaches what she hoped for. In the scene, she also speaks from and experiences from the perspective of Middle Alison, a narrated-I who does not yet know that this will be the last time she can speak openly with her father, who does not yet know that she and her father will not ever fully see each other. This is a kind of double-voiced perspective that amplifies the emotional experiences of both Alisons for the audience. Such a double-voiced perspective is certainly present in the graphic memoir as well; we "hear" from both the narrating-I and the narrated-I throughout that text and in close proximity to each other, and that accounts for much of the book's affective power. What the musical can do that the comic cannot, though, is place these two distinct perspectives into one person, one voice. Here those two perspectives are embodied by one actress, one human being whose performance focuses rather than disperses the audience's attention, and our experiences of her emotions are magnified. We see the different kinds of *presence* we experience in a performance where the narrative levels of the memoir, the clear distinctions between a narrating-I and the narrated-I, can be brought closer together and even located within one individual; and because of the suspension of plot time in favor of lyric time in this moment, we pause to experience with Alison in ways that are distinct from a reader's experience of the graphic memoir.

Beth Malone, the actress who played adult Alison in the musical's first two productions in New York City, sings these lines with great intensity. Earlier in the number, Malone's voice is quiet and seems to take on characteristics of Alexandra Socha's singing voice, the actress who plays Middle Alison. Here at the end she is nearly yelling in despair and panic as the moment slips away without the conversation she wished had happened.[4] Hearing these lyrics and watching this scene, even after a number of times, brought the emotions of the adult Alison to the very surface of my body. There in the library, intently focused on the two characters inside the screen, I had that familiar feeling that creeps into your nose and your face as your eyes fill with tears. In Erin Hurley's estimation, theatrical productions move us in part by tightening our focus on actors performing: "The feeling-technologies of lighting, architecture, and audience control," she writes, "orient the spectator's senses—notably, her vision and hearing—to the action onstage by effectively reducing the number of stimuli competing with the onstage performance" (28). Hurley does not discuss musical theater at length, but we can see that what McMillin calls "lyric time," a feature common to the musical form, and Bechdel's narrating-I as adapted by Kron both function as powerful "feeling-technologies" for the musical.

Hurley describes affect as "unruly": "It exceeds us by happening against our will.... Affect happens *to* us.... Feelings ... extend our perception beyond our own body" (14, 22, 23). Matthew Reason describes affective experiences during performances in a similar way: "These are not so much experiences we have, but experiences that have us" (84). This aptly captures my experience of watching the recording of *Fun Home* and seems to do so as well for Bechdel's experience represented in "Play Therapy." The formal elements of the scene, one that was so tightly controlled and regimented into its evenly spaced panels in Bechdel's memoir, the song and its lyrics, and the adult character bodily reliving her past experience and voicing her memories—all cohere into a more "unruly," affective experience that asks the audience to feel intensely with this character, to feel in our bodies what she feels in hers.

Well before she published *Fun Home* in 2006, Bechdel wrote a short illustrated essay, "The Wonderful World of Me," about her experiences writing autobiographical comics. In that essay, she describes moments in her comics when she writes and draws details from other people's stories alongside hers: "The best material happens when my story collides with someone else's" (*Indelible*, 42). She refers here to the story of a young man at Oberlin College who happened to enter her life just when she was discovering that she was gay, but this line could just as easily refer to the way that *Fun Home* plays on the collisions between her stories and those of her father. It could also refer to what is happening here when Lisa Kron and Jeanine Tesori bring their vision to stories in *Fun Home*. We don't see their personal stories in this musical—none of Kron's experiences with her own parents are explicitly visible, for instance—but their perspectives, brought to bear on this story, and the musical medium, unearth new affective, highly emotional avenues into Bechdel's experiences.

NOTES

1. Sidonie Smith and Julia Watson provide a thorough discussion of these and many other critical terms in autobiography studies in their *Reading Autobiography*.

2. *Fun Home* won in the following categories: Best Musical, Best Performance by an Actor in a Leading Role in a Musical (Michael Cerveris), Best Original Score Written for the Theatre (Lisa Kron and Jeanine Tesori), Best Book of a Musical (Lisa Kron), and Best Direction of a Musical (Sam Gold) (Pedersen).

3. A few notable drawings of this narrating-I appear in *Fun Home*. When Bechdel reproduces the photograph of Roy lying on a hotel room bed, she also draws her own hand holding the photograph on the left-hand page (*FH*, 100–101). But where some of her earliest autobiographical comics did include full drawings of her present-tense self (the multipage "Coming Out Story," published in *Gay Comics* #19 in 1993, features many frames with drawings of the cartoonist herself, explaining aspects of the surrounding frames [reproduced in *Indelible*, 35–46]), the narrating-I of *Fun Home* is almost exclusively textual.

4. I thank Jill Stevenson for alerting me to this detail about Malone's singing in "Telephone Wire," shared with her by a student of musical theater at Marymount Manhattan College.

WORKS CITED

Anderst, Leah. "Feeling with Real Others: Narrative Empathy in the Autobiographies of Doris Lessing and Alison Bechdel." *Narrative* 23, no. 3 (2015): 271–90.

Bechdel, Alison. "Play Therapy." *Vulture*, April 10, 2015. Accessed March 14, 2018.

Collins, Sean T. "Alison Bechdel on *Fun Home*'s Tony-Award Triumph." *Rolling Stone*, June 18, 2015. Accessed March 14, 2018.

Hurley, Erin. *Theatre and Feeling*. Palgrave, 2010.

Keen, Suzanne. *Empathy and the Novel*. Oxford University Press, 2007.

Knapp, Raymond. *The American Musical and the Formation of National Identity*. Princeton University Press, 2004.

Kron, Lisa. *2.5 Minute Ride and 101 Humiliating Stories*. Theatre Communications Group, 2016.

Kron, Lisa. *Well*. Theatre Communications Group, 2006.

Kron, Lisa, and Jeanine Tesori. *Fun Home*. Samuel French, 2015.

Massumi, Brian. *Parables for the Virtual: Movement, Affect, Sensation*. Duke University Press, 2002.

McMillin, Scott. *The Musical as Drama*. Princeton University Press, 2006.

Paulson, Michael. "'Fun Home,' the Musical, Takes Alison Bechdel's Life to Broadway." *New York Times*, April 8, 2015. Accessed August 30, 2018.

Pedersen, Erik. "Tony Award Winners 2015 Full List: 'Fun Home,' 'Curious Incident of the Dog in the Night-Time' Lead the Way." *Deadline*, June 7, 2015. Accessed March 14, 2018.

Phelan, Peggy. *Unmarked: The Politics of Performance*. Routledge, 1993.

Reason, Matthew, and Anja Molle Lindelof, eds. *Experiencing Liveness in Contemporary Performance*. Routledge, 2016.

Smith, Sidonie, and Julia Watson. *Reading Autobiography: A Guide for Interpreting Life Narrative*. University of Minnesota Press, 2010.

"'Fun Home' with Lisa Kron, Jeanine Tesori and Alison Bechdel." CUNY TV's *Theatre Talk*, April 17, 2015. Accessed March 18, 2018.

Warhol, Robyn. *Having a Good Cry: Effeminate Feelings and Pop-Culture Forms*. Ohio State University Press, 2003.

GENERATIONAL TRAUMA AND THE CRISIS OF *APRÈS-COUP* IN ALISON BECHDEL'S GRAPHIC MEMOIRS

NATALJA CHESTOPALOVA

Autobiographical and memoir narratives stand out as authorial projects dedicated to the drive of knowing the self across temporal and affective planes. In an interview with the *Paris Review*, Alison Bechdel described her graphic memoir *Are You My Mother? A Comic Drama* as a self-reflexive autographic narrative that negotiates the dangers of exposing intimate details of family life in public space. It is a continuation of *Fun Home: A Family Tragicomic*, inspired by a complex and on occasion tumultuous relationship between Bechdel and her parents. These narratives reveal Bechdel to be an artist who recognizes an internal longing for emotional clarity and reconciliation between her past and her present. To an extent, the concern with public and private exposure of familial and domestic trauma forms only one of the dialogical backbones of the memoirs. As far as the symbiotic psychological work contained in the two narratives is concerned, the focus lies with the deeper uncovering of Bechdel's origins as a daughter, as a lesbian, and as a victim of internalized PTSD symptoms. This process of uncovering comes through as highly retrospective as well as shaped by intersecting themes across generations.

Fun Home and *Are You My Mother?* function together as a narrative space for an examination of multiple intersecting themes including mourning, melancholia, nostalgia, gender diversity, sexuality, and particularly cross-generational and familial trauma. This essay suggests that both autographic memoirs are indicative of the multiplicitous potential that exists in graphic narrative to provoke new dialogues with regard to how we approach, interpret, and interact with generational and familial trauma that stems from dysfunctional relationships with parental figures. This essay also looks at the two autographical memoirs by tracing out some of the narrative trajectories and storytelling methodologies that sustain Bechdel's texts. Bechdel's self-healing and therapeutic writing is framed by the memoir and diary traditions and plays with the capacity to uncover generational trauma that taps into a number of narrative methodologies, such as diary keeping, memoir traditions, and the practice of writing-as-healing.

Enclosed by the idea of an affective archive, *Are You My Mother?* builds on the juxtapositions of the father-daughter bond in *Fun Home* by shifting the focus toward Bechdel's traumatic relationship with her mother. This uneasy shift is a key transformational moment in Bechdel's writing and is contingent on a set of transitions: from past to present, paternal to maternal, internal to external, and unconscious to conscious. I argue that these transitions, and Bechdel's capacity to portray and address generational and familial trauma retroactively, rely on explicitly weaving the narrative around a backdrop of psychology and psychoanalysis. Bechdel intentionally situates the "reader in the position of the analyst" (Terzian), by embedding her storytelling within the network of theories and concepts developed by D. W. Winnicott, Freud, Jung, and Lacan. On the one hand, this allows Bechdel to experiment with the task of taking on both the role of patient and the role of analyst. On the other, the reader is called on as a rhizomatic entity taking on the functions of the analyst, observer, and witness all in one. With each chapter, Bechdel invites the reader to examine her trauma through a series of crises, narrated both textually and visually and enacted through the Freudian concept of afterwardness or, as Lacan coined the term, *après-coup*. Both a narrational and a therapeutic method, the psychological process of returning to the sites of past traumatic experiences in *Fun Home* and *Are You My Mother?* allows Bechdel to use *après-coup* to regain a formalized connection to her mother-daughter and father-daughter bonds.

Joan Didion wrote that we tell ourselves stories in order to live (11). Ellen Forney's *Marbles: Mania, Depression, Michelangelo, and Me* (2012) and Nicole Georges's *Calling Dr. Laura* (2013) share Didion's perspective by conveying and questioning the traumatic, as well as regenerative, processes that allow the authors to capture the connection between mental health and creative subjectivities. In Bechdel's graphic works, her traumatic personal and familial histories collide with the autobiography, memoir, and diary genres within the dimensions and temporalities of the comics medium. The disparate images of Bechdel's past, bound by panels, pages, and gutters, are likewise framed by the need to account for *le pacte autobiographie*, or the autobiographical pact of the memoirs (Lejeune, "New Genre," 160), which finds its basis in truth and how a truth-based narrative can be therapeutic.

Psychological healing through memoir writing is thus intimately connected to a self-reflexive negotiation and acceptance of the experience of growing, aging, and living. William L. Randall and A. Elizabeth McKim elaborate on these experiential phenomena by arguing that "narrative activity is rooted in the most basic form of consciousness, and that consciousness itself is a narrative process" (22–23). In fact, our life story, or the narrative that we compose from within, can be approached as a literary story (41). The development of our narrative identity is based on this internalized and continually evolving life story, which in turn expands into a self–story line (65–66). Randall and McKim further state that this process involves a paradoxical activity where a subject has to take on the dual functions of a self-reader and self-author (69). This process of self-healing through autobiographical writing requires a sophisticated reading of one's own conscious as well as unconscious self, a type of acquired self-literacy (94).

Bechdel's authorial and narrative voices showcase this type of self-literacy through an intently reflexive reading of her familial histories and a recurrent concern with psychological self-analysis, compelling her to return to past traumatic experiences and memories. We can observe the evolution of Bechdel's self-literacy in her obsessive-compulsive symptoms around the time she started her first diary. In particular, she began to experience an existential hesitation that caused her to add the phrase "I think" to every statement in her diary notes. Reflecting on this behavior, Bechdel later comments that those "I thinks were gossamer sutures in that gaping rift between the signifier and signified" (*FH*, 142). She further adds that "to fortify them, I perseverated until they were blots" (142). This remark invests a sense of genuine urgency and violence into the desire to figure out how to return to and then read one's own self–story line. The subject's mundane daily activities and encounters suddenly gain an existential dimension and become the site of struggle for subjectivity. In Lacan's take on Saussure, the signified and signifier become trapped in an "incessant sliding of the signified under the signifier," continuously set to "demonstrate that no signification can be sustained except by reference to another signification" (Lacan, 419, 415). Bechdel's obsession with introducing "I think" into her permanent diary records is an act of self-preservation against this incessant sliding and against the vertigo of self-literacy. It is likewise an uncanny doubling of the slanted bond between younger Alison and her father Bruce. The diary, which began as a sign of parental affection and concern, becomes a sacred personal space, a type of "amulet, warding off evil from [Alison's] subjects" (*FH*, 142), and preparing her for transforming chaos into regenerative order.

The distinction between authorial and narrative voices allows Bechdel to create an uncanny otherness between the drawn subject on the page and the author's subjectivity in search of an ontological ground. Although this reflects an emotive writing methodology, such a dynamic likewise helps to establish the patient-analyst frameworks critical to the narratives of the memoirs. When visiting Carol, her therapist at the time of writing, in chapter 4 of *Are*

You My Mother?, Bechdel emphatically states that throughout her life she has been "pitting" herself against each of her psychoanalysts, but "What I really want is to cure myself. To be my own analyst" (*AYMM*, 149). This observation is key to understanding both memoirs and the kinds of psychological unpacking that such writing can offer Bechdel as a subject and an author. Part of the healing potential of the memoir genre lies in its capacity to offer a unique space where, as Mary Evans suggests, "individual chaos" can be projected as a "desire for social order" (1).

The emphasis of the memoirs on self-healing, as well as the distinction between Bechdel, the author, and Alison, the narrative voice, is likewise valuable to the narrative return to her childhood and teenage years. The storytelling merges Bechdel's memories, interpretative reflections, and various meticulously re-created memorabilia. In fact, the extent to which both graphic narratives rely on the insertion of the redrawn journal entries, letters, newspaper clippings, passages from literary books, and photographs into the narrative transforms the storytelling into an accidental multimodal "archive-of-feeling," echoing Ann Cvetkovich's notions of fluidity and emotional affect. Although the inclusion of letters, photographs, and other ephemera is a common method for integrating and legitimizing familial histories in autographic narration, Bechdel emphasizes the need to return and assess her collected memorabilia as one would an object or childhood memory in a clinical case study. That is, each drawn photograph, letter, and page from a book is contextualized with an aura of autoethnographic inquiry. For example, in chapter 1 of *Are You My Mother?*, a full-bleed splash laid out in a two-page spread features a layered narrative based on drawn photographs of Helen, Bechdel's mother, holding baby Alison, and a re-created set of the drawing instruments used to produce them (*AYMM*, 32–33) (fig. 8.1).

Items including the ink pen, pencil, ruler, eraser, and even a Gerber baby food container set the stage for Bechdel's dive into her family's photo archive. The two-page bleed spread features three types of text bubbles that are temporally and thematically disjointed: signifying the narrator's voice in the present, the narrator's inner dialogue about Bruce Bechdel and Sylvia Plath, and the author's close reading of the photographs. Laid out like crime scene evidence, the panel functions as a site of multiple emotional economies, one primarily concerned with the difficulty of experiencing afterwardness through objects that conjure up memories of parental abandonment, depression, and inability to cope. This panel reflects the same deep preoccupation found in D. W. Winnicott's primitive emotional development work on the pre-Oedipal stages of the infant's development that, on the one hand, cannot exist outside the infant-mother relationship and, on the other, is cognizant of the infant's absolute dependence and the mother's depressive potential ("Primitive," 145–56).

Fig. 8.1. Alison and her mother (*AYMM*, 31–32).

At the center of Bechdel's second autographic memoir is an exploration of the affective economies that define a mother-daughter bond as an imperfect, intimate, and psychologically tense phenomenon. The narrator of *Are You My Mother?* interacts with the figure of the parent in a way that begins a dialogue about Bechdel and the various influences that inform and stem from her dysfunctional mother-daughter relationship. The intensity of this autobiographical unpacking rests on a symbiotic understanding of where the audience fits into this dialogue. By weaving the narrative around a backdrop of psychology and psychoanalysis, especially the thinking of Winnicott, Freud, and Jung, Bechdel situates the reader in the position of the analyst. She allows the reader to examine the figure of the mother as a shifting entity that mutates and molds itself onto substitute transitional objects and experiences, including Bechdel's therapists and romantic attachments. Alternating between transcribed audio dialogues, diary entries, counseling sessions, dreams, letters, photographs, and memories, Bechdel's second autographic memoir's unpacking uses the *après-coup* to return to the emotional sites of memory.

Freud's afterwardness or Lacan's *après-coup* in both memoirs offers a retroactive understanding and revisitation of the instances of previous suffering, anxiety, and trauma. To begin with, Bechdel's search for a mother figure in her second book is based on the desire to acknowledge and repair traumatic moments of failed affection, reciprocity, connection, and acceptance. Negotiating the boundary between a writing cure and an appeal for parental acknowledgment, the memoir also appraises the efficacy of *après-coup* in mending the mother-daughter bond and marking the ambiguity of defining and distinguishing between a mother and a mother figure. For instance, within the first few pages of *Are You My Mother?* the reader encounters Bechdel as narrator, driving alone and engaging in an imaginary conversation with her mother Helen about the need to create *Fun Home*, the desire to give her father a "proper funeral" (*AYMM*, 6). At the outset, the narrative applies a particular tone and perspective that position the reader as a critical observer of a dialogue between a depressive mother figure and, as Bechdel puts it, a "smarmy, self-indulgent, solipsistic piece of shit" of a daughter (5)—a relationship bound by the same needs and expectations already present in Winnicott's infant-mother bond that by definition escapes finitude and remains forever open to suffering.

Contextualizing the narrative perspective as a framework that builds on *Fun Home*, *Are You My Mother?* is bound by Bechdel's return to the struggle of writing her first memoir, while navigating an ongoing traumatic relationship with Helen through moments of *après-coup*. This doubled retroactive journey serves as one of the multiple instances of *après-coup* at the sites of traumatic pain; as she puts it, "This story begins when I began to tell another story" (*AYMM*, 4). *Are You My Mother?* sets the audience up for a rhizomatic engagement with a dual purpose of both writing a new narrative and addressing the toll of the first one. The reader-as-analyst has to traverse the storytelling terrain where each chapter begins with a dream, followed by a dream interpretation, and is partitioned with scenes from Bechdel's therapy sessions, glimpses of her romantic relationships, and theoretical passages focused on psychoanalytical concepts she uses to make sense of her past and present. In terms of the graphic style, dream sequences stand out as bleeds with pitch-black background appropriate for subconscious and sublimated narratives that find their sources in forgotten or repressed anxieties. The black, gray, and red color scheme in the second memoir, versus the black, gray, and blue-green in *Fun Home*, helps draw the reader's attention to certain memorabilia or similarities, especially in the panels re-creating phone conversations between Bechdel and her mother. In fact, the sporadic use of red throughout the memoir helps sustain the sense of a disruptive motherly presence, such as in the episode where Bechdel admits, "Whatever it was I wanted from my mother was simply not there to be had," and "it was not her fault" (*AYMM*, 228). The red phone cord, acting as a physical connection for this reenactment of the infant-mother bond, resembles the umbilical cord that has failed to provide Bechdel with a sufficient environment in which to grow and thrive.

Part of the memoir's uncovering of Bechdel's aim to reestablish a more balanced and satisfying relationship with her mother figures finds its counterpart in the therapy sessions with Jocelyn and Carol. To an extent, both therapists prepared Bechdel for the engagement with a number of Winnicott's concepts, including the transitional object (*AYMM*, 59), transitional behavior, true and false self (96–97), and the good-enough mother (61, 131). The last concept is of particular relevance to Bechdel's return to the sites of original familial trauma, since it aids the narrator in creating a system of emotional references that sustain rather than jeopardize the mother-daughter bond. In one of the episodes, Bechdel considers the dysfunctional mother-daughter bond in correlation to a memory of Helen suddenly rather than gradually ending breast-feeding (60–61) (fig. 8.2).

From Winnicott's perspective, this withdrawal does not allow the child to gain the necessary subjectivity and adaptability to his or her surroundings in time to process this maternal denial. However, with a better understanding of the good-enough mother and the facilitating environment, the narrative's return to the site of childhood distress can offer a regenerative instance of afterwardness—the mother did her best, considering the circumstances and the father's complicity in them.

Within the panels of Bechdel's regular phone conversations with her mother in the second memoir, we see a reflection of the good-enough mother who is imperfect, but reasonably consistent, predictable, and reliable. At certain points in the autographic narrative, the figure of the mother begins to mutate and shift, eventually being substituted with transitional objects and experiences, including Bechdel's therapists and relationship partners. One of these transitional objects and behaviors is Bechdel's attachment to her therapist Jocelyn, whom she locates as an uncanny source of warm and motherly connection. Bechdel keeps re-creating and returning to this transitional attachment by taking long, almost tranquilizing, walks at night to Jocelyn's house (*AYMM*, 58–59). Another illustration can be seen in Bechdel's childhood teddy bear Beezum, which functions as a traditional transitional object and a special possession that permits the subject to learn that she is separate from the motherly figure (56). Moreover, "Beezum" was adopted as a pet name between Bechdel and her girlfriend Eloise, a source of protective affect and motherly emotional economies. Here the autographic memoirs themselves can be considered as special possessions, at the time of writing and in their form as published works that circulate and replay the pain of an infant-mother bond.

It is worthwhile thinking about how the psychoanalytical concepts included by Bechdel function within the framework of afterwardness or *après-coup*.

pleasure principle to the reality principle or towards and beyond primary identification (see Freud, 1923), unless there is a good-enough mother. The good-enough 'mother' (not necessarily the infant's own mother) is one who makes active adaptation to the infant's needs, an active adaptation that gradually lessens, according to the infant's growing ability to account for failure of adaptation and to tolerate the results of frustration. Naturally, the infant's own mother is more likely to be good enough than some other person, since this active adaptation demands an easy and unresented preoccupation with the one infant; in fact, success in infant care depends on the fact of devotion, not on cleverness or intellectual enlightenment.

Fig. 8.2. The "good-enough" mother (*AYMM*, 60).

Although Freud's take on afterwardness continued to develop over time, and then further through the works of Lacan, what structures *après-coup* as a psychic mechanism is the idea that experiences related to various types of affect "are registered in the psychic apparatus, which is, a system that exists in space and time," and these experiences are "re-experienced and externalized through the analytic process" (Perelberg, 1201). The overwhelming majority of these types of experiences are based on affect and emotional economies that stem from generational and parental trauma or conflict.

In *Studies on Hysteria*, Freud introduced the idea of afterwardness as a conceptual continuation of the relationship between trauma and symptom. As Freud notes, trauma does not act as merely an "agent provocateur in releasing the symptom, which thereafter leads an independent existence"; rather, "the physical trauma—or more precisely the memory of the trauma—acts like a foreign body which long after its entry must continue to be regarded as an agent that is still at work" (Freud and Breuer, 6). As such, Bechdel's work derives much of its storytelling precisely from this continuous remembering, reexperiencing, renarrating, and reembodiment through the comics medium, the process of drawing, and the multimodal framework. The fact that in creating her memoirs, Bechdel chose to reenact the narrative, take photographs of herself in character, and then draw the comics based on the immersive image makes her experience of *après-coup* that much more visceral. Freud stresses the necessity of a vivid recollection of the original trauma that is supplemented with genuine affect and a careful recollection through narration. Within the original context of *Studies on Hysteria* and the cases Freud considers, this emotive recollection can take the form of verbal utterance, since Freud already began to recognize the intrinsic link between trauma and symptom as a potentially cathartic one (Freud and Breuer, 8). He wrote that "language serves as a substitute for action," and "by its help, an affect can be 'abreacted' almost as effectively" as through a physical interaction (8). The introduction of *après-coup* into Bechdel's storytelling tests the capacity for healing despite, as well as because of, traumatic parental relationships that structure her desire to recollect and recontextualize the past.

There is a certain expectation that the narrator of these memoirs is attempting to take control of her past experiences of suffering and discomfort; however, it is the utterance through visual and textual language that in itself becomes a form of therapy. A powerful example of such regenerative *après-coup* comes at the end of *Are You My Mother?* when Bechdel's style of drawing transitions from a paneled memory of a "crippled child" game she used to play with her mother (*AYMM*, 286), to a bleed depicting a "mutual cathexis" (287). Against the pitch darkness of solid black, young Alison lifts her imaginary crippled feet, and her mother responds by playing into the infant-mother scenario where "she could see my invisible wounds because they were hers, too" (287). This instance of *après-coup* reflects the emotional complexity of the smallest gestures and interactions that can act as a stimulus for a point of return. The reader-as-analyst has to consider Bechdel's experiences of afterwardness within specific contexts, including her understanding of the Freudian unconscious and its functions in everyday life (46–49). In the second chapter, the reader follows a series of panels in which Bechdel talks about the psychopathology of everyday life and how it can be retroactively applied in her self-analysis. She notes that the psychopathology of the everyday is "all about how our mistakes reveal the contents of our unconscious" (46). The psychopathology of the everyday is also correlated to Jung's concepts of patient-analyst transference, transformation dreams, and rebirth (81). Next to a series of panels depicting Helen mending little Alison's jeans, the text boxes state that the day she read about Jung's mother archetype and its basis in "goodness, passion, and darkness" (80), she experienced a transformational nightmare. In this case, a conversation with her therapist Carol signals a potential desire to justify the need for expression through autobiographical writing and an even deeper desire to understand how the mother-daughter bond can be reclaimed as a source of healing. In another episode, a wooden plank hits her right between the eyes, the "third eye, or brow chakra in Indian medicine," "where we look not out, but in" (48). Bechdel's self-analysis concludes that "perhaps my unconscious was telling me to pay more attention to my unconscious" (49). On the pages, however, this memory is paired with a redrawn section of Bechdel's journal written during her obsessive spell, and pointing to the need to return even further back into her past where some of the sources of her anxieties lie, that is, her relationship with the father figure.

In Bechdel's autobiographical writing, the sets of *après-coup* narratives are woven around the violent incoherence of her parents and their respectively traumatized and traumatizing identities. In fact, each *après-coup* memory is primarily in dialogue with either the mother or the father figure, keeping the parents in separate storytelling spaces and instantiating Bechdel's sense of fissured familial ties. *Are You My Mother?* uses the story of the writing of *Fun Home* to return to the subject of dysfunctional parental bonds as introduced in that first memoir; the writing of *Fun Home* sets the psychological stage for a dialogue between Bechdel and her mother that could only occur once she has returned to her past and reformulated the childhood traumas she has incurred because of Bruce's obsessive temperament, domineering personality, and possible suicide.

For Bechdel, the father figure, and in an extrapolated manner any parental figure, is an elusive object that exists in a continuous state of flux. Driven by the desire to know her father and to know her own self through a return to parental bonds, in *Fun Home* Bechdel lays out the ways in which her father struggled to maintain the duality at the core of his ongoing process, set on preserving a sense of normalcy in a dysfunctional familial and cultural setting. The title of the first chapter, "Old Father, Old Artificer," and later references to Bruce as "an alchemist of appearance, a savant of surface" (*FH*, 6) orient the autographic narrative around a father figure incapable of offering a stable emotional model for his daughter. In *Fun Home*, we find Bechdel in the process of continuously formulating and reformulating her identity and assigning meaning to the internal and external, conscious and unconscious, experiences of her childhood and early adulthood. Specifically, this progression is shaped by unstable emotional economies developed and sustained by the psychological boundaries Bruce has constructed as a way of coping with the double life he was leading as a gay man with a heteronormative family.

A father who felt the need to hide his sexuality for most of his life, Bruce's bond with Alison as a child and adolescent is an unbalanced and traumatic relationship punctuated with sporadic moments of paternal familiarity. In *Fun Home*, the physical and emotional distance between Bechdel and her father is occasionally interrupted by instances of tenderness and confidence. For example, Bechdel carefully describes the times when Bruce played the "icarian games" (*FH*, 3) or washed her in the tub. These interactions offer rare instances of physical intimacy as well as a sense of discomfort, since they highlight the intensity of the failing child-parent bond. One of the techniques Bechdel developed in *Fun Home* as a result of her repressive upbringing was the practice of accessing emotions vicariously. In chapter 2 of *Fun Home*, she describes the difficulty of talking emotionally about Bruce's suspected suicide and notes that "for years after my father's death, when the subject of parents came up in conversation I would relate the information in a flat, matter-of-fact tone . . . eager to detect in my listener the flinch of grief that eluded me" (*FH*, 45). This need to engage in grief, even if vicariously and retroactively, reflects Bechdel's journey to acquire the methods necessary for regenerative engagement with traumatic memories and experiences, especially in instances that emphasize the need to return to the affect-ridden sites of psychological discomfort and strain. Toward the end of *Fun Home*, Bechdel returns to the awkward conversation she had with Bruce not long before his suspected suicide—a conversation about her sexuality. Narrated on two pages, each with twelve identically sized panels, the conversation is not the "sobbing, joyous reunion of Odysseus and Telemachus" (*FH*, 220–21) but rather an experiment in reverse parenting. Instead of locating a Winnicottean good-enough parent in this afterwardness, the memoir returns to this moment as a harsh realization that the father figure and its failure is in some vital ways irredeemable.

Part of Bechdel's progression through her self-story line in *Fun Home* includes a return to her childhood home as a precarious space, the domain of a domineering and inaccessible father figure incapable of providing a proper facilitating environment for a child. In chapter 1, multiple memories turn to the restoration of the Victorian house and Bruce's compulsion to preserve the domestic space through a facade of normalcy and sophistication. The house and its emotional economies reflect an uncanny traditional space within imposed heteronormative contexts. As far as Bechdel's memories are concerned, being part of this household was similar to being raised by Martha Stewart (*FH*, 13). The family home thus functions as a stage for the unraveling Bechdel family and an embodiment of the domestic boundary constraining the familial emotions within an enclosed, hidden, and uncanny area. In a panel depicting one of the numerous instances where Alison had to help Bruce with his curatorial projects around the house, she notes, "I grew to resent the way my father treated his furniture like children, and his children like furniture" (14). On another page, the Bechdel family is decorating the house for the holidays, with Alison and her brothers sitting around the Christmas tree in a pose she refers to as "still life with children" (13). In this telling panel, the festivities are aestheticized under the guided supervision of the father, who appears as a dark shadow (13) (fig. 8.3).

Reflecting on this problematic setting, Bechdel's depiction of her father and the tensions he introduced into her childhood draws an affective parallel with Tolstoy's *Anna Karenina*, as a reminder that all happy families are alike, and each unhappy family is unhappy in its own way. To use Bechdel's phrasing, "It's tempting to suggest, in retrospect, that our family was a sham. That our house was not a real home at all but the simulacrum of one, a museum. Yet we really were a family" (*FH*, 17).

The experience of afterwardness in the first autographic memoir includes episodes when Bruce helps Bechdel situate her own developing subjectivity within a storytelling framework by introducing her to literature and Greek mythology. To an extent, Bechdel's return to those childhood moments is defined by a sense of opposition and aggressive counternarrativity, or as she writes, "I was Spartan to my father's Athenian. Modern to his Victorian. Butch to his Nelly. Utilitarian to his Aesthete" (*FH*, 15). On the other hand, both Bechdel and her father share the lack of emotional coherence and a Sisyphean impulse to continually negotiate their approaches to gender, sexuality, and fulfillment. The forms of such a fulfillment become a key concern in both of Bechdel's autographic memoirs, especially in the later relationships with romantic partners and psychoanalysts that function as transitional objects.

The transformational potential of returning to the memory sites of original familial disharmony takes on a new dimension toward the end of *Fun*

Fig. 8.3. Still life with children (*FH*, 13).

Home where the reader encounters a discernible change in tone and narrative perspective. In addition to the constrictive settings of the funeral parlor and Victorian house symptomatic of the authority of the father, the childhood scenery in the latter part of *Fun Home* is diluted with an occasional image of Bechdel in open and unfamiliar spaces, where she appears at ease and in charge of her physical and mental state. On one page, the Alison figure takes a bike ride to watch the sunset, calm and composed as her mind contemplates Bruce's death and its connection to a sense of displaced grief (*FH*, 196). In a speech bubble, she ponders, "Maybe I'm trying to render my senseless personal loss meaningful by linking it, however posthumously, to a more coherent narrative. A narrative of injustice, of sexual shame and fear, of life considered expendable" (196). The episode shows a greater sense of control over her subjectivity, and an acceptance that it is inevitably bound by her experiences as a daughter, a lesbian, and a subject of internalized trauma. It likewise illustrates Bechdel's developing narrative voice and allows her to experiment with the genre boundaries of the autobiographical framework and engage in self-healing through *après-coup* and fantasizing.

A noticeable emotional shift in the storytelling occurs as Bechdel writes: "It's tempting to say that this is my father's story. There is a certain emotional expedience to claiming him as a tragic victim of homophobia, but that's a problematic line of thought" (*FH*, 196). Such a therapeutic sense of control through retroactive storytelling and fantasizing enables Bechdel to visualize the traumatic father figure transformed from an obsessive, melancholic, and overbearing parent into a man proudly embodying his gender identity and successfully navigating the boundary between the internal and external, conscious and unconscious desires (197). This reimagined father sharply contrasts with Bechdel's memories of Bruce as a towering emblematic figure habitually intruding on the domestic space with an imposition of order and dread, sometimes taking over the space of an entire panel. However, such a domineering father figure serves a critical purpose in terms of the psychological and emotional unpacking that the memoirs perform as a whole. *Fun Home* works through the idea of a father as a dysfunctional and "lowering, malevolent presence" (197) so as to create sufficient emotional space to properly engage with the mother-daughter relationship. The second memoir builds on those initial emotional economies as it discloses some of the regenerative sites where familial healing is possible—in a present that accepts the past through conscious afterwardness.

Bechdel's autographic storytelling develops a space for psychological work that uncovers her origins as a daughter and a critical reader of her own life narrative. It likewise functions as a vehicle through which she can return to temporal moments with an identifiably different narrative aim, psychological self-reflexivity, and psychoanalytical perspective. This process entails the sophisticated use of *après-coup*, as traces of memories, experiences, and impressions can be revisited only once the subject reaches a new stage of internalized maturation. The process of uncovering also implies that both progressive and regressive movements will take place simultaneously. From the psychological standpoint, this calls for affect-rich phenomena like repression, repetition, fixation, compulsion, and multiple returns to the sites of the repressed trauma. Both *Fun Home* and *Are You My Mother?* permit the reader to trace this intimate, personal, and tension-ridden process as each memoir shifts between past and present, maternal and paternal, pain and healing. The sites of parental anxiety and trauma that remained inaccessible before the creation of *Fun Home* begin to resurface in a manner that lends itself to the narrative model of *après-coup*. Although reading Bechdel's second memoir is possible without the context of *Fun Home*, the overlapping of the two autographic works affords an opportunity for an engagement that takes into account not only the depth of traumatic affective economies in mother-daughter relationships but also the ongoing, continuous, temporal nature of this bond and its capacity to reinvent itself. By accepting the relevance of concepts such as a good-enough mother and transitional objects, through the *après-coup* framework, Bechdel finds an alternative to the linear-time view of parental trauma. The reader-as-analyst is placed in a privileged position of accessing circular time where the mending of the mother-daughter bond through storytelling is possible, and new memories open up a crucial space for an active, recurring, and therapeutic engagement. Bechdel's autographic memoirs are a form of rare communication that mends familial wounds by voicing, rather than silencing, the dysfunctions within the always already emotional and always already present mother-daughter closeness and dependence. To use Winnicott's poetic metaphor for the child's communion with the mother, which echoes in Bechdel's own journey: "I find you; / You survive what I do to you as I come to recognize you as not-me; / I use you; / I forget you" ("Communication," 80).

WORKS CITED

Cvetkovich, Ann. *An Archive of Feeling: Trauma, Sexuality, and Lesbian Public Cultures.* Duke University Press, 2003.

Didion, Joan. "The White Album." In *The White Album*, 11–48. 1990. Reprint, Farrar, Straus and Giroux, 2009.

Evans, Mary. *Missing Persons: The Impossibility of Auto/Biography.* Routledge, 1999.

Forney, Ellen. *Marbles: Mania, Depression, Michelangelo, and Me.* Gotham-Penguin, 2012.

Freud, Sigmund, and Josef Breuer. *Studies in Hysteria.* In *The Standard Edition of the Complete Psychological Works of Sigmund Freud: Volume II (1893–1895)*, trans. James Strachey. Vintage Books, 2001.

Georges, Nicole. *Calling Dr. Laura: A Graphic Memoir.* Houghton Mifflin Harcourt, 2013.

Lacan, Jacques. "The Instance of the Letter in the Unconscious, or Reason since Freud." In *Écrits: The First Complete Edition in English*, trans. Bruce Fink, 412–44. Norton, 2006.

Lejeune, Philippe. "A New Genre in the Making?" *Auto/Biography Studies* 32, no. 2 (2017): 159–61.

Miller, Nancy K. "The Entangled Self: Genre Bondage in the Age of the Memoir." *PMLA* 122, no. 2 (2007): 537–48.

Perelberg, Rosine Jozef. "The Controversial Discussions and *après-coup*." *International Journal of Psychoanalysis* 87 (2006): 1199–220.

Randall, William L., and A. Elizabeth McKim. *Reading Our Lives: The Poetics of Growing Old.* Oxford University Press, 2008.

Terzian, Peter. "Family Matters: Alison Bechdel on 'Are You My Mother.'" *Paris Review*, May 9, 2012. Accessed September 20, 2017.

Tolstoy, Leo. *Anna Karenina: A Novel in Eight Parts.* Trans. Richard Pevear and Larissa Volokhonsky. Penguin, 2006.

Winnicott, D. W. "Communication between Infant and Mother, and Mother and Infant, Compared and Contrasted." In *Winnicott on the Child*, 70–84. Perseus Books, 2002.

Winnicott, D. W. "Primitive Emotional Development." In *Collected Papers: Through Paediatrics to Psycho-Analysis*, 145–56. Basic Books, 1958.

THE EXPERIMENTAL INTERIORS OF ALISON BECHDEL'S *ARE YOU MY MOTHER?*

YETTA HOWARD

Before Alison Bechdel became widely read with the publication and subsequent Tony Award–winning Broadway production of *Fun Home*, her *Dykes to Watch Out For* comic strip—recently and occasionally resurrected as a response to the presidency of Donald Trump—was circulated primarily in queer cultural contexts and, despite its eventual reach beyond these contexts, is situated within the legacies of underground comix. At a certain remove from both *Fun Home* and *DTWOF*, Bechdel's *Are You My Mother? A Comic Drama* is an avant-garde memoir that all at once turns its attention to, and moves away from, a strict focus on the author's relationship with her mother and is, significantly, her most experimental work to date. Following *Fun Home* but departing from its more mainstream impulses, this second graphic memoir demonstrates a resistance to normative narrative sequence and, by extension, psychic navigability. This essay dwells in these textual resistances as what I argue is an invocation of interior space as queer space that depends on the implementation of experimental comics-associated methods. That is, all at once narrative and mental, corporeal and spatial, the queerness of these interior spaces becomes defined as lingeringly liminal, unpredictable, and unresolvable states of being and representing.

    I locate such states as erotically directed text-image play with the graphic form that productively revises understandings of the text beyond reading exclusively for its psychoanalytic elements. In turn, the queerness of the text's interiority is detectable in features that are infinitely open-ended, resist closure, and ultimately signify for both Bechdel and her readers a counterintuitive "way out" (*AYMM*, 289), observable, for example, in the text's ending as its own beginning, which can also be thought of as an incessant revision of a conclusion. Accordingly, it is necessary to turn to lesser-expected ways into the text and the features associated with its experimental interiors: the role of the auditory and of disability, the queer objects/objecthood of the text, and frameworks of narrative unorientability all become a constellation of possibilities for visualizing the queerness of the memoir's graphic form. Queerness therefore comprises interior textual-spatial-psychic-bodily instances that I broadly designate as loosening putative distinctions between interiority and exteriority epitomized in the statement "the space between me and not-me" (*AYMM*, 58).

Susan Rubin Suleiman's feminist approach to the avant-garde offers a way to situate how the figure of the mother in Bechdel's text becomes a transitory entity that may call up a psychoanalytic maternal while discarding it: "The mother denied or displaced, played with and over and on, the object of apparently endless inventions in the perverse game of transgressive sons; the mother repudiated by rebellious daughters, or else idealized" (xvi). For Suleiman, the political imperative of avant-garde practices operates in tandem with the radical gestures of aesthetic experimentation for a politics of difference. At stake along these lines is how the experimental qualities of *Are You My Mother?* queerly exceed and complicate the intersubjective frameworks that it displays via depictive strategies that I show readily account for the disruptive queerness of the text's graphic form in relationship with its narrative content. I accomplish this by turning to a range of formal and relational contexts identifiable within the nonlinearity of the text's narrative as imbricated in the aesthetic qualities of the text. The investment in the avant-garde aligns with both its modernist historical application in reference to Bechdel's incorporation of Virginia Woolf's *To the Lighthouse* (1927) and contemporary experimental approaches attending to the queer feminist erotics that underwrite the text's inclusion of Adrienne Rich's lesbian literary poetics and prose.[1] Without reducing the text to these metanarrative inclusions, I seek to think queerly and graphically about sexual minority difference.

Are You My Mother? positions itself within methodological innovations that readily reflect queer intimacies outside orthodoxies of clinical, relational, or authorial practice. While Lisa Diedrich, who grounds her analysis in Winnicott and Bechdel in tandem, contends that the text's "[(re-)creation of] space and time to begin in formlessness" (184) is crucial for psychoanalytic as well as creative practice, Genie Giaimo discusses the text's "[failure] to produce meaning" (38) in the context of autobiographical writing that is remedied by turning to interdisciplinary neuroscientific contexts. Such approaches are certainly generative for thinking about the ways that attention to form can extend beyond the disciplinary boundaries that come with a focus on life writing and the strictures of its generic conventions. What Giaimo theorizes in terms of the text's "autobiographical uncertainty" (45) and what Diedrich describes as Bechdel's being "concerned with the process, as much as the product, of making" (185) are relevant to how this essay works through the text's experimental queerness.

But the text's experimental aesthetics invite an untidier way into experiencing its queerness, which the attention to Winnicott's object relations theory or even to psychoanalysis writ large may have the effect of circumventing. As Tammy Clewell argues, Bechdel's book "rejects the classic notion of a psychoanalytic cure based on the analyst's interpretation of the patient's symptoms and the dissolution of the patient's resistance to this interpretation" (53). Using a range of interdisciplinary methods from queer cultural studies, this essay departs from a psychoanalytic focus and instead moves toward reading for how the experimental interiors of Are You My Mother? explicitly and implicitly depend on erotic differences that characterize the narrative's textual antistructures. An overreliance on Winnicott and other psychoanalytic elements, I suggest, has the effect of emptying out the text's queerness and the centrality of Bechdel's sexual identity that informs a large part of it. We may borrow the title of the text to ask it of the text itself: is it merely about the relationship with her mother? While the text does, of course, make this familial relationship crucial, I want to abandon a strict account of how it may or may not resonate with clinical and kinship conventions and instead see Bechdel's innovative craft of graphic form in light of sexual minority difference and as an opportunity to work through complex aesthetic reflections of queer subjectivity that move beyond Winnicott and the associated psychoanalytic theories with his work regarding Bechdel's relationship with her mother. This essay does not discount their importance in the text but rather seeks to emphasize what is queer about the text in modes that are not beholden to clinical psychoanalytic perspectives.

The Auditory and Disability as Markers of Difference

While placing together the auditory forms of Are You My Mother? and the references to disability in the text may seem like questionable juxtapositions, I believe that their inconsistent treatments are necessary ways into the queerness of the text's experimental palpability. In regard to interior space in the instances of their textual inclusions, I group them together because they maintain oblique yet potent markers of difference in the minor instances of their appearances in the text. We could even make the claim that the minority status of their appearances is coextensive with their roles as onomatopoetic and non-able-bodied expressions that transmit Bechdel's sexual minority difference. Here their status as minor is key: the reader may all at once acknowledge but ignore them. Since just as their appearances are sporadic, so they become visible manifestations of nondominant identificatory and aesthetic realms that exceed the norms that come with dominant ways into textual analysis, that is, interests only in major themes and standard narrative features.

Bechdel's choice to use a red watercolor wash—rather than turquoise, as in *Fun Home*—for *Are You My Mother?* is significant in its affective suggestiveness. Red signifies love, anger, and passion, and the text capitalizes on the indistinct combinations of these emotive states through the visual presence of the watercolor's aesthetic imperfections and messiness of its execution as readable signifiers of Bechdel's unresolvable relational negotiations. This is particularly noticeable in one of the chapter-ending pages, each of which are uncomfortably and unevenly centered as a single-panel, two-page spread with a black-fill background, sustaining a restrained splash-page effect.

At the end of the "Mind" chapter, the sound of a phone constantly ringing with no answer, onomatopoetically displayed as the sound effect "IIINNNGGGDRRRIIINNNGGGDRRIIIN" (*AYMM*, 158–59), brutally bisects the isolated panel with its forcefully thick, dark burgundy-red all-caps typographic rendering, which thrusts its jagged harshness with a reverberating effect (fig. 9.1). This image follows Bechdel's recounting of when she came out as a lesbian to her mother, the letter received from her mother as a nonresponse to it, and a phone conversation a couple of months after receiving the letter. Rather than just focusing the scene on the discussion of her parents' impending divorce with no follow-up conversation about the revelation of her sexual identity, Bechdel chooses to give prominence to their conversation about the difficulty that her mother had in reaching her by telephone, since she had apparently been dialing an old number and letting it ring over and over again. Marking a suspended state of unworkable neglect and lack of interest in supporting her daughter's queerness, the previously described image ends the chapter. In a series of text box insets, Bechdel turns the blame on herself—"I wasn't there when she needed me" (*AYMM*, 158)—while simultaneously calling up the ongoing futility of attempting to achieve full acceptance by her mother.

As an expression of such ambivalence, the watercolor in the background shows the traces of where the colors have bled into each other while still wet, a visible unevenness that mirrors the unfinished quality of their conversation. The auditory framework of the panel follows suit: "One ring reverberating into another." "And another." "And another" (158–59). The pinkish bleed outside the fine lines of a door image next to the phone (mis)communicates passion as straddling the negative/positive divide of anger/love that is indeterminately placed in time: "The phone ringing in the empty room. I couldn't get it out of my head" (158). The exterior constancy of the audible ringing is visually projected outward via the onomatopoetic graphic form as a distinct invasion of her psychic space, an aesthetic-sonic negotiation of queer affective surrender.

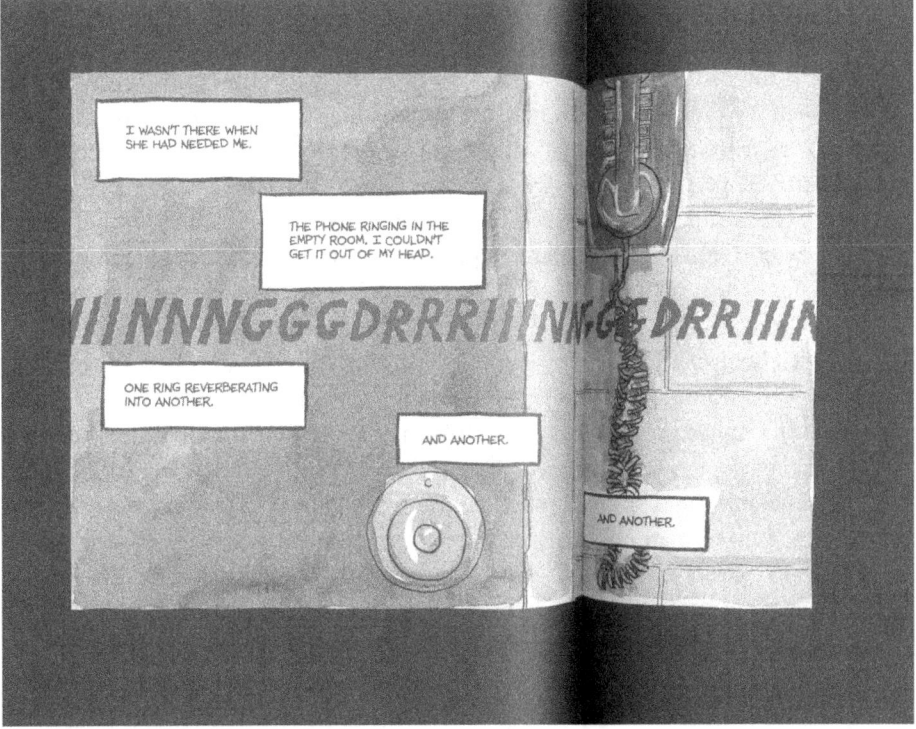

Fig. 9.1. Phone ringing (*AYMM*, 158–59).

Somewhat similarly, at the beginning of the "Mind" chapter, which opens with a dream sequence (as do the rest of the book's chapters), Bechdel dreams of abject bodily fluid—"The body is gone, but an awful sign remains—blood, or vomit, or something" (*AYMM*, 120)—that has been left behind on a dorm room floor. I will briefly return to this fluid later, but in this moment, appalled by her indifferent roommates, the college-aged Bechdel figure in the dream urgently and unsuccessfully attempts to call for help on what appears to be the same hall phone imagined as ringing incessantly in the context of her mother's dialing the wrong number to reach her as discussed earlier.

What is equally significant, however, is the role of the auditory in this moment. In the dream, Bechdel attempts to navigate the campus phone system to dial out but is unable to. One of the panels depicts an angrily frustrated Bechdel, whose bodily signifiers fittingly communicate her frustration: one arm stretches out to lean against the wall, and her facial features show her looking down impatiently as she fails to get help. But in the panel and what follows it, her frustration is executed sonically. A spiked speech balloon hovers between Bechdel and the phone and contains an illegible, miscommunicative scribble indicating that she has indeed reached someone but it is a wrong number. As reader-listeners, we are not privy to the voice at the other end of the line, but instead we experience the moment as a visual display of sonically directed frustration. This moment is instructive not only in how it uses illegibility but also in how it resonates with the sonic dimensions that address sexual minority difference and gender nonconformity. As J. Jack Halberstam writes in reference to James Scott, "Illegibility may in fact be one way of escaping the political manipulation to which all university fields and disciplines are subject" (10). The unpredictable possibilities in the autonomy that illegibility yields, what Halberstam explains as "undisciplined knowledge" (10), become useful ways to situate the queerness of the moment outside psychoanalytic disciplinarity and, by extension, generic conventions, especially in regard to its sonic framing in the "silent" medium of graphic narrative.

The image that follows is Bechdel manically punching the number keys on the telephone, which are "sticky and unresponsive" (*AYMM*, 121). Bold, exclamatory 1s and 8s loudly surface as auditory effects of her protracted efforts, which more than obliquely call up a later moment when she describes herself as "paralyzed with self-consciousness" (156) when rationalizing her social awkwardness at a younger age with her sexual identity. The visually illegible voice on the other line—the scrawls in the context of the wrong number—operates in the same scope as the encounter between sound and image in comics aesthetics. This encounter places itself as a congested form of oppositions that links with a question posed by Bechdel's therapist Carol, "Who's the authority you're appealing to?" (123), in analyzing the significance of the dream as a series of exterior displacements among her authorial voice, Carol's, her mother's, and her girlfriend's.

And yet the selection of the word *paralyzed* to address her budding sexuality and gender nonnormativity is significant. It points to the spare moments when Bechdel refers to the "crippled child game" she played with her mother, a game that involved pretending to be disabled. This game has been read as "therapeutic space" (Diedrich, 201) and self-entrapment (Giaimo, 52–53), but we might also extend this game, specifically the visualization of transgressive bodily integrity, as coinciding with Bechdel's queerness. The moment in the text that stands out in relationship to gender and sexual difference is less about the game but is notable when Bechdel ponders, "How much of me is me?" (*AYMM*, 140) alongside an image of herself with one leg missing and a speech balloon that simply says, "Me" (140), executed in a wavy panel, indicating a thought or dream state. Following this panel is a series of panels bordered with wavy lines that increasingly show Bechdel losing more and more extremities—both bodily and textual—and eventually reduced just to her head, shown smiling, connected to a life-support machine. As she moves further and further away from normative embodiment in the dream-thought

Fig. 9.2. Fragmentation/bodily integrity (*AYMM*, 140–41).

panels, the speech bubbles within them counterintuitively confirm integrity with each repetition: "Me." "Still Me." "Me!" (141) (fig. 9.2). Instructive here is Alexandre Baril's work on transability, a term otherwise known as body integrity identity disorder (690), which he connects with trans identity: those who "see themselves as disabled individuals whose bodies do not reflect what they feel" (690) and experience "dysphoria caused by differences between the physical body and body image often compared with the experience of transgender/transsexual people" (690). While it might be questionable to claim that Bechdel's text displays any clear representation of her in terms of trans identity—whether transabled or transgender—the interiority of her thought process in articulating her fragmentation collides with the visible exteriority of how she presents herself as a gender nonnormative queer person to the world. Her statement, expressed in another panel displaying her wide-eyed contemplation in bed, "I'm in my brain" (*AYMM*, 141), therefore develops as an unexpected yet solidified state/ment of outward physical being.

Queer Objects

Winnicott's transitional object, "neither internal nor wholly external to the child" (Diedrich, 187), is perhaps the dominant object in question when approaching the text, even as it is, for example, reworked so that the figure of Winnicott becomes the transitional object that Bechdel uses to write the book (192–93). Of course, the text itself is a queer object that relies on its self-referentiality, what Diedrich deems "a meta-obsessive-compulsive documentation of the process of documentation itself" (186), and what Heather Love describes as "*Are You My Mother?* is in large part about the difficulty of writing *Are You My Mother?*" In other words, it is a book that simultaneously is and is not about Winnicott's object relations in terms of Bechdel's relationship with her mother. Similar to Diedrich's and Love's references to its postmodern qualities, the text's experimental objecthood is detectable in visual-narrative sequencing that mobilizes objects in seemingly random, sometimes chaotic, fashion, so that the objects isolated for repetition in the text mark its queerness by redirecting lines of division between interior and exterior states.[2]

Such repetitions and reproduced objects are noticeable even when implicitly structured.[3] As mentioned earlier, the mysterious abject bodily fluid that could be either blood or vomit in the dream that initiates the "Mind" chapter is anything but neutral. It reemerges as a small amount of fluid that Bechdel vomits on the linoleum (*AYMM*, 260). While Bechdel's mother's tone is described as "kind, sympathetic" (260) in this moment, her disappointment with Bechdel's failure "not [to] need anything from her" (260) translates as the traces of objects her father threw in the kitchen, such as the gouge left behind from a plate and marks left on a wall from a mayonnaise jar (263), posthumous signs of marital frustration or a quarrel. In these instances, the bodily traces of various forms of parental rejection materialize as the vomited food and liquid as much as the thrown objects—things that that body has rejected or projected and with which it cannot reconcile. As Ramzi Fawaz writes in his reading of *The Fantastic Four*, visually displaying the physicality of bodies and objects "[disorients] the arrangement of normative heterosexuality, becoming a locus for unpredictable, queer desires" (84). In the queerly dispersed arrangement of repetitions in *Are You My Mother?* objects are often bodily, such as the vomit, while internal affective states and kinship relationality become physically enacted and extend outward.[4] The absence of the thrown objects lingers in their exterior traces as erotic dislocations, as "substitute[s] for intercourse" (*AYMM*, 265).

But in the context of queer sex, lesbian sex, and other nonheteronormative sexual practices, hands are body-objects beyond the conventionally corporeal. When interacting with other objects or body parts, hands signify an erotically manifested response to Bechdel's question, "Why *can't* my life and my work be the same thing?" "My work is *about* my life!" (*AYMM*, 152). Bechdel's words here, when routed through Adrienne Rich and Virginia Woolf in light of Bechdel's sexual identity in the text, position her work—particularly her work tools—as the same thing, indeed. The instruments she uses to write and draw are also staple genital objects in lesbian sexuality. SDiane Bogus's prose piece "Dyke Hands" is fitting to bring up as illustrative: "dyke hands are the sexual organs of lesbian love" and "are the private source of lesbian pleasure

Fig. 9.3. Reading Adrienne Rich (*AYMM*, 170).

and a constant betrayer of it" (198). The private source of pleasure—enacted practices that may be interior or hidden from public view—becomes exteriorized as public objects that betray their sexual force in not being conventionally thought of as sexual objects but are instead exposed for all to see. When Bechdel recalls her college years, she includes a moment when she and a lover are reading Adrienne Rich together. In a seduction scene, her lover reads to Bechdel, "'Your strong tongue and slender fingers reaching where I had been waiting years for you in my rose-wet cave'" (*AYMM*, 170) (fig. 9.3). The queerness of this moment is not reducible to the explicitness of Rich's words. Instead the queer body-objects are routed through the words in the book, which, as the object that they are reading, continuously displaces the erotic object in question beyond phallic sexuality. Accordingly, the genital interiority of the "rose-wet cave" should be thought of in its persistent interaction with queer sexual organs—fingers, tongue—whose status as exterior is always deceptive.

Unorientable Relationality

The question that the text takes as its title—"are you my mother?"—becomes an apt way to situate its continuous workings through relational contexts that perpetually stray from normative orientation, which characterizes its aesthetic-narrative properties. Like its queer objects, Bechdel's documentation of the interactive qualities of those with whom she surrounds herself serves as guideposts to the larger stakes of the text's intimacies and eroticism that necessitate experimental expression. When Bechdel's therapist Carol tells her, "You relate to your own mind like it's an object . . . like it's an internalized parent or lover" (*AYMM*, 152), Carol connects these relations to Bechdel's work, to which Bechdel duly and self-referentially responds with wanting to write them down. As Carol's assessment in this exchange suggests, the desire for a maternal object is in a near-constant state of deferral in the text. At one point Bechdel wants Winnicott to be her mother (21), while at another point, she wants Jocelyn, her therapist from an earlier moment in her life, to take on the role (51). When she refers to her own inhabitation of the role, what she describes as "the strangely inverted relationship I'd always felt I had with my mother . . . this sense that I was her mother" (53), the accompanying images are those of herself with a girlfriend, Eloise. This substitutive framework not only represents a transgressive take on erotic-kinship structures—structures that the text is intent on depicting while also dismantling—but also further characterizes the unorientable trajectories that its objects of desire follow. As Sara Ahmed writes, part of what makes an object desirable is its lack of readiness to be an object: "Getting what you want can be terrifying because what you want is not simply 'ready' as an object" (31). What Ahmed theorizes as the promise of happiness—of happy families in particular—pertains to the fulfillment of expectation and those who may be alienated from such promises (49), such as the "unhappy queers" who "might have to minimize the signs of queerness" if required to approximate the signs of happiness (94).

Bechdel's narrative-psychic strategies of deferral, then, are crucial and the erotic-kinship substitutions that inform the relationships with her therapists follow suit. She characterizes her therapists as if they were ex-girlfriends: "Long before Carol, there was Jocelyn. I started seeing her when I was twenty-six" (*AYMM*, 19); the platonic intimacies that encompass these relationships run awry and reframe their contextual boundaries. This is observable, for instance, in being denied a hug from Jocelyn, who translates Bechdel's request purely therapeutically: "I wish you'd brought that up earlier. We'd need to talk about it, and there's no time now. Let's start here next week" (271). At another point, Jocelyn—whom we do see hug a surprised-looking Bechdel—admits, "I *like* you" (105), which is set in a horizontal panel that includes Bechdel's confession to us/Jocelyn, "I hated being just another client. I lived for weeks on her reply" (105). The inconsistencies of the relational circumstances find unlikely graphic form in the consistency of the replicated horizontal panels that take up the page as well as the two pages that precede it and the one that follows it.

Perhaps more imperative as far as "boundaries" are concerned is the reader-author relation and the book's own relationship to itself, to which the physical exteriority of the book, specifically its dust jacket, provides key access.

Love writes that, in the hardback edition, the book's cover is "soft and textured," showing "everyday items in sensuous detail," and "situates the reader at eye level, looking at the mother's dressing table." In turn, Clewell discusses how the dust jacket *reflects* "the mutual recognition of common suffering" as a reparative experience in having the question that the book takes as its title "printed in the mirror atop her mother's dresser" (68), so that readers inhabit, if only temporarily while reading, the psychic-spatial dwelling of Bechdel's mother vis-à-vis Bechdel's forms of self-reflection. If Love and Clewell are correct, we may extend their notions to notice that the mirror on the dust jacket is opaquely cast in shiny but matte silver ink that nonetheless offers erotic possibilities as an avant-garde mirror. In other words, we have no clear reflection, and the visual effect aligns with the text's narrative pointing back to itself as an endless mirroring.

The closing image of the "Mirror" chapter visually corroborates this idea, as it includes the young Bechdel figure standing with her back to a mirror: the image corresponds to holding a mirror up to a mirror, with the unlimited yet contained impossibility of a stable reflection. The inset text boxes communicate that Bechdel is both "trapped" and "opening out, in an infinite unfurling," and she introduces these states as equally "one way" and "in another way" (*AYMM*, 244). The simultaneity here, beyond its links with Winnicott's mirror-role or Lacan's Imaginary, is significant in terms of the unbounded effect of play with the mirror-image as much as with the image of the mirror itself. Rather than the funeral home's shorthand as *Fun Home*, *Are You My Mother?* functions more as a funhouse mirror, reminiscent of John Barth's postmodern *Lost in the Funhouse*, which includes stories rhetorically and aesthetically structured like a Möbius strip, where the question of straightforward, orientable interior and exterior space is undetermined, thus reflecting what Charles Hatfield writes about the problem of authenticity in autobiographical comics: "The representation of time through space, and the fragmentation of space into contiguous images, argue for the changeability of the individual self" (126).

But as a queer text, the erotics of *Are You My Mother?* are intimately connected with such experimental qualities. Instructive here is Irigaray's theory of the speculum, which invites corporeal aesthetics of interiority in dialogue with the genital interiority revealed earlier. For Irigaray, in reference to the vicissitudes of the object-mirror, "The speculum is not necessarily a mirror. It may, quite simply, be an instrument to *dilate* the lips, the orifices, the walls, so that the eye can penetrate the *interior*. So that the eye can enter, to see, notably with speculative intent" (*Speculum*, 144; italics in original). While bordering on the gynecologically cisnormative, this dilation of interiority is perhaps a more suitable way to think about the erotic interaction between reader and

Fig. 9.4. Infinite mirror (*AYMM*, 244–45).

text. When Bechdel writes about Woolf's writing, she remarks that "language gets very confusing as it approaches this place where outside and inside touch ... Or fail to" (*AYMM*, 257). Confusion, like the dilation of interiority, is the fun place to be: it is the erotic imperative that is central to the text and the promise of its queer experimentations. Its beginning and ending "touch" each other so that the reading experience compels an anti-essentialist account of queer female sexuality that revises and extends what Suleiman writes as an element of the avant-garde, "where the reader expects the sense of an ending, it offers merely a stop" (36).[5] In *Are You Mother?* the difficulty of deciding if the text has ended is actually expressed early on when Bechdel admits that "there's a certain relief in knowing I am a terminus" (7). The way into the text, then, is to embrace the terminus as "the way out" (289) (fig. 9.4).

NOTES

1. Clewell writes that Bechdel "[grants] Woolf something of the status of a comics artist" (63).

2. The text's "[drawing] together [of] seemingly unconnected events of her life" (Clewell, 52) offers significant potential in situating queerness as a randomness that points to the nonnormative interaction of body-objects, similar to what Suleiman describes as "avant-garde fiction [offering] repetition or else the juxtaposition of apparently random events" (36).

3. For Giaimo, "Reproduced objects and theories fail to account for or explain Bechdel's autobiographical story" (38).

4. Significant here are also the affective contexts of proximity: as Ahmed writes, "Orientations register the proximity of objects, as well as shape what is proximate to the body" (24).

5. Irigaray's vaginal imagery can be invoked here once again: "Woman 'touches herself' all the time, and moreover no one can forbid her to do so, for her genitals are formed of two lips in continuous contact. Thus, within herself, she is already two—but not divisible into one(s)—that caress each other" (*This Sex*, 24).

WORKS CITED

Ahmed, Sara. *The Promise of Happiness*. Duke University Press, 2010.
Baril, Alexandre. "'How dare you pretend to be disabled?': The Discounting of Transabled People and Their Claims in Disability Movements and Studies." *Disability and Society* 30, no. 5 (2015): 689–703.
Bogus, SDiane. "Dyke Hands." In *Erotique Noire/Black Erotica*, ed. Miriam Decosta-Willis, Reginald Martin, and Roseann P. Bell, 198–99. Doubleday, 1992.
Clewell, Tammy. "Beyond Psychoanalysis: Resistance and Reparative Reading in Alison Bechdel's *Are You My Mother?*" *PMLA* 132, no. 1 (January 2017): 51–70.
Diedrich, Lisa. "Graphic Analysis: Transitional Phenomena in Alison Bechdel's *Are You My Mother?*" *Configurations* 22, no. 2 (Spring 2014): 183–203.
Fawaz, Ramzi. *The New Mutants: Superheroes and the Radical Imagination of American Comics*. New York University Press, 2016.
Giaimo, Genie. "Psychological Diffusions: The Cognitive Turn in Alison Bechdel's *Are You My Mother? A Comic Drama*." *European Journal of Life Writing* 2 (2013): 35–58.
Halberstam, J. Jack (published under Halberstam, Judith). *The Queer Art of Failure*. Duke University Press, 2011.
Hatfield, Charles. *Alternative Comics: An Emerging Literature*. University Press of Mississippi, 2005.
Irigaray, Luce. *Speculum of the Other Woman*. Trans. Gillian C. Gill. Cornell University Press, 1985.
Irigaray, Luce. *This Sex Which Is Not One*. Trans. Catherine Porter. Cornell University Press, 1985.
Love, Heather. "The Mom Problem." *Public Books*, October 2, 2012. Accessed March 18, 2018.
Suleiman, Susan Rubin. *Subversive Intent: Gender, Politics, and the Avant-Garde*. Harvard University Press, 1990.

INCHOATE KINSHIP

Psychoanalytic Narrative and Queer Relationality in *Are You My Mother?*

TYLER BRADWAY

In "Is Kinship Always Already Homosexual?" Judith Butler observes that psychoanalytic theory has yet to rethink its narration of kinship from the perspective of "those who live outside of normative kinship or in some mix of normative and 'non-'" (*Undoing*, 128). While queer theory and anthropology have begun to conceptualize "post-structural kinship," psychoanalytic theory remains beholden to an Oedipal plot that—despite its queer potentialities—presumes the nuclear family.[1] Hence Butler wonders what a psychoanalytic narrative of kinship might look like from the perspective of nonheteronormative subjects, such as LGBTQ people, adoptees, and children produced through surrogacy and IVF. She calls for a queerer consideration of the narrational practices that structure the child's psychic and social emergence:

> Must the story that the child tells about his or her origin, a story that will no doubt be subject to many retellings, conform to a single story about how the human comes into being? Or will we find the human emerging through narrative structures that are not reducible to one story, the story of a capitalized Culture itself? How must we revise our understanding of the need for a narrative understanding of self that a child may have that includes a consideration of how those narratives are revised and interrupted in time? (*Undoing*, 128)

Here Butler unravels the retrospective temporality of psychoanalytic narration, which invariably seeks the subject's origin in the past. A queerer narrative would grasp the inchoate nature of kinship—how narratives of relationality are revised and proliferated across time. It would also understand narrative itself as an active force in the epistemic and affective negotiation of kinship.

To capture the queerness of kinship narration, then, we must attend to the plurality of narrative structures for self-understanding that do not conform to—or that actively resist—an Oedipal plot.

It is within this nexus of queer narrative form and familial belonging that I want to turn to Alison Bechdel's "comic drama" *Are You My Mother?* Bechdel's work centers on a figure of "mixed" kinship absent in Butler's account—namely, the queer child who remains vitally, if ambivalently, attached to their ostensibly heteronormative "blood" family. Bechdel's narratives ironically foreground the absence of a relation otherwise presumed by heteronormative culture. In a queer twist on Simone de Beauvoir, for Bechdel, *one is not born, but rather becomes, kin.* Her life writing narrates what I call *inchoate kinship*—a mode of queer belonging in which even blood bonds are unfinished, open-ended, and susceptible to being rewritten as queer bonds. Bechdel's narratives thus provide a staging ground for the conflicting cultural pressures of heteronormativity and queerness as they compete over the terrain of belonging. *Are You My Mother?* visualizes the double binds of heteronormative kinship that impinge on the lesbian author, particularly the heterosexist pressure to properly "mirror" the maternal figure. The comic's disruption of the mimetic logics of kinship and memoir—that the narrative accurately reflect reality—opens new ground to narrate kinship queerly.

Many scholars have examined Bechdel's relationship to psychoanalytic theory.[2] Yet the conversation overlooks how psychoanalysis converges with Bechdel's experimentation with the narrative forms for parental relationality. Bechdel not only unties and reties the bonds knotted through the Oedipal plot. Her work fundamentally remaps the narrative structures through which kinship becomes thinkable and inhabitable. It is key, then, that *Are You My Mother?* turns to D. W. Winnicott. Whereas Freud "saw the individual as an isolate, an ego seeking satisfaction of primary instinctual drives," Bechdel discovers in Winnicott a relational model of subjectivity (*AYMM*, 22). The subject comes into being through affectively dense and irreducibly intersubjective relations, and there is no end point for this process of relational becoming. Through Winnicott, Bechdel reimagines her kinship narrative as a parental object relation, nonteleological and, most importantly, situated within the "area of illusion" that constitutes the transitional space of the object (57). Modeled on the relationship between mother and child, this transitional space lies in a "territory between the subjective and the objective" (56).[3] Locating her memoir within transitional space, Bechdel frees herself from the burden to represent the "truth" of her mother and external reality itself. Insofar as this shift queers the aesthetic logic of memoir, it also opens a new understanding of the queerness of narrative within psychoanalysis. Psychoanalytic theorists such as Leo Bersani, Lee Edelman, and Teresa de Lauretis position queerness in opposition to the conservative forces of narrative, which consolidates and entraps subjects within heteronormative closure.[4] By contrast, *Are You My Mother?* offers narrative as an ambivalent scene of relationality where similarity and difference can energize each other without being resolved into a telos of identification or disidentification. As a genre, graphic narrative offers a particularly dramatic visualization of this ambivalence as a spatial and temporal relation.[5] In Bechdel's hands, it also reroutes the cultural narrative of kinship away from the daughter's reproduction of the maternal figure. Indeed, *Are You My Mother?* affords a visual and textual narrative scene for the emergence of a queerer mode of parental kinship, dynamized by intersubjective relationality.

Queering Literary Kinship

Few graphic narratives have been as anticipated as *Are You My Mother?* Yet the memoir, published six years after the critically acclaimed *Fun Home*, received a tepid response. It has not garnered anywhere near the amount of praise or public debate as *Fun Home*. While reviews praise its artistry, they invariably compare *Are You My Mother?* to its predecessor and find it lacking. Laura Miller, for example, prefers *Fun Home*'s "grotesque Victorian pile fit for Miss Havisham." "There's a bit too much therapy," Miller laments, arguing that "psychology boils away the particulars of individual experience to arrive at abstract generalities. It may get at the same truths that art does, but the trip isn't nearly as fun." Joanna Scutts similarly critiques the lack of narrative pleasure in *Are You My Mother?* While she suggests that the memoir is "perhaps the more challenging examination of family," she contends that, unlike *Fun Home*, "no such inherently dramatic discovery and quest for answers structures this story." Scholars such as Tammy Clewell have responded that *Are You My Mother?* uses psychoanalysis to offer a "transformative experience" for readers (53). For Clewell, the memoir configures public space to work through and repair mother-daughter relationality. Despite the insights of Clewell's analysis, I want to underline the dissatisfaction expressed by critics and readers. Their reactions do not evince a failed understanding of Bechdel's project. Rather, they attest to the success of Bechdel's effort to complicate the interpretive desire to compare *Are You My Mother?* to *Fun Home*. Bechdel disrupts the expectation that *Are You My Mother?* can and should be read primarily as a corollary to *Fun Home*—a "mom" book to complement the "dad" book. By troubling this hermeneutic framework, Bechdel loosens a literary kinship narrative that binds the two memoirs together in a way that would uncritically reproduce the heteronormative nuclear family.

To be sure, Bechdel beckons readers to see *Fun Home* and *Are You My Mother?* as visual complements. For example, the very first image of *Are You My Mother?* depicts Alison in a dream, engaged in a "home improvement" project, lifting a large wooden board (*AYMM*, 1). This image cannot help but recall the figure of her father, Bruce, the "old artificer," posed as Christ, carrying a spindle at the outset of *Fun Home* (7). Yet note that Bechdel is turned in the opposite direction from her father, and when she turns to look in his direction, she "block[s] [her] exit" (*AYMM*, 2). Bob, Helen's boyfriend, interprets Alison's dream as related to her struggles with "creativity" (10). This image also offers a performative metacommentary on reading *Are You My Mother?* At first, "The only way out [of the basement] is to squeeze through the small, spidery window" (2). Later, the spider web signifies Alison's fascination with Freudian psychoanalysis and its conceit of a "skillful and designed" pattern hidden beneath consciousness (47). Just as she turns from Freud to Winnicott, so Alison turns from the window to a door that did not exist before; it appears as if spontaneously, and Alison is surprised at this discovery. In effect, Alison turns away from the ornate intertextual web of *Fun Home* as the primary hermeneutic frame for *Are You My Mother?* and asks readers to turn with her. Undoubtedly this turn signifies a shifting of identification from father to mother; her subsequent plunge into the "deep and murky" pool of "dirty water" evokes her ambivalent embrace of the maternal (3). But more importantly, Bechdel figures her leap into water as a "sublime feeling of surrender," holding her breath and closing her eyes as she sinks into the unseen depths. Surrender allows for new relations to emerge immanently from the transitional space of maternal narration. It calls for us to let go of what we think we know about—and what we think we want—from this text, so it can forge a space for difference.

Bechdel's loosening of *Fun Home* as a hermeneutic frame for *Are You My Mother?* works against the temporality of paranoid reading. After all, as Eve Sedgwick argues, paranoia has a "distinctly rigid relation to temporality, at once anticipatory and retroactive, averse above all to surprise" (146). Yet paranoid temporality draws its aversion to surprise from a "generational narrative that's characterized by a distinctly Oedipal regularity and repetitiveness," which forecloses the emergence of queer possibilities. This foreclosure occurs through a narrative chain that assumes: "It happened to my father's father, it happened to my father, it is happening to me, and it will happen to my son, and it will happen to my son's son" (147). The tenses shift, but nothing changes. Inherited along the narrative chain—between men—is a lockstep of fatalistic heteronormative certainty. This is why *Are You My Mother?* revises and interrupts, to borrow Butler's phrasing, a temporality of heteronormative kinship that would position the text as parallel or sequential to *Fun Home*. Indeed,

Fun Home is simultaneously finished and unfinished within the diegesis of *Are You My Mother?* As Alison explains, "This story begins when I began to tell another story" (*AYMM*, 4). Her statement sets the stage for the recursive temporal relations between the two texts. In some moments, *Fun Home* has been published; in others, Alison is unable to complete the drawings for *Fun Home* and shifts to working on *Are You My Mother?* The memoir also resists plotting Helen's story in a way that smoothly converges with *Fun Home*'s chronology. The recursive structure makes it exceedingly difficult, if not impossible, to map the two narratives—and their composition—in sequential time. Pushing the queer temporality of conception, composition, and reception further, Alison sends Helen the first four chapters of *Are You My Mother?* before completing the text (284). It is impossible to say where this text begins or ends, whether it is complete or incomplete, frustrating any expectation that it clearly complements *Fun Home*.[6]

By troubling this expectation, Bechdel questions the impulse to figure kinship between these two memoirs. By extension, she foregrounds the constraints of heteronormativity in the queer child's narration of kinship relations. This tension is evident when Alison discovers that a photograph of her mother holding her as a child is actually part of a sequence of five images that had been "scattered about in different albums and boxes" (*AYMM*, 31) (fig. 10.1).

Lacking the negatives, Alison realizes that "there's no way to know their chronological order. But I've arranged them according to my own narrative" (*AYMM*, 32). Her narrative is strikingly Oedipal, beginning with a joyful "rapport" between mother and child, which is then "shattered" when the child "notice[s] the man with the camera" (33). This arrangement mirrors the Lacanian Oedipal plot, in which the symbolic law of the father interrupts the primordial maternal imaginary. As Butler notes, this is an overdetermined moment in psychoanalytic narrative, precisely because it stands in for the child's inauguration into the heteronormative and patriarchal symbolic order.[7] Undoubtedly, Bechdel's arrangement stresses the child's apprehension of the father, underscoring the implicit violence in the Oedipal interruption of the maternal. But more radically, Bechdel clarifies that this is just one possible ordering of the sequence; her fearful gaze might begin the sequence or appear in the middle. So much is unknown about the temporal gaps between these five photographs, about the photographs that may have been lost, and about the surrounding dynamics that may escape visualization. Alison understands her "search for meaningful patterns" in the photographs as part of a "mission" inherited from her mother—a hermeneutic quest that binds them as intellectuals and as women. Yet the memoir also presses back against this desire for interpretative order, stressing its reliance on heteronormative plots of belonging.

Fig. 10.1. Alison, her mother: images and objects in relation (*AYMM*, 31–32).

What falls outside these "meaningful patterns," Bechdel suggests, is the materiality of visualization that mediates kinship narration itself. The structure of this two-page spread—a full-bleed splash—creates an antinomy between narrative sequence and graphic space, emphasizing the means of representational practice that cannot be gathered into the sequential pattern: the eraser, the artist's glasses, her brushes and pens, the ruler. Layered on top of these details is Alison's admission that "for a long time I resisted including my present-day interactions with Mom in this book precisely because they're so 'ordinary.' Then I started seeing how the transcendent would almost creep into the everyday" (*AYMM*, 32–33). Interspersed with the photographic sequence and the space of visualization is Helen's mundane commentary on Lady Gaga and Sylvia Plath, details plucked from an unremarkable phone conversation. It is tempting to cohere these snippets of dialogue into a meaningful pattern, one that mirrors Bechdel's narrative of maternal communion and interruption. Yet even these snippets are detached from a clear grounding in temporal sequence. In the same way that this page denaturalizes the Oedipal triangle, we cannot triangulate the temporal relations between the long past of the photographs, the recent past of maternal conversation, and the present-tense figuration of these events. It is apt, then, that a Helix brand ruler is split across the spine of the page; its linear geometry becomes distorted and bent, less triangular and more akin to the shape that inspires its name, three-dimensional and twisted. Of course, "helix" also evokes the double-helix structure of DNA, a form that is key to its transmission and reproduction of genetic information. This page thus condenses the problem of kinship as a problem of graphic narrative itself. While the linearity of narrative beckons for an Oedipal ordering, the spatiality of comics interrupts that temporal sequence, cleaving space for a queerer figuration of kinship to emerge.

No Relation and the Maternal *Mise en Abîme*

The Oedipal plot is not the only narrative form that constricts the lesbian artist as she attempts to queer maternal kinship. Bechdel stresses that the very assumption of a foundational maternal relation is underwritten by a logic of heteronormativity. To contest that assumption, *Are You My Mother?* visualizes the bond between mother and daughter as a *nonrelation*. For example, Alison illustrates herself within Helen's womb as she writes poetry on a typewriter (fig. 10.2).

She narrates: "The womb is an environment that adapts absolutely. Nothing impinges because there's no outside or inside. No separation. And if there's no separation, then properly speaking, there's no relation either. As they say, all is one" (*AYMM*, 138). This panel exemplifies Bechdel's intertextual entwinement of the womb and the "Plexiglas dome" from Dr. Seuss's *The Sleep Book*. This figure condenses Alison's "fantasy of self-sufficiency," which derives from Helen's emotional unavailability (134). While the figure suggests maternal absence, it also expresses her overwhelming presence as she subsumes the child's subjectivity into her own. The panel thus evokes a suffocating fusion of mother and daughter. As they fold into each other, in what Bechdel experiences as a "dizzying, infinite regress," there is no separation—and thus no transitional space for difference—between them (7). Of course, Alison also lacked a relation with her father. Yet *Fun Home* crafted a "sort of inverted Oedipal complex" to retrospectively narrate a relation with Bruce (*FH*, 230). Oedipal inversion destabilized heteronormative and patriarchal orders of sexual difference, and it engendered transversals of queer identification—between daughters and fathers, between queer children and queer parents—that are culturally foreclosed.[8] No analogously subversive potentiality lies in the Oedipal narrative for *Are You My Mother?* because Bechdel must not only repair an absent paternal relation but also first demystify a narrative of maternal

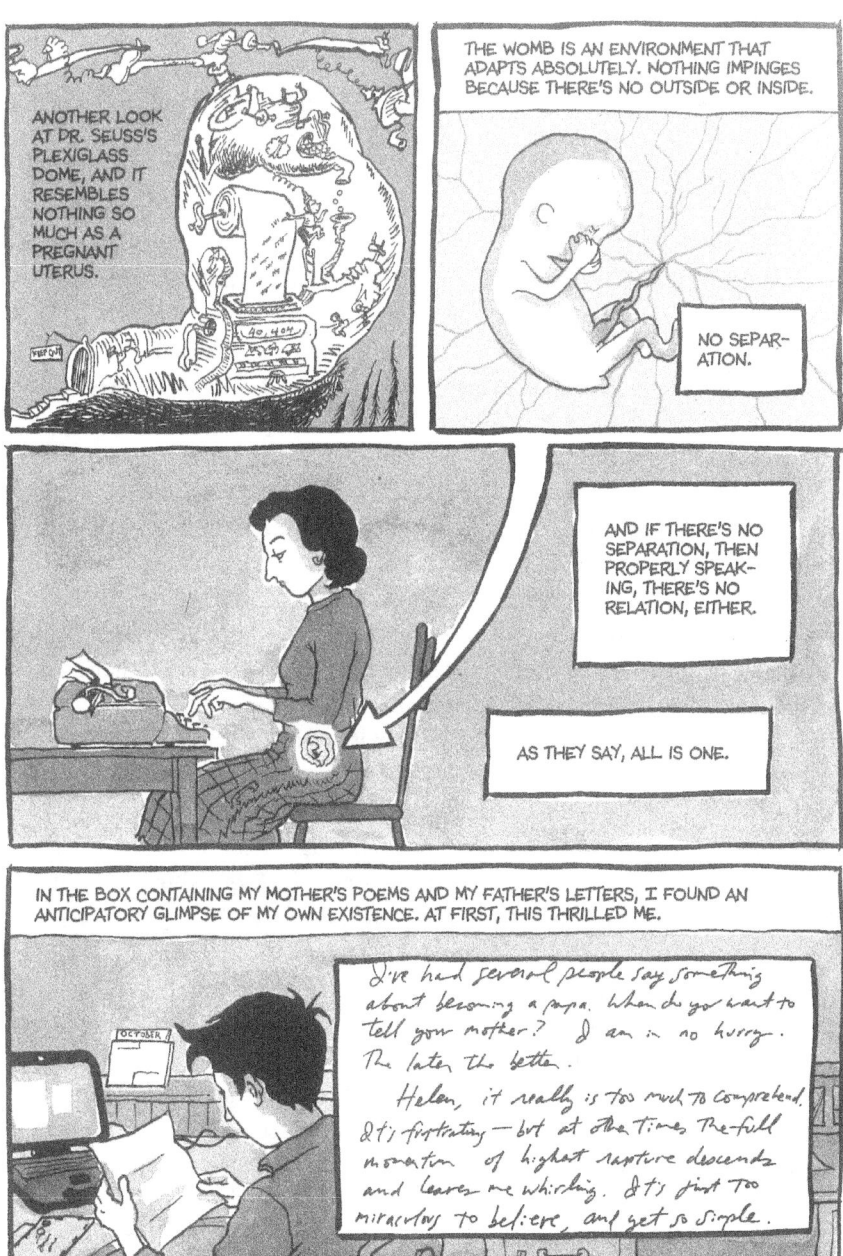

Fig. 10.2. The womb and *The Sleep Book* (*AYMM*, 138).

relation, naturalized by psychoanalysis and heteronormative culture, that grounds kinship in reproduction. That narrative is succinctly captured in Alison's childhood understanding of "human reproduction": "I was an egg inside my mother when she was still an egg inside her mother, and so forth and so on" (*AYMM*, 7).

Alison's *mise en abîme* echoes Sedgwick's paraphrase of the Oedipal chain, but note the arrow that stresses the simultaneity of Helen's writing and gestating. Here Bechdel grafts two distinct modalities of creation—reproductive and aesthetic—onto each other. Her grafting opens the possibility for Helen and Alison to identify with each other as writers, but it simultaneously enacts heteronormativity's collapse of literary creation into a discourse of reproduction.[9] Bechdel wryly comments on that collapse: "Even if I'd ever had the slightest urge to reproduce, it's too late now. I'm running out of eggs. My clockworklike menstrual cycle skipped its first beat the very week, in my forty-fifth year, that I sat down to begin writing about my mother" (*AYMM*, 7). Of her struggle to write, Bechdel tells her therapist, "I can't tell whether it's normal creative strife or menopausal insanity" (21). By aligning menopause with creative incontinence, *Are You My Mother?* reroutes aesthetic creation through the queerness of menopause. It is not that writing about her mother suspends menstruation; rather, Alison must step outside the hetero-gendered temporalities of reproduction to rewrite maternal kinship as artistic kinship. After all, Alison's lack of reproductive desire stigmatizes her as "not a woman," and this stigmatization is intensified by her queerness and her entrance into menopause. Within this liminal space, essentialist discourses of women's reproduction become suspended—literally "paused." A queer temporality for kinship subsequently emerges that is akin to the temporality of the queer child who, according to Kathryn Bond Stockton, "grows sideways" (1–57). The generational hierarchy between mother and daughter becomes horizontal, and kinship can be threaded around the mutual creation of art rather than an essentialism of linear reproduction.

Yet this queer kinship is thwarted by Helen's criticism of her daughter's artwork, which disrupts Alison's creativity and pressures her to bracket the queerness that is the content of her art. A fan of Helen Vendler and of the ideology of formalism, her mother believes that "the self has no place in good writing" (*AYMM*, 200). As she observes, "Wallace Stevens wrote transcendent poetry and never used the word 'I'" (202). Helen's resistance to subjectivity leads her to criticize Alison's chosen genre. Alison notes, "My mother considers memoir a suspect genre" (11). Helen's criticism disguises a psychic and political dilemma as a debate over form. Indeed, she worries how Alison's revelation of the family's most "intimate secrets" reflects on her (63). More fundamentally, she is ashamed by Alison's imbrication of art and sexuality.

Fig. 10.3. An infinite unfurling (*AYMM*, 244).

She admits, "I would love to see your name on a book but not on a book of lesbian cartoons" (182). Here Helen marks queerness as the stain on the mirror that prevents her ability to identify with Alison as an artist. Crucially, Alison does not internalize her mother's homophobia; in fact, she contends that "being a lesbian actually saved me. . . . If it weren't for the unconventionality of my desires, my mind might never have been forced to reckon with my body" (*AYMM*, 156). In other words, queerness breaks apart her solipsistic subsumption into the maternal *mise en abîme*. Yet Alison nonetheless finds herself trapped by "the extent to which [she has] internalized [her] mother's critical faculties" (11). The question she faces, then, is how to break through the *mise en abîme* in a way that fosters kinship, engendering a relation with difference that does not reify (hetero)sexual difference. Alison literalizes this tension when she reflects on the two mirrors that face each other in the vestibule of her childhood home: "In one way, what I saw in those mirrors was the self trapped inside the self, forever. But in another way, the self in the mirror was opening out, in an infinite unfurling" (244) (fig. 10.3).

This divided path appears on a page that maddeningly divides Alison's portrait. The panel is set off-center, so that most of her face is folded into the spine of the book; the text boxes defuse our gaze of the apparently unmediated side of her face. This image intensifies and disrupts the reader's desire to see Alison's face reflected in the mirror. As such, it forces us to reckon with our investment in the representational logic that understands *memoir as a mirror*, a logic that further entraps Alison within the maternal *mise en abîme*. Alison is also invested in this logic, confessing, "I have taken to transcribing what [Helen] says. . . . I want to capture her voice, her precise wording, her deadpan humor. I don't think I could possibly re-create it on my own" (*AYMM*, 11–12). Here memoir "capture[s]" truth; art becomes transcription, a faithful reproduction untainted by writerly subjectivity. Alison claims, "I am not ultimately interested in writing fiction. I can't make things up. Or rather, I can only make things up about things that have already happened" (28). Notably, this pronouncement arrives after the virtuosic sequence in which she speculates on the possible convergence of Winnicott and Virginia Woolf in Tavistock Square in 1924 (24–27). Bechdel comes close to outright fiction in this sequence, but she remains bound by an intense fidelity to the reproduction of reality.

Yet this representational logic converges with the heteronormative pressure for daughters to properly "mirror" their mothers—to faithfully reproduce the mother and thereby enter a generational sequence of maternal kinship. Bechdel foregrounds this double bind of representation and reproduction on the cover of the first edition of *Are You My Mother?*[10] On the front and back covers, an older woman photographs a child. Presumably Alison and Helen are the children, but it is not immediately clear which is which. Notably, both children wear clothes that match their photographer's, stressing the compulsory nature of visual similitude within the gendered scene of performativity, as well as the performative nature of maternal representation. The contrast between cameras and cars suggests a generational lapse between front and back (or back and front), but the salient point is that the scenes underscore the literal and figurative role that visual representation plays in codifying the *mise en abîme* of heteronormative kinship. After all, as Elizabeth Freeman argues, "Photographic media participated in the emergence of a highly heterogendered, middle-class discourse of family," specifically through a "representation of collective longitude" (*Time Binds*, 22). Located in nature, with the child's feet planted in grass, these scenes of photography contribute to the merging of "secularized, quasi-sacred time of nature and family with the homogenous, empty time across which national destiny move[s]" (22).

While this merging fuses subjects into a longitudinal genealogy, it also, as Freeman suggests, fosters queer potentialities that disrupt heteronormative sequence. Note that on the inside covers, Bechdel reproduces the photographs of these two children (fig. 10.4).

Less in the style of comics art, these images are rendered with heavy brush strokes that foreground the shadows and lines of the faces. These are

Fig. 10.4. Two children (*AYMM*, inside cover).

melancholic portraits of children withdrawn in a moment of compulsory gender performativity; they gaze back at the camera's maternal gaze—if not in radical defiance, then in apprehension at their visual inscription into heteronormative kinship. With their short, butch haircuts, both girls could pass for boys, and this effect is intensified on the inside cover, which excises the dress on the girl in the back cover. The inside covers also reverse the positions of the children: the child on the front appears on the inside back cover, and vice versa. This swapping indexes the pressure to reproduce the mother, to take up her role in the maternal chain. But it also visualizes the queer potentiality of rerouting kinship through other modalities of similitude, such as a shared ambivalence about, and disidentification from, gender normativity. Indeed, their eyes look toward each other across the interleaved pages of the book, and their visual and affective confusion opens room for queer kinship. To narrate such kinship, however, Alison must discover a figural logic for memoir that is not overdetermined by the heteronormative conflation of representation and reproduction but instead premised on an "infinite unfurling" of relationality.

Object Relations and the Transitional Space of Writing

Bechdel discovers this logic in Winnicott's theory of object relations, which enables her to narrate kinship beyond the Oedipal plot and the maternal *mise en abîme*. Indeed, Bechdel delights in Winnicott's claim "There is no such thing as a baby" (quoted in *AYMM*, 22). The "baby" exists within a dense web of relations, such that it cannot be individuated from the outset. As such, "The development of a baby's ability to use an object is not given" (*AYMM*, 266). In other words, relationality cannot be assumed from the start; it must be facilitated within an affectively charged scene of care. For Bechdel, this concept underscores her trauma in lacking a "good-enough" parent to facilitate a holding environment. But it also highlights how transitional phenomena—art, dreams, and play—contribute to the development of relationality because they exist in a liminal space between subjectivity and objectivity. This transitional space underlies Winnicott's distinction between merely "*relating*" to and fully "*using*" others (*AYMM*, 262; italics in original). Alison explains, "We progress to *using* another person—to being able to fully assimilate what they have to offer us—only when we understand that they're separate from us" (262; italics in original). To understand this separation, "The subject must destroy the object. And the object must survive this destruction. . . . If the object doesn't survive, it will remain internal, a projection of the subject's self. If the object survives destruction, the subject can see it as separate" (267). The affective "destruction" of the object opens a pathway out of the *mise en abîme* of projection, cleaving a space for relationality to emerge, and relationality becomes redefined as dynamically intersubjective, energized by difference.

Object relations enables Bechdel to reinterpret the work of memoir as relational rather than representational. Now understood as a transitional object, memoir is unbound from the reproduction of reality and alternatively invested in creating new relational possibilities. Hence Alison delights in Winnicott's reversal of Freud's reality principle: "Reality doesn't make us feel aggression. . . . Aggression makes us feel real" (*AYMM*, 268). Reality does not preexist and justify the work of memoir; rather, reality emerges *through* memoir's appropriation and revision of the world. This reversal creates new room for Alison's aesthetic agency—for her to write without compliantly succumbing to her mother's representations of reality. Note Alison's joy in Helen's feedback to the first four chapters of *Are You My Mother?* Helen states, "Well, it coheres. There are clear themes. . . . It's . . . It's a metabook" (285). Alison proclaims, "At last, I have destroyed my mother, and she has survived my destruction" (285). Her joy derives not from Helen correctly interpreting the text, or in feeling understood by her mother. Rather, Alison has written her own interpretation of her mother and their relationship—aesthetically "destroying" her—and her narrative can now exist in productive intersubjective tension with Helen's. That Helen calls the book a "metabook" aptly stresses their movement toward intersubjectivity. In postmodern literature, metanarrative often signifies solipsism.[11] This is exemplified in Alison's opening address to "Mom," which initially reads as a dialogue with Helen but is revealed to be a monologue to herself. Yet, as Robyn Warhol argues, metanarration is also a "convention for interrupting the reality effect of narrative, or for disrupting mimesis with reminders of the diegesis which makes it possible" (64). As a "metabook," then, *Are You My Mother?* interrupts and disrupts the heteronormative logic that has constricted Alison's narration of maternal relationality.

At the same time, metanarration affords a queer style to figure the inchoate kinship that can emerge within the transitional space of intersubjectivity. The queerness of this style becomes apparent in the final scene, which Bechdel calls "the moment my mother taught me to write" (*AYMM*, 287). Alison recalls the "crippled child" game they played together, in which Alison pretends to be disabled, and her mother fashions braces and shoes so that she can walk. Alison admits, "I don't remember the particulars of our play. I'm inventing this dialogue wholesale." Indeed, she notes, "I'm sure Mom indulged many such play scenarios with me," and wonders, "Why is this the one that I recall?" Rather than pursue an answer to this question, Alison foregrounds the pleasure and agency that emerge in the space of their play: "What I remember is a feeling of inebriation. The further I moved into this imaginary space, the more it opened up" (*AYMM*, 287). In its Lacanian register, queer theory has often critiqued the imaginary as a narcissistic lure that obliterates the queerness of difference.[12] By contrast, Bechdel rewrites the imaginary as a queerly transitional space that gives rise to aesthetic agency. Through this game, Helen has "given [Alison] the way out" (289).

If this gift is the affective space afforded through writing, then Alison has rewritten writing itself; it is no longer modeled on the *mise en abîme* of maternal documentation—condensed in Alison's compliant transcription of Helen's phone conversations or in Helen's transcriptions of Alison's diary. Instead writing becomes an inebriating space for relationality. I agree with Clewell that this panel reads as a "birthing scene," evidenced by the overhead angle of the illustration and the position of the two figures (66). Yet the image also queers the logic of birth, stressing, as Winnicott does, that one is not born, but becomes, related. This becoming occurs across a void of difference—literalized here by the book's spine, which carves a gap between mother and daughter—and operates in a temporality that cannot be mapped along a heteronormative generational sequence. This panel thus depicts a *becoming-kin* that comes into being through an act of narration untethered from mimesis, through a mode of writing that creates space for affective exchange. Seen from this vantage, the birth image condenses not so much the emergence of queer kinship as its aesthetic conditions of possibility, which will become realized in and through *the labor of graphic narrative*.

Becoming-Kin

Queer theory often expresses skepticism about narrative because it seems to cohere and stabilize the unruly negativity of queerness. Yet Bechdel charts a different relationship between narrative and queerness. She offers graphic narrative, in particular, as a means to figure and foster queer relationality. If, as Hillary Chute argues, graphic narrative "reveals the complex creation of subjectivity and unfinished selves," it also, in Bechdel's hands, creates new modes of intersubjectivity and unfinished relationality (206). Indeed, Bechdel does not narrate queer kinship as a teleological achievement; rather, it is *inchoate*: an endless process of *becoming-kin*, even with those that heteronormative culture has already designated as family. As Alison insists, "The story has no end. But now it's five years later, and I must manufacture one" (*AYMM*, 284). Through her metanarration, Alison stresses the artificiality of any "ending" that kinship narration might offer. In the breakdown of a sequential telos, however, kinship narration becomes a space that can be left and reentered, a transitional space of revision that creates new relations. In this sense, Bechdel answers Butler's call for a queerer "consideration of how those narratives [that a child may have about kinship] are revised and interrupted in time" (*Undoing*, 128). Undoubtedly, *Are You My Mother?* reveals the complex revision and interruption of the queer child's narratives about maternal relationality. But perhaps more radically, Bechdel suggests that narrative might serve as a queer means for forging kinship. From this vantage, kinship does not preexist us but rather moves from the outside in through an endless revision of our relations.

NOTES

1. On queer kinship, see, e.g., Eng; Freeman, "Queer"; Rodríguez.
2. See, e.g., Clewell; Love; Diedrich; Giaimo.

3. On "transitional phenomena" in *Are You My Mother?*, see Diedrich; on transitional objects and phenomena, see Winnicott, 1–34.

4. For critiques of this approach, see Huffer; Bersani and Phillips.

5. On graphic narrative, see Chute and DeKoven. My argument about narrative form draws on their claim that "graphic narrative does the work of narration at least in part through drawing—making the question of style legible—so it is a form that also always refuses a problematic transparency, through an explicit awareness of its own surfaces" (767).

6. For example, Bechdel interrupts and revises *Fun Home*'s undecidability about Bruce's sexuality and death when she mentions his "bisexuality" and "suicide" (*AYMM*, 6).

7. Butler, *Undoing*, 118–27.

8. Butler, *Psychic*, 132–50.

9. For Bechdel's perspective on her mother as a writer, see Swisher.

10. The paperback edition of *Are You My Mother?* literalizes this theme in an illustration of a mirror on Helen's vanity. On the import of "peritextual" elements to Bechdel's work, see Watson, 33–34.

11. See McHale.

12. See Edelman.

WORKS CITED

Bersani, Leo. *The Freudian Body: Psychoanalysis and Art*. Columbia University Press, 1986.
Bersani, Leo, and Adam Phillips. *Intimacies*. University of Chicago Press, 2008.
Butler, Judith. *The Psychic Life of Power: Theories in Subjection*. Stanford University Press, 1997.
Butler, Judith. *Undoing Gender*. Routledge, 2004.
Chute, Hillary. "The Space of Graphic Narrative: Mapping Bodies, Feminism, and Form." In *Narrative Theory Unbound: Queer and Feminist Interventions*, ed. Robyn Warhol and Susan S. Lanser, 194–209. Ohio State University Press, 2015.
Chute, Hillary, and Marianne DeKoven. "Introduction: Graphic Narrative." *Modern Fiction Studies* 52, no. 4 (2006): 767–82.
Clewell, Tammy. "Beyond Psychoanalysis: Resistance and Reparative Reading in Alison Bechdel's *Are You My Mother?*" *PMLA* 132, no. 1 (2017): 51–70.
de Lauretis, Teresa. *Freud's Drive: Psychoanalysis, Literature, and Film*. Palgrave Macmillan, 2010.
Diedrich, Lisa. "Graphic Analysis: Transitional Phenomena in Alison Bechdel's *Are You My Mother?*" *Configurations* 22, no. 2 (2014): 183–203.
Edelman, Lee. *No Future: Queer Theory and the Death Drive*. Duke University Press, 2004.
Eng, David L. *The Feeling of Kinship: Queer Liberalism and the Racialization of Intimacy*. Duke University Press, 2010.
Freeman, Elizabeth. "Queer Belongings: Kinship Theory and Queer Theory." In *A Companion to Lesbian, Gay, Bisexual, Transgender, and Queer Studies*, ed. George E. Haggerty and Molly McGarry, 293–314. Blackwell, 2008.
Freeman, Elizabeth. *Time Binds: Queer Temporalities, Queer Histories*. Duke University Press, 2010.
Giaimo, Genie. "Psychological Diffusions: The Cognitive Turn in Alison Bechdel's *Are You My Mother? A Comic Drama*." *European Journal of Life Writing* 2 (2013): 35–58.
Huffer, Lynne. *Are the Lips a Grave? A Queer Feminist on the Ethics of Sex*. Columbia University Press, 2013.
Love, Heather. "The Mom Problem." *Public Books*, October 2, 2012. Accessed October 17, 2017.
McHale, Brian. *Postmodernist Fiction*. Routledge, 2001.
Miller, Laura. "*Are You My Mother?* by Alison Bechdel—Review." *Guardian*, May 24, 2012. Accessed October 17, 2017.

Rodríguez, Juana María. *Sexual Futures, Queer Gestures, and Other Latina Longings*. New York University Press, 2014.

Scutts, Joanna. "'Are You My Mother?,' a Comic Drama by Alison Bechdel." *Washington Post*, June 1, 2012. Accessed October 17, 2017.

Sedgwick, Eve Kosofsky. *Touching Feeling: Affect, Pedagogy, Performativity*. Duke University Press, 2003.

Stockton, Kathryn Bond. *The Queer Child, or Growing Sideways in the Twentieth Century*. Duke University Press, 2009.

Swisher, Kara. "Full Transcript: Alison Bechdel, Onstage and on *Recode Decode*." Recode.net, February 13, 2017. Accessed August 23, 2018.

Warhol, Robyn. "Giving an Account of Themselves: Metanarration and the Structure of Address in *The Office* and *The Real Housewives*." In *Narrative Theory Unbound: Queer and Feminist Interventions*, ed. Robyn Warhol and Susan S. Lanser, 59–77. Ohio State University Press, 2015.

Watson, Julia. "Autographic Disclosures and Genealogies of Desire in Alison Bechdel's *Fun Home*." *Biography* 31, no. 1 (2008): 27–58.

Winnicott, D. W. *Playing and Reality*. Routledge, 2005.

Part III

PLACE, SPACE, AND COMMUNITY

DECOLONIZING RURAL SPACE IN ALISON BECHDEL'S *FUN HOME*

KATIE HOGAN

Place Matters

The myth of rural America as both emblem of the nation and symbol of backwardness fuels the continuing—and deepening—rural-urban divide in the United States. Ironically, LGBTQ culture has its own rural-urban binary separation, which rural queer studies has spent over a decade challenging. Historically, LGBTQ culture has been linked to urban space, with rural space typically cast as a pathetic, inhospitable closet stuffed with suffering rural queer and trans people who must "get thee to a city," as the anthropologist Kath Weston captured the message in her famous essay on the city and the gay imaginary. The trans scholar Susan Stryker's experience of relocating from Oklahoma to coastal California included regular encounters with "the dismissiveness and condescension that many of the people whose social values I share feel toward the demographic that I come from." Despite critical interrogation of metrocentric attitudes, Lucas Crawford points out that the city remains the place "where queers *do* queerness," and "the country is where things *are done* to queers" (917). Given this stark binary, no self-respecting queer person would willingly choose to reside in the countryside. As Stina Solderling explains, "Those who are stupid enough to not leave for the city are to blame for their own death" (343).[1]

The field of rural queer studies rose to challenge urban-centrism, and some of the scholars who have created the field grew up in rural areas. They draw on the theoretical concept of metronormativity, a term coined by Jack Halberstam in 2005, to refute the urban bias in queer culture, including commercial culture, politics, activism, and academic theory. Metronormativity, like a colonizing ideology, casts small towns and farmland communities as backward and "nowhere."[2] This colonialist view of rural queer life reflects dominant ideas of what counts as "out" and visible, assumptions that typically render rural queer and trans people as closeted and pitiful. As Mary Gray explains, metronormativity exists because "rurality itself is depicted as antithetical to LGBT identities" (12). The complication, as Halberstam puts it, is that "some queers need to leave home in order to become queer, and others need to stay close to home in order to preserve their difference" (27).

Staying close to home to preserve difference is a central focus in Alison Bechdel's highly acclaimed graphic memoir *Fun Home*. Based on Bechdel's experience growing up in Beech Creek, a small Appalachian town in central Pennsylvania, in the 1960s and '70s, *Fun Home* explores the complexities of rural queer place by unknowingly employing a strategy that the queer historian John Howard calls "a precise regionalist methodology" (*Carryin' On*, 9). *Fun Home*'s uncanny use of this method is apparent in the hundreds of drawings of the tiny rural town where Alison and her father, Bruce Bechdel, were born and raised. Maps and images of mountain ranges, trees, flowers, yards, streams, campsites, sunsets, tractors, the Bechdel dairy farm, and the Bechdel family home coincide with notable depictions of environmental degradation and the construction of local, state, and federal road systems—working in tandem to emphasize how physical place and nature are central to the book.

Readers have picked up on the significance of place to the text; a *New York Times* book reviewer, Sean Wilsey, was prompted to drive to Beech Creek to compare the memoir's meticulous drawings and maps to actual locations in the town and its nearby surroundings. In an interview with the comics scholar Hillary Chute, Bechdel is quick to point out how *Fun Home* "is very much about place," mentioning its focus on a "particular part of rural central Pennsylvania, on the edge of the Allegheny Front" (1005). In *Fun Home*, place is not a side issue, an inert, passive backdrop, or a lapse into sentimentality; it is how the book explores rural culture from a queer perspective and delineates Bruce Bechdel's complicated rural queer desires. Panels and text portray Bruce's deep alienation and despair over his life as a sexually nonconforming man in rural America, with its traditional family life, religious conservatism, and enforced heterosexuality. But other panels depict him—despite his "unnatural" sexual and gender practices—as belonging to Beech Creek, even suggesting how rural life suits him. For Bruce, rural queer existence is both excruciating and a source of resiliency; his rural family attachments and same-sex and gender nonconformity are not problems to be solved but contradictions to be endured and, when possible, embraced. What is more, this regional methodology captures Bruce's complicated rural queer commitments without idealizing them. By drawing Beech Creek as both life affirming and toxic, the memoir presents a nuanced vision of rural life instead of an urban-centric indictment; the compromises, trade-offs, and difficulties that make up Bruce's life suggest how loving a place that is both beautiful and inhospitable is possible. Beech Creek is no queer idyll, and the countryside is often a contentious and violent space, yet *Fun Home* shows that commitments to rural queer place happen and that they matter.

Queering Kinship, Nature, and Culture

Born and raised on a dairy farm in Beech Creek, Bruce Bechdel had his first same-sex experience with a farmhand when he was a teenager. As an adult, his nonnormative sexual activity was not openly discussed until his arrest for providing an alcoholic beverage to a minor, the younger brother of one of his older high school students. Bruce's arrest threatens his reputation, livelihood, marriage, and family, and Alison believes it may have driven him to suicide. Because Bruce is white, male, and college educated and belongs to a family with deep roots in Beech Creek, he escapes prison but is ordered to begin sessions with a psychiatrist for his "disorder." Had Bruce been a person of color or an immigrant, he would probably have been treated very differently by the criminal justice system. Nevertheless, Bruce's arrest alters his life; it impels his wife, Helen, to file for divorce, and soon after, Bruce is hit by a truck and killed.

Bruce's untimely death haunts almost every page of the memoir, and it inspires one of the book's central questions: why Bruce, a sexual and gender nonconforming man with interests in literature and antiques, stayed in a small town that probably drove him to suicide. How did "staying," to borrow again from Halberstam, "preserve [his] difference" (27)? Bechdel's text suggests that she finds her father's place attachment perplexing: "It's puzzling why my urbane father, with his unwholesome interest in the decorative arts, remained in this provincial hamlet" (*FH*, 125). In an email interview with the author, Bechdel explained that "sorting out that contradiction was one of the things I set out to explore in the book." A good deal of the memoir espouses an antirural view, portraying Bruce as "stuck in the mud" (40–41); after Bruce dies, Bechdel visits his grave in Beech Creek and declares he is "stuck in the mud for good" (54). Yet, near the end of the book, Bechdel arrives at a startling conclusion: "In the end, although the anonymity of a city might have saved my father's life, I can't really imagine him anywhere but Beech Creek" (144). This conclusion rejects the dominant spatial narrative of the countryside as unlivable for queers. The image of Bruce as "stuck in the mud" in Beech Creek is replaced with a new image of him as being "planted deep" (145). Bruce's depressions, rages, and probable suicide are juxtaposed with the idea of Beech Creek as a viable place, evident in drawings throughout of Bruce's embrace of rural kinship, nature, a farm boy work ethic, and a nonconforming rural masculinity.

Beech Creek boasts a population of approximately eight hundred people, and the Bechdel family has lived there for several generations. A panel portrays Alison's great-grandfather and grandfather standing outside the family business (the Bechdel funeral parlor), and another explains that "26 Bechdel families [are listed] in the phone book" (*FH*, 126). Alison's grandmother was a Bechdel "even before she married my grandfather" (126), and family members live within walking distance, represented in a map that illustrates the proximity of the Bechdel household to Bruce's many relatives (31). Beech Creek wields staying power, too: the offspring of aunts and uncles, instead of leaving home for the "wider" world, remain in Beech Creek—depicted in a panel portraying a cousin's prefab house being delivered to the backyard of the family home (31).

However, while *Fun Home* depicts Bruce's investment in rural kinship, it does so unromantically. In the panel showing the delivery of the cousin's prefab house, Alison's mother, Helen, warns her, "After you graduate from high school, I don't want to see you again" (*FH*, 31). Other drawings and text imply that Bechdel's parents felt thwarted in the small town, expressing contemptuous attitudes toward rural conventions and the paucity of big-city culture. In our interview, Bechdel said that she "got the clear message from both my parents that I needed to get out of Beech Creek." Not surprisingly, in the memoir Alison makes disparaging remarks about Beech Creek, referring to her "dull, provincial life" there (*FH*, 153).

In a key rural queer studies text, *Another Country: Queer Anti-Urbanism*, Scott Herring interprets Bechdel's parents'—and Alison's—condescending attitude about rural place as the inevitable result of urban colonization: the Bechdel family, like many Americans, including LGBTQs, have internalized a dominating metro-chauvinistic ideology. But, as Herring also notes, Bechdel complicates the inevitable metronormativity of her memoir in a map that marks the milestones of her father's life: his grave, the location where he died, the house where he raised his family, and the farm where he was born. Bechdel writes, "This narrow compass suggests a provincialism on my father's part that is both misleading and accurate" (*FH*, 30). Herring also interprets the "misleading and accurate" paradox as an expression of mourning and grief over the loss of her father, which is also a loss of connection to rural culture. But another meaning of this paradoxical statement is Bechdel's unease with dichotomous thinking—including her own. Characterizing the map as both "accurate" *and* "misleading" challenges dichotomous assumptions, showing that place-based dissatisfaction coexists with place-based pleasure, a stance not to be confused with metronormativity.

While Bruce Bechdel appears to be an urbane closeted gay man unsuited for the countryside, he says he sees himself as a "country boy," an identity he claims in a letter he wrote to Alison while she was attending college. Identifying with the rural characters and landscape in William Faulkner's *As I Lay Dying*, Bruce writes, "Faulkner IS Beech Creek. The Bundrens ARE Bechdels—19th century perhaps but definitely kin. How about that dude's way with words[?] He knows how us country boys think and talk" (*FH*, 200). The allusion to Faulkner is significant; literary allusions in *Fun Home*, from classical Greek myth to the works of Oscar Wilde, Marcel Proust, Ernest Hemingway, F. Scott Fitzgerald, and Albert Camus, develop the idea of Bruce as an educated, closeted gay man languishing in a rural backwater. The reference to Faulkner, who thought of himself "as a farmer, not a writer" (Faulkner, interview with Hutchens, 59), and was known for creating characters that the literary world labeled "white trash" and "nasty people," indicates Bruce's ties to rural culture, quietly undermining the characterization of him as a disempowered victim of Beech Creek (Faulkner, interview with Mok, 38, 39). In the same letter to Alison, Bruce not only acknowledges his rural roots but queers Alison's gender, extending the "country boy" identity he is claiming for himself to her—"*us* country boys" (*FH*, 200; my italics).

This agrarian sensibility emerges in Bruce's many interactions with rural nature throughout the book. In a letter to Helen before she and Bruce marry, he writes, "I want to work in the earth," a statement supported by the many drawings depicting Bruce engaged with the physical environment (*FH*, 145). In the same letter, he refers to sites he wants to show her when she visits Beech Creek for the first time: "There are places I will show you. The farm, The jungle, The old canal. Do you understand?" (145). And in a different letter to Helen, Bruce describes a "winter scene" on the canal, one of the places he plans to take her:

> Yesterday we skated on Beech Creek for miles through the silvery grey woods. How can I explain the creek? There are holes and crusty spots and solid mirrorlike passageways. It's dark bluish green under the iron bridge. Then on down between the island and the locks of the old canal the ice is like crystal and pale green weeds wave back and forth over blue rocks. (*FH*, 145)

Bruce's affection for Beech Creek, evident in these lines, presents rural nature as central to his everyday life, an outlook that the rural queer studies scholar Will Fellows also found in the oral histories he conducted with gay men from family farms and small towns in the American Midwest. One interviewee explains: "Our farm was in a valley and we had pastureland that extended into the woods on the sides of the bluffs. I was in heaven when I was in the woods; it was an escape" (Bauer, quoted in Fellows, 67). Another of Fellows's interviewees talks about nature as facilitating—instead of preventing—queer sexual experimentation, aligning nature with "unnatural" queers instead of the ancient claim that queers are "against nature": "Our farm sat at the edge of a heavily wooded area, twelve to fifteen acres. Oftentimes we'd just hike into the woods. That was real safe, because there were lots of places where nobody would find you. We made a number of hideaway places. We'd get a bunch of leaves and make it like a bed" (Cross, quoted in Fellows, 78).

Jenna Goldsmith explores the idea of queer sexual desire and rural landscape as a "hideaway" in *Fun Home* by analyzing the contrast between Bechdel's drawings of the home's front porch and patio. The patio, strategically removed from public view, acts as a retreat from the heteronormative world of the front porch and is therefore more conducive to expressing nonnormative sexual desire. On the patio, Bruce's attraction to Roy, and Roy's attraction to Bruce, is portrayed in the comic through a long panel positioning Bruce and Roy at opposite ends with their eyes locked. The "shared gaze of Bruce and Roy" occurs in the context of nature—a more welcoming realm than the normative world of domestic heterosexuality (Goldsmith, 14). In another patio scene, Bruce hands Roy a beer while the kids happily play nearby; the outdoor speakers blast the lyrics "The feelin's the same as bein' outside of the law," words that capture Bruce's "outlaw" sexuality and the nonnormative "gay" family he, Roy, and the kids symbolize (Bechdel, 94; Goldsmith, 16). As with Fellows's respondents, nature facilitates nonconforming sexuality and gender instead of preventing it.

Yet Bechdel's linkage between nature and rural queer desire is evoked to be critiqued, spelling out how Bruce's queerness and rural commitments create tension and alienation in the family. In several sections of *Fun Home*, Bechdel draws Bruce, Helen, and Alison coping with the emotional distance in their lives by turning to isolated pursuits. A powerful panel depicting cutouts in the house, with each family member shown as a silhouette, absorbed in reading, drawing, playing music, or engaged in some other solo activity, illuminates the idea of an emotionally barren home; "Ourselves were all we had," as Bechdel puts it (*FH*, 134, 139). But these somber drawings and their commentary are complicated by alternative depictions of landscape and kin. Readers see Bruce wearing shorts and work shoes and teaching Alison how to operate a tractor; in one panel, Bruce and Alison drive the tractor together. Alison's references to positive memories in nature with her father, including images of their shared love of sunsets and a poignant image based on a dream Alison had the night before her father's apparent suicide, undermine a one-dimensional view of the family as monolithically dysfunctional (123).[3] These intimate scenes between father and daughter, often hearkening back to the land, imply a connection despite the feelings of dissatisfaction and displacement they both experience. These nuances counter the simplistic stereotype of the rural as a one-dimensional, primitive space and resonate instead with Bechdel's overall method of questioning dichotomies.

While Goldsmith suggests that the Bechdel front porch—as well as the entire house—represents the power of oppressive heteronormative patriarchal domesticity, a rural queer perspective also shows how the front porch, the house, and the yard are Bruce's "farm," exposing his profound internalization of rural masculinity, with its pronounced work ethic and almost constant physical labor. More than eighty panels depict Bruce at work, often shirtless, wearing cutoffs and sneakers, engaging in hard physical labor. Even after Bruce leaves his parents' family home and dairy farm to attend college and join the army, he still feels responsible for chores at home. In the letter to Helen about her first visit to Beech Creek discussed earlier, Bruce mentions the tasks he must accomplish while on leave: "I have things to do at home. A Dogwood to put in the front lawn. Sawdust to put around the foundation plantings" (*FH*, 145). Fellows's research documents a gay farm boy work ethic that resembles Bruce's: "I'm not afraid of work, and I'm not afraid of getting my hands dirty, so I get a lot done" (Lindholm, quoted in Fellows, 91); "We very rarely did anything other than work. . . . [Dad] was up and gone by the time we got up, so we had to go out and help" (86). These sentiments echo Bruce's work-focused attitude, one he probably developed as a child growing up on the family's farm.

Once married to Helen and living in Beech Creek, Bruce assumes the role of family patriarch, treating his wife and children as farmhands to whom he doles out daily chores. Bechdel says, "My brothers and I were free labor. Dad considered us extensions of his own body" (*FH*, 13). Although Bechdel refers to the family's farm-like work-centeredness disparagingly, and the children resent the daily chores, it is striking how each member of the family seems to have internalized a strong work ethic (134). In an interview with Rachel Cooke of the *Guardian*, Bechdel says, "I don't feel I deserve to exist unless I'm working." In fact, Bruce's exacting farm boy work ethic may have played a role in Bechdel's own meticulous standards for her artistic work.

Although assumed to be incompatible with normative rural culture, Bruce's "farm boy" persona includes gender nonconformity. In a memorable scene with Alison near the end of the memoir, Bruce admits that when he was a child, he would "dress up in girls' clothes" (*FH*, 221). In other words, while one can read Bruce's notable focus on the physical home and landscape as a sign of his repressed homosexuality, from a "farm boy" and rural queer studies perspective, his nonstop activity is a rural work ethic in action. Bruce's paid professional work as a teacher, mortician, and funeral parlor director takes up a good deal of his time, but his labor related to rehabilitating houses—his own and others'—and his endless landscape and interior design work were "his passion" (*FH*, 7).

Fellows's research similarly documents how rural men challenge expected gender roles in the context of traditional rural masculine cultures. Although tricky to negotiate in many families and communities, farm boys with gender-nonconforming interests are sometimes accommodated—especially by mothers, aunts, and sisters. One respondent tells Fellows, "I got into embroidery in my early teens.... Dad didn't like that I was doing it—it was sissy—so I didn't make a show of it. My mother bought it for me in the first place, so it must have been okay with her" (Lindholm, quoted in Fellows, 86). Another explains, "Sometimes, when Mom and Dad would go away for a couple hours, I would go up in Mom's closet and dress up in her high heels and dresses" (Reed, quoted in Fellows, 118). Bruce's adult interests in home decoration and flower arrangement—activities labeled "women's work"—suggest how his "masculine" farm boy work ethic exists side by side with his interest in "feminizing" pursuits. Drawings of him engaging in typical rural masculine farm-like activities are juxtaposed with scenes of him polishing a newly purchased chandelier or rearranging knickknacks, enacting a complicated rural masculinity.

This complex portrait of Bruce's labor resonates with what scholars in feminist rural studies call "multiple models of masculinity" (Little, 115). New feminist research on rural space, inspired by Judith Butler's theories of gender as performance, argues that there is no stable, singular, static masculine rural identity—just as there is no stable, static rural place or region (Pini, Brandth, and Little, 9). Julie Keller's essay "Rural Queer Theory" explores how "places can be infused with degrees of both queerness and heteronormativity," and argues that these seemingly irreconcilable positions "can be braided together into the social landscape" (158). *Fun Home* exemplifies this argument, linking the rural and the queer together instead of casting them as eternal enemies. Bruce's rugged appearance meshes—rather than conflicts—with his interest in antiques and cross-dressing, challenging the typical assumption of a monolithic masculine rural type. His "delicate" interests, coupled with his cross-dressing practices and "farm boy" work ethic, enact a nuanced theory of rural masculinities—and of rural space overall.

Geographies of Ambivalence

Fun Home's ambivalence toward Beech Creek remains one of the text's most pronounced and interesting aspects. Bechdel skillfully avoids replacing the typical view of rural space as a totalized nightmare for queers with an equally delusional vision of it as a queer paradise. This strategy resonates with Angelia Wilson's ethnographic research on rural lesbians and gay men from the 1950s to the 1970s who withstood the contradictions that came with rural territory by adopting a self-determining "getting on with life" attitude. "Getting on with life" may seem like defeatism, assimilation, or capitulating to rural heteronormativity (going down without a fight), but Wilson's research suggests that it is an action rooted in resilience and the ability to embrace conflicting desires—for queer sex, rural kinship, rural place, and nature.

bell hooks's *Belonging: A Culture of Place* also offers a nuanced analysis of place focused on rural minorities. Born and raised in a self-governing rural black community in Kentucky, hooks lays out the ways that rural black communities negotiate white supremacy as they carve out rich place-based cultures of belonging in hills and rural towns. While the ever-present trauma of racial terrorism in the South was—and is—a daily reality, hooks identifies transformative memories and practices of a black agrarian past, "one that helped us understand that we are always more than our pain" (182).

hooks's perspective resonates with Mary Gray, Colin Johnson, and Brian Gilley's observations that country queers try to "reconcile their deep connection to or pride in their hometowns with the popular representation of their communities as backward, ignorant, and unlivable—not just for queer folks, but for anyone with taste or class" (15). Bruce knows that Beech Creek is understood as a limiting place for queers and that he is supposed to live in a city; his attachment to a tiny rural hamlet is, from an urban-centric perspective, embarrassing. In a letter to Alison, he expresses shame about his inability "to take sides" and "take a stand" when it comes to his conflict over his life in Beech Creek, admitting, "I am not a hero" (*FH*, 211). He even confesses to being "somewhat envious of the 'new' freedom" on college campuses, telling Alison that in the fifties being open about nonnormative sexuality "was not even considered an option" (212). Bruce speaks in political terms, too, referring to queer oppression and other civil rights issues, writing that he saw "Colored and Whites on drinking fountains in Florida in elementary school" (212). But what Bruce is also indicating in these confessional lines is his desire to be "more than [his] pain" (hooks, 182). Although his attachment to Beech Creek conflicts with the expectation that to be "gay" is to be urban, Bruce "gets on with life" because it is what he desires.

How Bruce achieves this goal emerges in the same letter mentioned earlier, sent to Alison before his death: "I was never even in New York until I was about twenty. But even seeing it then was not quite a revelation. There was not much in the Village that I hadn't known in Beech Creek" (*FH*, 212). Bruce's observation that the sexual subcultures of Beech Creek and Greenwich Village were not very different is striking. As Bruce explains, what distinguishes

Beech Creek from the Village is not access to inventive queer sex, since Bruce has been engaging in this kind of queer sex since his early teens, but the cultural norms about talking about queer sex. In the city, queer identity and culture are more openly expressed than in Beech Creek. As Bruce explains, "In New York you could see and mention it but elsewhere it was not seen or mentioned. It was rather simple" (*FH*, 212). The similarities and differences between Beech Creek and the Village suggest that queer cultural and sexual expression varies with geography, and urban cultural expressions are not "superior" to rural ones. Bruce's rural-based queerness is site specific instead of evidence of a pitiful rural-imposed "closeting."[4]

Drawing on insights from Brian Horton's research, it may be that Bruce deliberately fails to ever be fully queer or fully normative. Instead he "inhabit[s] contradictions" as "the substance central to [rural] queer experience" (Horton, n.p.). It is in rural Beech Creek where Bruce's multiple and conflicting desires are most fully legible; in the city, he loses access to nature, rural kin, and rural culture even though he can speak openly about his desire for sex with men. Since queer metronormativity positions "out, loud, and proud"—an urban-centric model—as the only authentic expression of queer desire and culture, rural queers like Bruce can easily be overlooked, scolded, or pitied. Being at once queer and normative is considered an oxymoron, yet Bruce embraces this contradiction to express rural cultural desire.

Ultimately, Bruce's "failure" to reconcile his same-sex practices with rural culture and hometown pride offers a unique lens on queer identity, one that resonates with Alex Ross's warnings about the confines of a fixed "queer ethos." Insisting on a monolithic LGBTQ ethos "reduce[s] the dizzying variety of gay lives to an ideal condition: either you're prowling the bars or you're gardening in the Berkshires" (Ross, 50). Using "ideals" as a yardstick for the lives of rural queer peoples erases how "queerness can endure even through attachments to respectability" (Horton).[5] *Fun Home* poignantly suggests how being both normative and respectable *and* queer does not necessarily rule out resilience in the countryside. This is what makes *Fun Home* such as complex and compelling text: it brings conflicting rural queer desires, contradictions, and dichotomies into view instead of ignoring them.

Alison Bechdel and Beech Creek

"Will this place hurt us?" "Can we love it?" The eco-critic Steve Mentz uses these questions to generate a nuanced analysis of place. When applied to *Fun Home*, the answers depend a lot on gender. Until Bruce's arrest for providing alcohol to a minor, he goes about his same-sex nonconformity in Beech

Creek nonchalantly—and with little regard for how his actions cruelly affect his wife and family. Steeped in white patriarchal male privilege, Bruce inhabits a space of intricate contradictory desire more easily than Helen or Alison; Beech Creek works for him in ways it can never work for them.

Nevertheless, like her father, Alison develops her own complex rural place attachment, evident in the many drawings that show love for the "particular, intimate contours of the landscape itself" (*FH*, 144). As a young lesbian, Alison internalizes a get-out-of-the-sticks mentality—an outlook she clearly learned from both of her parents, US culture, and the lesbian and gay movement. She rages about Beech Creek and says her father killed himself because of where he lived ("He couldn't face living in this small-minded small town one more second"), espousing ideas about rural space as lifeless and hostile (125). However, at thirty, Bechdel did a "reverse migration." After living in several big cities, she moved to rural Vermont, a far more progressive place than rural central Pennsylvania, but a place where, as she commented in an interview with the author, she could "live in the country" with "ready access to nature."

Bechdel's affection for rural culture also surfaces in *Fun Home*, not only through her in-depth and complex portrait of her father but in specific drawings of her childhood. As a young girl, Alison's favorite page in a *Wind in the Willows* coloring book was a map of the Wild Wood and surrounding county, which inspired her to painstakingly map out Beech Creek and note parallels between the two. Other drawings depict her childhood encounter with environmental destruction, signaling Bechdel's retrospective environmental awareness of how Beech Creek was negatively altered through mountaintop removal during her childhood. As a teenager, even as she hated Beech Creek, she also felt ambivalent about the city. In a powerful image of Alison and Bruce, with the impressive New York City skyline behind them, they look frozen and unimpressed: the city fails to liberate them, even though it is a seemingly far more hospitable place for queer people. After Alison graduates from college, she moves to New York City, yet the images in the memoir depicting this time often show her as isolated: riding her bike through the streets, mourning the death of her father, and encountering what will become the large-scale devastation of AIDS.

From a metronormative point of view, Bruce Bechdel's life seems sad and unfulfilled, and Alison's trajectory to the city seems like liberation. But Alison returns to rural culture, and as much as she mourns her father's circumscribed life and tragic death, she cannot imagine him anywhere but the countryside, suggesting, to quote again from Keller, that "rural queers are [not] rendered powerless by virtue of their geographic location" (162). Living in Beech Creek makes Bruce and Alison vulnerable, but they are not immobilized—at least not in any totalized way. A cool, detached, ironic analysis of life in Beech

Creek permeates *Fun Home*, with images of the father's seemingly fastidious behavior paralleling young Alison's affliction with obsessive-compulsive disorder. But the same images coexist with hand-drawn scenes of poignant intimacy, love, and place attachment, capturing the complexity of Bruce's and Alison's allegiance to rural place.

Decolonizing rural place in *Fun Home* reveals how home, place, kinship, and nature are essential components of this memoir, challenging readers to move past the idea of rural place as backward and unlivable and urban space as the only authentic place to be queer. The difficulties and challenges that queers encounter in rural space are formidable, but they are neither totalizing nor unique. As the Appalachian author Silas House writes, "Homophobia lurks in the hollers and slithers along the ridges of Appalachia. The reason why is because Appalachia is in America" (quoted in Catte, 124).

NOTES

1. Amos Lassen's online book review of *Queering the Countryside: New Frontiers in Rural Queer Studies* reproduces metronormative ideology—even though the point of *Queering the Countryside* is to challenge entrenched metrochauvinism in all forms of queer work. Lassen portrays rural areas as devoid of queer culture and encourages urban LGBTQs not to "forget that we have LGBT brothers and sisters in rural areas" who need help. He urges metro LGBTQs to do "some kind of outreach to our gay friends in those areas. I do not believe that I am speaking only for myself when I say that I have no desire to live in a rural area." Lassen's post implies that there is no rural queer organizing. Southerners on New Ground (SONG), a queer people of color liberation organization with a regional and rural focus in the South, addresses attitudes such as Lassen's by challenging the ways in which rural areas—and the South as a whole—have historically been written off as pathetic and doomed: "Our efforts have often been looked on with pity, and our organizing and infrastructure too often under-resourced, abandoned, and not taken seriously. While we live in states deemed 'red and left for dead,' in towns and cities that have been forsaken and entire communities left to fend for ourselves, we've *learned a thing or two about what it means to survive, to fight back, and to build culture and power in these places.*"

2. The distorting effects of metronormativity on conceptions of rural queer people in the United States recall Abu Lughod's analysis of problematic representations of Muslim women in Western discourse. Lughod shows how Western feminist (and nonfeminist) discussions consistently position Muslim women as pitiful and in need of saving. The result, she explains, is that Muslim women become people "for whom [Western feminists] can feel sorry and in relation to whom they can feel smugly superior." Lughod's insights resonate with William Spurlin's observation that the field of queer studies is deformed by a "Eurocentric, and therefore imperialistic gaze" that ignores complex queer cultures beyond metropolitan centers.

3. Friends of the family note a strong bond between Alison and her father: "On our final evening, a family friend remarked admiringly to Joan [Alison's girlfriend] on the close relationship between my father and me" (225).

4. In *Men Like That: A Southern Queer History*, John Howard documents how southern men, instead of claiming a gender and sexual core identity, *practice* gender and sexual identity in the context of rural and urban sexual networks in contrast with men in cities. Urban centers are more likely to have larger concentrations of "gay" people in neighborhoods, a spatial formation

more conducive to claiming a core "gay" identity. Amin Ghaziani categorizes urban gay men and lesbians who—like rural and Southern queers—decenter their sexual and gender identity as having "postgay" identities. In an urban context, postgay identities are linked to progress in LGBTQ civil rights and greater societal acceptance, allowing sexual and gender identity to recede from the forefront of one's life. However, this same kind of decentered identity in rural contexts is typically interpreted as "closeting." Although Ghaziani believes sexuality does not have a singular spatial expression, decentered identity is interpreted differently depending on the geographic region in which it takes place. In the city, a decentered identity is a sign of progress; in the countryside, it's a sign of backwardness.

5. Ryka Aoki expresses similar discomfort with the demand for idealized notions of transgression and subversion in approaches to gender and sexuality (150). Aoki offers encouragement for moving beyond the "prowling the bars" or "gardening in the Berkshires" stranglehold: some people want both, some people want neither, and idealizations don't tell us much about the complexity of gender and sexuality.

WORKS CITED

Abu Lughod, Lia. "Do Muslim Women Need Saving?" In *Women Worldwide: Transnational Feminist Perspectives on Women*, ed. Janet Lee and Susan Shaw, 597–607. McGraw-Hill, 2011.
Annes, Alexis, and Meredith Redlin. "Coming Out and Coming Back: Rural Gay Migration and the City." *Journal of Rural Studies* 28 (2012): 56–68.
Aoki, Ryka. "On Living Well and Coming Free." In *Gender Outlaws: The Next Generation*, ed. Kate Bornstein and S. Bear Bergman, 143–52. Seal, 2010.
Bauer, Henry. "Henry Bauer." In *Farm Boys: Lives of Gay Men from the Rural Midwest*, ed. Will Fellows, 59–67. University of Wisconsin Press, 1996.
Bechdel, Alison. Interview with author. February 4, 2015.
Butler, Judith. *Gender Trouble: Feminism and the Subversion of Identity*. Routledge, 1990.
Catte, Elizabeth. *What You Are Getting Wrong about Appalachia*. Belt, 2018.
Chute, Hillary. "An Interview with Alison Bechdel." *Modern Fiction Studies* 52, no. 4 (2006): 1004–13.
Cooke, Rachel. "*Fun Home* Creator Alison Bechdel on Turning a Tragic Childhood into a Hit Musical." *Guardian*, November 5, 2017. Accessed February 10, 2018.
Crawford, Lucas. "A Good Ol' Country Time: Does Queer Rural Temporality Exist?" *Sexualities* 20, no. 8 (2017): 904–20.
Cross, Jim. "Jim Cross." In *Farm Boys: Lives of Gay Men from the Rural Midwest*, ed. Will Fellows, 76–88. University of Wisconsin Press, 1996.
Faulkner, William. Interview with John K. Hutchens. In *Lion in the Garden: Interviews with William Faulkner, 1926–1962*, ed. James B. Meriwether and Michael Millgate, 59–60. Random House, 1968.
Faulkner, William. Interview with Michel Mok. In *Lion in the Garden: Interviews with William Faulkner, 1926–1962*, ed. James B. Meriwether and Michael Millgate, 38–41. Random House, 1968.
Fellows, Will, ed. *Farm Boys: Lives of Gay Men from the Rural Midwest*. University of Wisconsin Press, 1996.
Ghaziani, Amin. *There Goes the Gayborhood?* Princeton University Press, 2014.
Goldsmith, Jenna. "Landing on the Patio: Landscape Ecology and the Architecture of Identity in Alison Bechdel's *Fun Home: A Family Tragicomic*." *disClosure: A Journal of Social Theory* 23, nos. 1–2 (2014): 1–25.

Gray, Mary. *Out in the Country: Youth, Media, and Queer Visibility in America*. New York University Press, 2009.
Gray, Mary, Colin R. Johnson, and Brian J. Gilley, eds. *Queering the Countryside: New Frontiers in Rural Queer Studies*. New York University Press, 2016.
Halberstam, Judith [now known as Jack]. *In a Queer Place and Time: Transgender Bodies, Subcultural Lives*. New York University Press, 2005.
Herring, Scott. *Another Country: Queer Anti-Urbanism*. New York University Press, 2010.
hooks, bell. *Belonging: A Culture of Place*. Routledge, 2009.
Horton, Brian. "What's So 'Queer' about Coming Out? Silent Queers and Theorizing Kinship Agonistically in Mumbai." *Sexualities*, September 12, 2017.
Howard, John. *Men Like That: A Southern Queer History*. University of Chicago Press, 1999.
Howard, John. Introduction to *Carryin' On in the Lesbian and Gay South*, ed. John Howard, 1–12. New York University Press, 1997.
Johnson, Colin R. Introduction to *Just Queer Folks: Gender and Sexuality in Rural America*, ed. Colin R. Johnson, 1–24. Temple University Press, 2013.
Keller, Julie C. "Rural Queer Theory." In *Feminisms and Ruralities*, ed. Barbara Pini, Berit Brandth, and Jo Little, 155–66. Lexington Books, 2015.
Lassen, Amos. "'Queering the Countryside: New Frontiers in Rural Queer Studies' ed. Mary L. Gray, Colin R. Johnson, and Brian J. Gilley: The Rural Queer Experience." Book review. February 13, 2016. Accessed September 24, 2016.
Lindholm, Dennis. "Dennis Lindholm." In *Farm Boys: Lives of Gay Men from the Rural Midwest*, ed. Will Fellows, 84–92. University of Wisconsin Press, 1996.
Little, Jo. "The Development of Feminist Perspectives in Rural Gender Studies." In *Feminisms and Ruralities*, ed. Barbara Pini, Berit Brandth, and Jo Little, 107–18. Lexington Books, 2015.
Mentz, Steve. "Walking through Newtown Creek." Paper presented at the Modern Language Association Conference, January 4–7, 2018. New York Hilton, New York.
Meriwether, James B., and Michael Millgate, eds. *Lion in the Garden: Interviews with William Faulkner, 1926–1962*. Random House, 1968.
Phillips, Richard, Diane Watt, and David Shuttleton, eds. *De-centering Sexualities: Politics and Representation beyond the Metropolis*. Routledge, 2000.
Pini, Barbara, Berit Brandth, and Jo Little, eds. *Feminisms and Ruralities*. Lexington Books, 2015.
Reed, Norm. "Norm Reed." In *Farm Boys: Lives of Gay Men from the Rural Midwest*, ed. Will Fellows, 115–26. University of Wisconsin Press, 1996.
Ross, Alex. "Love on the March." *New Yorker*, November 11, 2012. Accessed February 1, 2018.
Soderling, Stina. "Queer Rurality and the Materiality of Time." In *Queering the Countryside: New Frontiers in Rural Queer Studies*, ed. Mary Gray, Colin R. Johnson, and Brian J. Gilley, 333–48. New York University Press, 2016.
Southerners on New Ground (SONG). "Queer South Rise Up: Organizing in the Time of Trump." February 7, 2017. Accessed February 11, 2017.
Spurlin, William. "Remapping Same-Sex Desire: Queer Writing and Culture in the American Heartland." In *De-centering Sexualities: Politics and Representation beyond the Metropolis*, ed. Richard Phillips, Diane Watt, and David Shuttleton, 182–98. Routledge, 2000.
Stryker, Susan. Response to 2016 Presidential Election. Facebook, November 9, 2016, 9:00 a.m. Accessed November 9, 2016.
Weston, Kath. "Get Thee to a Big City." *GLQ: A Journal of Lesbian and Gay Studies* 2, no. 3 (1995): 253–78.
Wilsey, Sean. "The Things They Buried." *New York Times*, June 16, 2006. Accessed February 2, 2015.
Wilson, Angelia. "Getting Your Kicks on Route 66! Stories of Gay and Lesbian Life in Rural America, c. 1950–1970s." In *De-centering Sexualities: Politics and Representation beyond the Metropolis*, ed. Richard Phillips, Diane Watt, and David Shuttleton, 199–216. Routledge, 2000.

FUN HOME AND *ARE YOU MY MOTHER?* AS AUTOTOPOGRAPHY

Queer Orientations and the Politics of Location

KATHERINE KELP-STEBBINS

Of Webs and Other Texts

The first page of *Are You My Mother?* depicts a cluttered basement room with a small window transected by a spider's web. This symbolic web performs many semiotic functions. Diegetically, it presages the "spiderweb dream" (*AYMM*, 42; fig. 12.1), which Bechdel historicizes as occurring "in the thick of writing the book about my father," a project that the reader may understand as *Fun Home*. Therefore, at a larger, intertextual scale, the web is a symbol weaving together Bechdel's oeuvre of memoirs—two explorations of parentage and filiation—occurring in the pages of the one and in the narrative "thick" of the other.

However, the web also signifies the comics form itself. Examined more closely, the small window on the first page of *Are You My Mother?* is split by the web into a form resembling a codex and is further dissected into geometric panels. This multivalent object—window and web, complication of visual surface and narrative depth—functions as a *mise en abîme* for Bechdel's practice of what Thierry Groensteen describes, in *The System of Comics*, as *tressage*, or braiding. For Groensteen, *tressage* denotes the basic model inherent to comics of shuttling between the synchronic "co-presence of panels" and the diachronic "reading, which recognizes in each new term of a series a recollection or an echo of an anterior term" (147). The image of the web represents the weaving together of numerous nodes of panels into one copresent yet spatially separated system of expression and narration while simultaneously serving as a node itself.

Fig. 12.1. The spider's web (*AYMM*, 1).

Mobilizing the web as the starting point from which to engage with Bechdel's work, I draw together a number of feminist theorists and comics scholars to analyze *Fun Home* and *Are You My Mother?* as works about locating the self in space and time. Although Bechdel has, in interviews, repeatedly referred to her belief that comics are like maps, the map is generally noteworthy for its flattening of space.[1] In contradistinction, the "maps" made by *Fun Home* and *Are You My Mother?* are noteworthy precisely for their thickness, how they weave together so many two-dimensional objects (pages of books, maps, journals, photographs, drawings, etc.) into a multidimensional text of warp and weft. As such, this essay considers Bechdel's deployment of cartographic, verbal, and visual regimes as forms of autotopography, Jennifer González's term for a "syntagmatic array of physical signs in a spatial representation of identity" (133). Bechdel's autotopographic work orients, disorients, and reorients the reader by positioning her amid a web of visual objects and representational spaces where selfhood becomes a condition of spatiality. Conceptualizing Bechdel's "autobiographies" as autotopographies highlights the ways in which her books do not simply write the self but compel the reader to question how the self is politically located.

The Politics of Location

Adrienne Rich's oft-quoted "Notes toward a Politics of Location" addresses the "confusion between our claims to the white and Western eye and the woman-seeing eye," which inhabits and inhibits the white feminist's responsibility to "recognize our location, having to name the place we're coming from, the conditions we have taken for granted" (219).[2] "Having to name the place we're coming from" does not merely correspond to a toponymic response—in Bechdel's case, writing Beech Creek, Pennsylvania, in a panel in *Fun Home*. Rather, as Rich avows, "I need to understand how a place on the map is also a place in history" (212). In Rich's terms, the text of the map, its toponymic indexicality, belies its texture in terms of temporality, as well as its status as an object in space and time. While the white Western eye depends on the "global linear thinking" that categorically demands the correlation between the textual signifier "Beech Creek" and a historical, biographical place, Rich challenges readers to resist the seductive pull of such semiotics maintained by the visual techniques of the cartographic imperative.

Within the study of visual media, the white and Western eye serves as the technical a priori for visualization practices like the cartographic grid, as well as quasi-visual practices like (phal)logocentrism. I argue that Bechdel's books deconstruct the authority of these practices, by deploying cartographic, verbal, and visual regimes to create autotopographies that queer the hierarchy of the white and Western eye over the woman-seeing eye. As a challenge to readerly expectations regarding locative media, many panels that a comics reader would expect to find filled with pictures are, in *Fun Home* and *Are You My Mother?*, filled with text or map fragments. Similarly, maps in these books are overlaid with critical and self-descriptive text or images, to show how Cartesian representations of space may be "both misleading and accurate," as Bechdel writes in a narrative box inset atop the circular map of her father's life as narrativized in map space (*FH*, 30). As such, Bechdel also reasserts the visuality of text and the verbality of images, while revealing the artificiality of distinctions like these that give meaning and authoritative weight to toponymic maps.

By amassing a multitude of different types of maps and mapping processes, *Fun Home* and *Are You My Mother?* refuse the epistemological authority of any particular way of writing, representing, or locating the self in place and time. Just as Bechdel's early journals in *Fun Home* show an "epistemological crisis" regarding whether things written are "absolutely, objectively true" (*FH*, 141), so the juxtaposition of various medial objects of self-location and their repetition attest to the "troubling gap between word and meaning" (143). As González asserts, between memory and history, an object's evidentiary status becomes paradoxical: "Memory allows the object to have changing and multiple meanings, whereas history demands of the object a specific and single identity" (147). In an autotopography, historical and memorial discourses cohere, much as how the circumscribed map of Beech Creek in *Fun Home* can make both misleading and accurate claims in the same narrative.

The Map Is the Text, the Autotopography Is the Texture

To unravel the implications of the locational technics of *Fun Home* and *Are You My Mother?*, I follow two threads. The first necessitates following the map as an object, one with a material history and position in space and time. The second involves understanding the map as the concatenation of a series of cultural techniques, some of which are also bound up in the medial structure of comics. These two approaches are interwoven. As the geographer Denis Cosgrove notes, "Geographical representations—in the form of maps, texts, and pictorial images of various kinds—are not merely traces or sources. . . . They are active, constitutive elements in shaping social and spatial practices and the environments we occupy" (15). Foremost among these elements is the "global linear thinking" that Carl Schmitt describes in *The Nomos of the Earth* as a type of schematic orientation to the earth inaugurated with the Treaty of Tordesillas (87). The lines that describe and circumscribe the whole world make it impossible to imagine the world outside of such lines, despite their artificiality and anthropological histories. Trying to reorient ourselves to a world whose representation is already delineated involves unraveling and reweaving geographical representations, as Bechdel does throughout both of her books.

Taking up Rich's call for a politics of location, scholars like Sara Ahmed have theorized how lines lead to physical, social, sexual, and psychic alignment. Following a certain line in space and time is also a way of being straight (Ahmed, 16), just as Bruce Bechdel's following in the family line of business or creating a line of progeny corresponds to a particular way of orienting the self. Heteronormativity, as a form of orientation, "can be redescribed in terms of the requirement to follow a straight line" (70). Such lines, like the lines on the map, correspond to dispositifs that dictate how we understand ourselves and the world. These lines recollect lines of inheritance and filiation within the family; they create a pressure to inherit the family line, but as Ahmed states:

> We need to ask what gets put aside, or put to one side, in the telling of the family story. What gets put aside, or put to one side, does not come after the event but rather shapes the line, allowing it to acquire its force. The family pictures picture the family, often as happy (the bodies that gather smile, as if the smile were the point of the gathering). At the same time, the pictures put aside what does not follow this line, those feelings that do not cohere as a smile. (90)

Alternately, as Ahmed points out, the word "queer" is etymologically a spatial term meaning "twist" (67). As Ahmed suggests, Bechdel's books function through myriad twists in space and time. These narrative or pictorial twists question what is left out of the family story and, in so doing, return to spaces where bodies gather—the home, the car, but also Beech Creek or London—while recollecting and rereading these spaces.

As the books reorient both the narrator and the reader in space, they also challenge what Judith Halberstam has called "reproductive temporality," or the logic of the normal, ruled by "the biological clock for women," in which inheritance in the form of "values, wealth, goods, and morals [is] passed through family ties from one generation to the next" (5). For Halberstam, "queer time" is a response to the normativization of reproductive longevity. Bechdel's books are noteworthy for the ways that they subvert reproductive lines as a hegemonic framework for narrative space and time. On the seventh page of *Are You My Mother?* the narrator announces that she has arrived at a terminus, a contradiction in terms, given that the book goes on for another 281 pages. She notes that she is "running out of eggs," thus acknowledging the pressure to inherit the monolith of reproductive time. However, because this acknowledgment comes at the beginning of the book, it paradoxically signals the fealty to, and the refusal to succumb to, the temporal logic of heteronormativity. Furthermore, both books end with a return to childhood; the final images are a child Alison with Bruce in *Fun Home* and Helen in *Are You My Mother?*, a clear disavowal of the time of reproduction, which would demand progression to adulthood, death, or childbearing. Bechdel's books do not reproduce the linear logic of the traditional autobiography. They circle back to events and places to twist them again and again in space and time.

While Ahmed and Halberstam, among others, have critiqued heteronormative and colonialist construction of space and time, the feminist geographer

Doreen Massey has also exposed how "currently widespread and significant ways of conceptualizing space and place are constructed in the same manner as, and both reflect and affect, the contemporary dominant western modes of conceptualizing gender" (13). Such an insistence on the dominance of the white Western eye as it inheres in maps and other forms is not a critique of the map per se as much as a demand for the contextualization of all maps and mapping forms. Maps are essential not only to finding oneself in space but to conceiving of space as it is known and knowable. The map's power lies in its abstraction, and its reductive and scalar potentialities. Thus the whole *mappa mundi* at its literal level is a cloth of the world or, more perversely, a cloth that can contain the image of the whole world. What is lost in this formulation is the cloth itself, a textile, a textured object capable of providing a space in which a representation of space may be drawn (alternately capable of providing a surface on which to serve a meal, as *mappa* also denotes a tablecloth or napkin). Consequently, a feminist approach to spatial representation insists on accounting for maps as objects in space and time, and objects that orient one toward a subjective reading of space and time.

Fun Home is so hyperattentive to location that Sean Wilsey, reviewing Bechdel's memoir for the *New York Times*, used the book to chart his own trip to Beech Creek. Exclaiming of the accuracy of the book, he called it "a memoir you can navigate by!" Yet there is a way in which this description misses the complexity of locational practices. The Beech Creek in *Fun Home* is always a lived place, a space for the crossing, recrossing, recollecting, and rereading of at least two prominent characters in the text. Hillary Chute calls the book "a map of the network of transversals for the two 'directions' embodied by Bruce and Alison Bechdel" (182). While the book itself may work as a particular type of orientation device, the maps within the book complicate and challenge the stability of geographical representations.

The map that we may understand initially as what the narrator deems a "misleading and accurate" map of Bruce Bechdel's life is first drawn on page 30, again on 31, and again on pages 140 and 146. The very repetition of the same map deterritorializes its paradigmatic function as a spatial representation by giving it a temporal function through that repetition. Furthermore, because the map is always partial and juxtaposed with other images and texts, it is deterritorialized in terms of its plane of representational space; it is reoriented as but one element of spatial representation among others. This reorientation is emphasized by the fact that all these maps share the same line weight, style, and drawing quality as that of the other images and text; that is, the same hand drew these maps and the gravestones, letters, characters, and panels surrounding them.[3] All these aspects demonstrate the map as a commingling of subjective and objective ways of seeing and locating selves in time and space.

On page 30, the map is overlaid by a shaded circle and diagrammatic letters referring to events and places explained in the narrative box on the left of the map. As the circle draws attention to the space of the map it circumscribes, it also deforms the map, creating another line within the space of representation and transecting a number of other topological lines. However, although I describe the image as if there were an originary map that had been drawn over, this is not the case in *Fun Home*; the entire map cum circle and letters is one representational system, which posits the capacity for drawing maps so as to orient a reader to particular ways of reading and interpretation. The following panel, at the top of the next page, zooms in further for a close-up of the map, reminding the reader that the subjectivity and objectivity of maps are negotiated through scalar politics. While the first map could show Bruce's grave, birthplace, place of death, and home, it could not at the same time illustrate the houses of each of his nearby relatives. Maneuvering scale to show more or less with the same map, Bechdel demonstrates that a map's objectivity will depend entirely on frames of reference.

A similar scalar transition occurs in *Are You My Mother?* with a shift in geographical focus across the Atlantic from Beech Creek to London. The ability of Bechdel's comics to recontextualize the mediality of maps is particularly evident on page 25 of *Are You My Mother?*, which visually situates the map of the London Underground under the ground of the rest of the image on the page, making a visual pun that refutes the perspectival logic of the other visual cues on the page (fig. 12.2). The vanishing point that was dead center in the similar image on the preceding page has, on page 25, been shifted upward to capture the image of Virginia Woolf, as well as the potential objects within her line of sight.

The central object in this line of potential (Woolf's gaze is not visible to the reader), vertically above the image of Woolf, is D. W. Winnicott, whose movement in diegetic space and the page itself is accompanied by a series of vertically stacked narration boxes staggered from top to bottom (or from the top of the page to the map). The textual reading of the page parallels the theoretical trajectory of Winnicott as image (i.e., his figural representation strolling across the street), and it provides a transverse or oppositional direction to Winnicott as symbol (i.e., the red arrow on the subway map indicating his movement to the station). While the arrow moves right to left, the text and the image of Winnicott move (or are captured in motion) from top to bottom. Both trajectories—image and arrow—converge toward the figure of Woolf, Bechdel's proxy in the scene, as verbally signaled by the narrator

Fig. 12.2a. Woolfian words and images (*AYMM*, 25–27).

Alison's authorial confession: "How I envy the involuntary torrent of words and images that came to Virginia Woolf that day" (*AYMM*, 23).

The fragment of subway map operates narratively as one more component of the word and image "torrent" oriented toward Woolf. Although the reader is aware that the map charts a potential pathway for Winnicott, he already appears in a different quadrant of the page as picture, complicating or enfolding the map's locative work within other visual techniques. Importantly, both symbolic Winnicott (on the underground map) and imagistic Winnicott (aboveground) are focalized through Woolf's perspective. Thus Bechdel orients Winnicott's extensive movement through urban space (a geographic

Fig. 12.2b. Woolfian words and images (*AYMM*, 25–27).

action long associated with masculine privilege) around and through Woolf as a far more domestic (she is walking the dog through the park) and also creative ("perhaps continuing to think about this new novel") figure of location in historico-fictive London (*AYMM*, 27).

The following pages of *Are You My Mother?* extend and expand the map's interweaving into the comic space and transform it in the process. On page 26, a street map takes up the top third of the page, and on page 27, an aerial close-up fills the top two-thirds of the page. From pages 25 to 27, maps take precedence on the space of the page, and each cartographic representation of space becomes more detailed and somewhat less abstract. Taken together, all three pages serve as an extended rumination on how maps mediate or weave together the fictional and the historical, as well as the invisible and the visible. The first map—a rendition of a 1920s pre–Harry Beck London Underground diagram—represents the ability of media objects to make the invisible visible. On maps made before Beck's iconic 1931 topological design, the underground lines were represented on the same space as London streets, thus using a representation of an aboveground (or visible) system to orient readers through a subterranean (or invisible) network. The fragment of the map that Bechdel draws on page 25 reproduces this visible-invisible dialectic and also represents a material artifact serving to bridge the real and the imaginary. Located in the midst of a speculative section of *Are You My Mother?*, the underground map lends credence to an imaginary network of authors and analysts unfolding in space. In weaving this network, the narrator speculates as to how Woolf and Winnicott may have literally and figuratively crossed paths.

This narrative of the possible is augmented by the underground map, as well as two other maps, which orient the reader to the space in which such a crossing may have occurred, while showing the tenuous historicity of such intersections of time, space, and visuality. Atop the second map on page 26—a fragment of a London street map—a narration box relates, "It's doubtful they know each other." This statement of uncertainty belies the systemic precision of the street map while gesturing toward the map's scale, at which London can be imagined as a featureless urban tangle. The final map—an aerial view of the space near Tavistock Square—is overlaid with another box that resolves the characters' speculative near encounter: "In a few minutes both of them have left the outside world" (*AYMM*, 27). Although two boxes with arrows indicate the locations of Woolf and Winnicott in the geography, neither character is visible, relegating these boxes to the status of makeshift toponyms. The sequence of pages ends with the narrator's assertion that "although I am enjoying this little foray into fiction, I feel the necessity of 'clinging as tight to the facts as I can'" (27), leaving the reader to question just how to orient fact and fiction among all these paths, networks, spaces, and maps.

Gridding and Weaving

Bechdel's comics do not merely represent the map as an object; they also reveal it as an accretive medium of spatial representation, as they partake of the graphic technologies of the map—another verbal-visual representative medium—while subverting its objective logic. The same global linear thinking that informs the map's flattening of topographic systems into lines in a grid also factors into the gridding of the page into the panels one finds in comics. These technical operations are not identical: the map uses its material substrate as a basis for continuous representation, while the comics page mobilizes the tension between the continuity of the page as a unifying space of enunciation and the panel as a unit of discontinuity within the space. US comics studies, following the model of Scott McCloud, have frequently discounted the spatial in favor of the narrative or the temporal. Yet Franco-Belgian comics theorists have for decades attended to the necessary interplay between the panel as an element of the spatial system of the page, and the panel as a narrative unit in a sequence of panels.

Continuing to pull on the thread of numerous textiles, we can understand the operation of comics according to the fabric of panels and texts. In addition to the terms "map" and "text," which both have their etymological roots in weaving and cloths, the Latin *pannus*, from which come both the words "pane" and "panel," also refers to a cloth and is cognate with the archaic Greek word πῆνος, or "web." In a metonymic transit into English, we find pane(l)—as in the comics panel—referring to a part of a surface, like a window.

Tracing *panel* to its etymological roots leads to a provocative insight into the image-making medium of comics: rather than see a window (or a panel) as an aperture onto objective truth, we might understand each panel as a division of a greater whole, its sole purpose to function as an image-making medium. Together these panels weave together to form an operational whole, as Groensteen has suggested. Yet a tension remains between the panel as a syntagmatic unit and the page as a surface. Bechdel both highlights and toys with the dynamic tension between aperture and surface in panels such as the two on the top of *Fun Home*, page 52, or the panels on the bottom of pages 86 and 139. On page 52, what appears as a continuous image is divided into two panels, reminding the reader of the structuring paradigm of the panel, and the plasticity of its divisions. On pages 86 and 139, a contiguous image is divided by the window separating characters from one another, showing how division even between interiority and exteriority is a function of surface. These types of panels occur continually in *Are You My Mother?*, as on pages 99, 102, 177, 216, 221, 274, and 281. On pages 122 and 123, 200 and 201, 261 and 262, and 266–68, the vacillation between Alison and mother or Alison and therapist as separated by panels or joined within a panel (or separated but joined by a bridging word balloon) is conspicuous to the point of producing narrative: the division between Alison and her (m)other generates a narrative strand regarding how she understands herself through her interlocutors, and the status of the panel showing Alison talking to her mother or therapist(s) denotes the status of this understanding at any given point in the story. The panel divisions refer explicitly to the questions of self and other, separation and identity. They also show the role of art in delineating such distinctions.

In these uses of panel distinctions and divisions on the page, Bechdel's work invites a critical reading practice that exceeds McCloudian approaches to comics. While McCloud privileges linear time and foregrounds the sequence of panels as the source of meaning in comics, Bechdel reveals that the sequence of panels may be inconsistent, aleatory, or impossible, and space itself precedes the phenomenon of sequence. As Franco-Belgian theorists such as Groensteen have shown in more spatially attuned reading models, "Comics are composed of interdependent images; and . . . these images, before knowing any other kind of relation, have the sharing of space as their first characteristic" (Groensteen, 28). Bechdel negotiates the shared space of the page to render the shared spaces of biographical habitation in graphic detail. Sustained narrative sequences emerge at specific locations, not only in time but also in place.

Insistence on the spatial component of the comics page does not discount the function of the sequence between panels; rather, it compels attention to the interplay between temporal and spatial reading models. Pierre Fresnault-Deruelle, in his essay "Du linéaire au tabulaire" (From Linear to Tabular), has argued that the comics page, as the spatial or tabular dimension of comic books, stands in dialectical relation to the temporal or linear dimension of the story. For Fresnault-Deruelle, this tension derives from comics as strip or its "stripological" syntagm, as opposed to comics as page, wherein the "composition of a page became a search for a way to integrate the variable aspects of the visual image (form, surface, value, colour) into the wider pane represented by the surface of the page" (129). Approaching the page as a composition, theorists like Benoît Peeters have used structural analysis to describe different forms of page layout, or *mise en page*. For Peeters, *mise en page* has four classifications that range from "conventional" to "productive" depending on how much the layout is constrained by the narrative. Because the page of comics is (almost without exception) a rectangular space, the orthogonal gridding (*quadrillage*) of the page into regular stripological units coincides with Peeters's "conventional" layout (41), which Groensteen instead calls "regular" layout (Groensteen, 95). Although the orthogonal aspect of the page inflects Bechdel's paginal compositions, her layouts are so heterogeneous as to entirely eschew the regular grid format—with one striking exception.

Bechdel's works subvert the operational logic of the grid, the technology that serves to make both cartography and comics legible by dividing available space linearly. German media theorists such as Bernhard Siegert have highlighted how the grid as a cultural technique combines an imaging process with ontological, operational, and epistemic potential (97). As a practice aligned with the white and Western eye, the grid has been essential for predatory and imperial forms of visual knowledge and mapping projects; it orders a person in her place because it is a mode of placing order on space. In contrast, Bechdel's constant play with spatial composition, as well as the image-text delineation of space, engenders disorientation for the comics reader by frustrating and reorienting expectations. As noted earlier, panels one "normally" expects to see filled with image are, in *Fun Home* and *Are You My Mother?*, taken up with text or map fragments. Further, because the books eschew "regular" *quadrillage* as a rhetorical technique of engaging space, the famous driving sequence between Bruce and Alison on pages 220–21 of *Fun Home* becomes an eruption of regularity within the text, as well as an irregularity that marks the grid as itself queer or out of place (fig. 12.3).

In this two-page spread, each page is segmented into a regular three-by-four or twelve-panel unified grid. The regularity of this format recalls Fresnault-Deruelle's qualification of the stripological as the familiar, which also speaks to the family, as it offers the "daily ration of idealized family life" (Fresnault-Deruelle, 123). Just as comics, in a linear, stripological fashion, symbolize a form of "idealized family life," so the conversation between Alison and Bruce in this sequence represents the closest the two come to an honest father-child bonding, or, as Bechdel calls it, "our Ithaca moment" (*FH*, 222). Likewise, the breakup of the page into twenty-four regular panels mirrors a standardized temporality that the rest of the book subtends. Rather than a day's worth of hours, this section extends a passage of minutes into twenty-four separate spatial nodes. Because the grid of panels on pages 220–21 is syntagmatically structured according to the stripological, it simultaneously evokes the familiar while twisting it or refusing to accord with the "conventional" or "regular" format of the familiar. The narrative content of these pages is at once the moment wherein the father-daughter relationship is both the most "normal" and yet also the most abnormal because the father reveals candidly what kept him from being a "normal" father.

The format of pages 220–21 resonates across the rest of *Fun Home* and extends into *Are You My Mother?* as well. By queering the grid, Bechdel's autotopography renders it as another object of subjectivity, which has, in Rich's words, been "taken for granted" as objective. Bechdel uses a conventional means of managing space in a way that is unconventional, pursuantly reorienting a reader's expectations of the comics page as a way of visualizing space. As Cartesian space ultimately becomes dislocated in her feminist mapping practices, Bechdel's works compel the reader to question the troubling dualisms at work in locating a white and Western self in time and space. Her use of the grid reveals the contingent and contextual aspect of how we come to know space as "conventional." The stripological grid may seem conventional in another context, but in the space of *Fun Home*, it is decidedly irregular. As Ahmed writes of being white in the world, this white world "extends the form of some bodies more than others and such bodies in turn feel at home in this world" (129); the same may be said of a heterosexual, heteronormative world, in which certain lines of inheritance and domesticity, convention and regularity, allow for some bodies to feel at home. The politics of location are also a politics of who gets to feel at home, and how much "feeling at home" is about "the making of worlds" (Ahmed, 20).

Groensteen's structural description of comics proposes a third component of articulation, beyond the page layout and the sequence of panels in

Fig. 12.3. Queering the grid (*FH*, 220–21).

syntagmatic arrangement. He calls this third level "general arthrology," and it corresponds to the function of braiding: how any panel or sequence exists in networked relation to all other spaces of the page, as well as the work as a whole. The panel, as it relates to other panels, is always, in Groensteen's terms, "a site," yet some panels may be enhanced through braiding to transcend the function of site and become "a place":

> What is a place other than a habituated space that we can cross, visit, invest in, a space where relations are made and unmade? If all the terms of a sequence, and consequently all the units of the network, constitute sites, it is the attachment, moreover, of these units to one or more remarkable series, that defines them as places. A place is therefore an activated and over-determined site, a site where a series crosses (or is superimposed on) a sequence. (148)

As Groensteen reminds us, our knowledge of a site (or a panel) changes in time and space. The knowledge that we have of a particular panel will shift based on what we have seen or how we orient ourselves to that particular space in time. While a map reduces a complex web of images, names, and topographies into an abstract text, Bechdel's works reinvest each place with texture. Comics operate through repetition and difference, and the panels in Bechdel's works, by repeating images, places, and events, weave these sites together and force the reader to account for the changing relations and knowledge that each panel provides, depending on the panels that have preceded it.

Although the places of *Fun Home* or *Are You My Mother?* may seem just as changeable or disorienting as they did at the beginning of the book, by the time the reader finishes, they have taken on material form—literally, as books glued together with many layers, and figuratively, as autotopographies. These books act as "orientation devices" in a manner that Ahmed describes, because as autotopographic archives they "are made up of paper and other things that 'matter,'" and they function as "'homes,' ways of gathering material, around which worlds gather" (Ahmed, 118). These worlds mark the bridging of the private and the public as much as they mark the epistemological regimes that hold such boundaries in check and relegate the domestic sphere (long considered the woman's place) as a world unworthy of discovery and mapping. In the reader's hands, these books act as orientation devices for exploring the shuttling between the limits of knowledge and the way that we politically locate ourselves in a place.

New orientations to place and visuality become possible when visual techniques for spatial epistemology are disoriented. By making, in Ahmed's words, "familiar [spaces of representation] strange" (177) as autotopographies, *Fun Home* and *Are You My Mother?* compel us to unwind the texts that map and extend white Western ways of locating a self in the world to construct new spaces of representation for representations of space.

NOTES

1. As Bechdel said in an interview in the *Comics Journal*, "I feel like cartoons function for me very much like maps, in that they take a complex or confusing three-dimensional reality and iron it out into a much more manageable two-dimensional version.... Also, maps combine words and images in the way cartoons do."

2. This essay by Rich is collected in the same anthology as "Blood, Bread, and Poetry: The Location of the Poet," a talk that Bechdel depicts herself and a partner attending in *Are You My Mother?*, thus allowing for Rich to have both theoretical and autobiographical relevance to Bechdel's own politics of location (*AYMM*, 186–87).

3. It is worth noting that the text is actually a digital font generated from a sample of Bechdel's lettering.

WORKS CITED

Ahmed, Sara. *Queer Phenomenology: Orientations, Objects, Others*. Duke University Press, 2006.
Cosgrove, Denis. *Geography and Vision: Seeing, Imagining, and Representing the World*. I. B. Tauris, 2008.

Chute, Hillary. *Graphic Women: Life Narrative and Contemporary Comics*. Columbia University Press, 2010.

Fresnault-Deruelle, Pierre. "From Linear to Tabular." In *The French Comics Theory Reader*, ed. Ann Miller and Bart Beaty, 121–38. Leuven University Press, 2014.

González, Jennifer A. "Autotopographies." In *Prosthetic Territories: Politics and Hypertechnologies*, ed. Gabriel Brahm Jr. and Mark Driscoll, 133–50. Westview Press, 1995.

Groensteen, Thierry. *The System of Comics*. Trans. Nick Nguyen and Bart Beaty. University Press of Mississippi, 2007.

Halberstam, Judith. *In a Queer Time and Place: Transgender Bodies, Subcultural Lives*. New York University Press, 2005.

Labio, Catherine. "The Architecture of Comics." *Critical Inquiry* 41, no. 2 (2015): 312–43.

Massey, Doreen. *Space, Place, and Gender*. University of Minnesota Press, 1994.

Peeters, Benoît. *Case, planche, récit: Lire la bande dessinée*. Casterman, 1991.

Rich, Adrienne. "Notes toward a Politics of Location." In *Blood, Bread, and Poetry: Selected Prose, 1979–1985*, 210–31. Norton, 1994.

Schmitt, Carl. *The Nomos of the Earth in the International Law of the Ius Publicum Europaeum*. Trans. G. L. Ulmen. Telos Press, 2003.

Siegert, Bernard. *Cultural Techniques: Grids, Filters, Doors, and Other Articulations of the Real*. Fordham University Press, 2015.

INSIDE THE ARCHIVES OF *FUN HOME*

SUSAN R. VAN DYNE

For Alison Bechdel, autobiography and biography were twinned in drafting her groundbreaking queer graphic memoir *Fun Home*. She recognized that unless she could write and draw the story of the father who defined her childhood and adolescence, she could not create the narrative of her own queer becoming. The dramatic tension of the memoir is produced by having her father's unsuspected queer sexuality revealed by her mother when Alison comes out to them in college, to be followed by his suicide five months later. If her father wasn't who she thought he was, then neither was she. I draw on the archives for *Fun Home*, part of the Alison Bechdel Papers held by Smith College, to map the stages in her creative process and trace her struggle to understand her father's sexuality in relation to her own to imagine a queer family history that could include them both.[1]

My approach draws on theorists of life writing who examine the creation of subjectivity through autobiography. John Paul Eakin proposed early on that "all identities are relational," and as a result, the first person of autobiography is never singular but plural (43). Others agree that memoir as an act of self-inquiry and self-knowing is "relational" and "routed through others," because subjectivities come into being through social relations. The concept of relationality, that our stories are always entwined with those of others, also implies that boundaries of an "I" are often porous and provisional rather than discrete and autonomous (Smith and Watson, 64). Nancy Miller, describing the field of autobiography studies in 2014, concludes that "in autobiography the relational is not optional" but an integral element of the genre (544). In reading the archives, I analyze several critical moments in which Bechdel entertains the possibility of speculatively aligning herself within her father's subjectivity, despite the divide of his death and the temporal differences of their embodied histories.

The Artist in the Archive

Amassed over six years, Bechdel's print archives bear the marks of her physical presence as she composed and edited. Although the most complete archive of *Fun Home*'s creation is stored only on her personal computer, the material Bechdel printed out and layered in rough chronological order for each chapter forms a record of moments when she edited by hand: "A lot of these drafts are just totally chaotic; either too much stuff there or not fleshed out," she told me in an interview. "I got to a certain point of clarity . . . to some state where I could work with it, and then I would print it out. . . . I had to see the physical thing, and I had to make written notes, I couldn't do that sort of thinking on the screen." In Bechdel's oeuvre, the *Fun Home* archive is especially valuable because it is the last of its kind: "That process has continued to evolve for me, and I feel I'm less likely to print stuff out now, I'm able to trust the screen more."

In the later stages of composition, when she began to sketch, to speed her drawing of individual frames, Bechdel often used reference shots taken with a digital camera mounted on a tripod. She posed, she told me, for "hundreds and hundreds" of these pictures. Repeatedly, she posed as her father, "looking out at things as if I were my father." She describes the consequence "that happens as I have to impersonate these characters. . . . It gives me an emotional intimacy that filters into my drawing" ("Public," 207). This massive shadow archive underlies all of *Fun Home*, but because she often worked directly from the camera or from a download to her computer, only a few of these photos of Bechdel as the visual prototype for the drawings exist in the print archive.[2] Once the size and relationship of panels and text were established, Bechdel drew rough sketches in heavy pencil on tracing paper overlaid on the layout page. For Bechdel, both features of her graphic practice are an intimate and porous connection between herself as cartoonist and her characters. In an interview, Bechdel acknowledges that because they are translated through her hand or style of drawing, her drawings "inevitably resemble or are a manifestation of the person making them" (quoted in Chute, *Graphic*, 186).

The artistic structure of *Fun Home* has been described as "recursive," demanding that we read backward as often as forward to comprehend its nonlinear progression (Chute, "Gothic," 2; Watson, 149; Van Dyne, 107). The archives demand an equally recursive analytical process, reading vertically through successive drafts of a single chapter, and horizontally across similar strata in different chapters. To identify patterns that emerge across multiple iterations in these sources over six years requires attention that embraces randomness and serendipity, and a willingness to suspend judgment about what evidence is central and what is peripheral for as long as possible. Rather than attempt a comprehensive account of what Bechdel kept, I have chosen to focus on a selection of key artifacts in the print archive and the evolution of central episodes in the narrative to demonstrate the strategies she used while composing. Each example isolates a different stage of the process, yet each reveals her desire to reinhabit her father's consciousness and to see herself through his eyes as a route to self-knowledge.

Working through the Father

During 1999, her first year of work on the book, Bechdel kept a daily work log. Much more than a record of her "daily progress," the space rapidly became a personal journal to acknowledge her insecurities about her authorial voice, her stamina as a cartoonist, the gaps in her knowledge of her family, and recurring anxieties about revealing her plans for the "Dad book" to her mother: "I could really get paralyzed. Instead, I have to just keep focusing on the node, the kernel that I feel sure about—I know that I have something to say about my relationship with my father."[3] The most consuming emotional work of the log, however, was dismantling the self-protective barrier she had constructed between herself and the memory of her father since his suicide. When she begins the project, she recognizes that "this summer is the 'halfway point'" between her father's presence in her life and his absence: "I'll have spent just as much of my life without him as I did with him." She fears that her analytical clarity about him ("yes, he was a charming sociopath, selfish, weak, cowardly, fixated with appearances, moody, a tyrant") has sealed off the emotional intimacy they shared. "I feel like I'm losing him," she notes, "that in all my therapeutic revelations about him over the years, I've lost the vital spark of him. . . . I want to miss him again, I want to resurrect my adolescent adulation of him" ("Daily Progress").

To counteract this loss, Bechdel invented a remarkable daily writing practice that would restore her father to her through his own words. Starting in March 1999, she began each work session by retyping a letter her father sent to her at college two decades before. In reproducing his letters, she hoped to resurrect as well the daughter who received them. The exercise proved to be freeing: in the associative, uncensored work log, she transcribes long excerpts from the letters and records the conflicted feelings of guilt, loss, alienation, and identification with her father they provoke ("Daily Progress"). The log produces a conversation across time frames between the memoirist she is becoming in her late thirties and the late adolescent self her father's letters constructed her to be.[4] In these earliest articulations of the material that would become *Fun Home*, Bechdel develops the doubling of subjectivities characteristic of memoir, alternating between reenactment of their earlier relationship and present retrospection. The conversation begun in the memory-work of the log becomes an invisible substratum that runs beneath the narrative of *Fun Home*. Five years later, in 2004, as Bechdel drafts the concluding chapter, several of her father's letters resurface as drawn images to haunt the final pages of the memoir.

By the end of 1999, Bechdel had produced six fragmentary drafts, all dated "12/29/99," that show she worked on several threads in the narrative at once without a clear plan for the overall structure.[5] These fragments each represent what Bechdel calls a "node" in her work log, associative clusters of emotions arising from vivid sense memories, whose meaning she knows she wants to understand ("Daily Progress"). I read these nodes as sites of tension, cognitive dissonance, hot spots in memory that are loaded with a volatile affective charge; the feelings embedded in them remain central and conflicted and are reworked, often over several years, in the composition process. "I have to find what resonates," Bechdel tells herself in the work log, "and one thing that resonates is that photo of Tom in his white jockey shorts in the hotel room in Ocean City" ("Daily Progress").

Drawing the Boy on the Bed

Bechdel identifies finding, in her twenties, the photo her father took of the family babysitter as the imaginative point of origin for the memoir. It will become the luminous centerfold, the eroticized, aestheticized, even sacralized centerfold at the heart of *Fun Home*. During our interview in the basement studio of her home off a dirt road in Vermont, Bechdel showed me the actual photo she found, a 3½ inch square, glossy black-and-white snapshot. It fit in the palm of her hand. Bechdel commented, "I can't tell you how much time I spent looking at that, trying to wonder, you know, is he awake, is he asleep, is he complicit or not."[6] In the interview, while we looked together at the tiny photo, Bechdel told me, "It was really this intense drawing challenge because it's just this muddy and gray and very hard to get any sort of definitive shapes out of it. It's like a metaphor for the whole book, that's all I have and I have to create something with hard outlines from it."

Bechdel first draws the photograph, more than twenty years after finding it, as part of an illustrated synopsis for the book in the summer of 2003. Her agent, Sydelle Kramer, urged her to create a proposal "in comic book form" for prospective mainstream publishers unfamiliar with the graphic medium.[7] As Bechdel told me in our interview, for her "it was wonderful to be forced to do that, everything started to come together then." For both, the success of the illustrated synopsis hinged on the photo of the young man who would become Roy: "If I know in my gut that the center is the centerfold, then we need to include that" ("Notes").[8] Bechdel remembers in our interview that the proposal in comic book form took her four full months to draw because "a big obstacle to getting the proposal done was getting *that* drawing done to my satisfaction." She began by digitally enlarging her father's underlit photo and then printed each half out separately and taped them together, making a 13 × 11 inch page to simulate the seam in a book layout. On another 8½ inch digital enlargement, Bechdel began inking the outline of the boy's head and torso, adding her hand as cartoonist to the material artifact of her father's desiring gaze. Even enlarged and digitally brightened, the boy's body below his waist is only a dark V-shape, contrasting with the white, slightly rumpled sheet behind him ("Sketches," chap. 4).

In the final proposal that Kramer sent to publishers in November 2003, the drawing of Roy is angled across two pages and features the elaborate crosshatching through which Bechdel translates the murky shapes of the original into the lush curves of the adolescent male body.[9] In the synopsis that accompanies the proposal, the single drawing serves as proxy for all of chapter 4, which was still under construction that summer: "This chapter, the core of the labyrinth, investigates the way that my childhood relationship with my father was shaped by our unspoken homosexuality."[10] The accompanying text in the proposal narrates some of the planned episodes but contains neither a prose description of the photo nor her own response to it. All the subsequent revisions to the centerfold attempt to render Bechdel's retrospective assessment of her relationship to her father's "unspoken homosexuality."

In 1999, she tabulated two decades of conflicted emotions:

> How did I feel at 20, finding these photos. Thrilled, a comrade in busting up the myth of the family. Subversive, also admiring the skill with which he dispatched himself. 10 years later, I was contemptuous of him, a weakling, a coward, a bully, afraid to compete in the world, preferring to terrorize his family, angry at how he killed himself, a classic coward's act. 10 years later, more balance. He's not a hero or a villain, just a fucked up gifted person doing some good stuff and some bad stuff . . . but how to identify, how to show that in voice I use? ("I Was at Stonewall")

From October through December 2003, when she works on chapter 4 most intensively, Bechdel tries to incorporate her volatile reactions in the dense text that wraps around the image angled on the page. In a rapid sequence of revisions at the end of November, red handwritten edits spill across the margins and bottom of both pages (fig. 13.1). Some reflect the euphoric twenty-year-old:

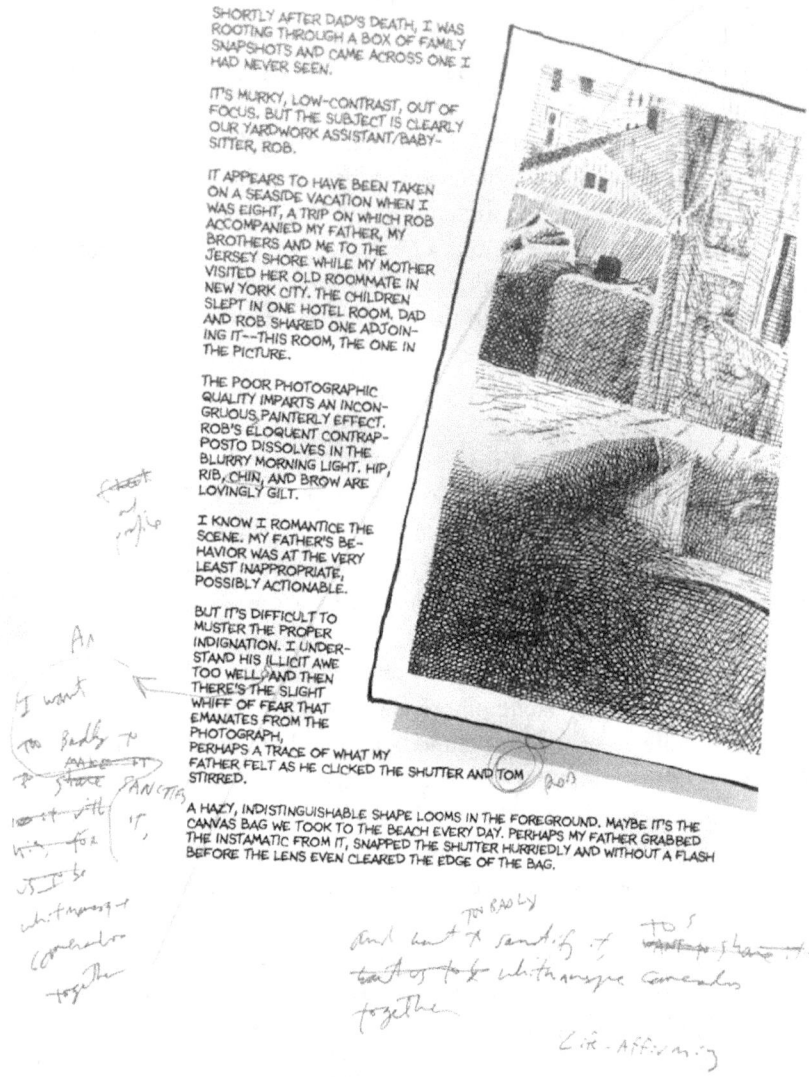

Fig. 13.1. Bechdel's edits to the centerfold.

"I know I romanticize the scene," "I want too badly to sanctify it, for us to share, be Whitmanesque camerados together." Bitter sarcasm marks her hostility at thirty: "He became unable to manage—when the exquisite Victorian satin brocade folding screen between his secret gay life and his public family life was knocked flat by his oafish lesbian daughter." Finally she enters the consciousness of both the boy and her father: "Is Rob's beatific languor that of sleep or satiety? Perhaps he's fully aware that he's being photographed. Or perhaps he's awake and feigning sleep? Has my father touched him, or not? Is he about to touch him? The ambiguity is palpably erotic."[11] Significantly, her alienation and her intimate identification with her father's desire are produced not through thought but through feeling: the outpouring of affect triggered by the image of the boy on the bed.

A year later, Bechdel's most significant alterations to the centerfold would not be textual but graphic. In an inspired decision in October 2004, Bechdel abandons the overcrowded, linear wraparound text and superimposes text boxes like graphic sticky notes over the photo to achieve temporal depth. The narrator recovers her earlier presence outside the frame of photo: "I remember the hotel room. My brothers and I slept in one adjoining it." She moves into the present tense of the father beholding the dozing boy in 1969: "Rob [revised to Roy in the published version] is gilded with morning seaside light. His hair is an aureole." Significantly, unlike her earlier edits from 2003, the narrator now inhabits her father's gaze and his desire without censure: "Perhaps I identify too well with my father's illicit awe." Bechdel's enlarged close-up in her final revision stages the almost compulsive looking we share with the narrator as we move back and forth between her notes and our increasingly detailed perceptions of the image. Her expected anger is replaced by affinity, her betrayal superseded by allegiance to her father's desire.

Sometime later, Bechdel adds a left hand holding the photo, and the narrator's embodied subjectivity enters the picture plane. The thumb overlaid on the photo may evoke equally the narrator's look when she finds it at twenty or Bechdel's, in her forties, creating the memoir. The gesture may also recover her father looking at the photo, perhaps when he gets the prints back from the camera shop in 1969, or when he revisits the hidden memento to look at the boy over the dozen years between taking the snapshot and his death. We also recognize our own thumb as we hold the book that holds the photo. Bechdel believes the intimate interaction between her physical presence, her drawings, and her readers is produced through "the very tactile physical medium" of comics. "I do think drawing is a form of touch for me," Bechdel commented in an interview with Hillary Chute. "I am trying to touch the people who are reading it . . . wanting them to touch me while they are holding this story about me ("Public," 211).

The comics theorist Scott McCloud might argue that the hyperrealism of Bechdel's drawings of photos impedes what he calls "closure," the rapid processing of separate cartoon images into narrative movement through time and space, by making her readers "particularly aware of the art" (91). We also become hyperaware of ourselves reading, our thumbs on the page, a kind of information within our visual frame as comics readers that Douglas Wolk contends we usually ignore (30). In all her graphic decisions about drawing

Roy's photo, Bechdel interrupts our immersion in the progress of the graphic narrative to focus explicitly on the acts of reading images. Yet in violating the conventions of reading comics, Bechdel nonetheless exploits in the centerfold the ability of comics to represent, in a two-dimensional space, several timescapes and competing ways of seeing, including our own. Ultimately the centerfold provides graphic testimony to the disavowal, preservation, and affective reproduction of queer desire in multiple embodied subjectivities occupying the same space over time.

The Missing Boyfriend

Initially Bechdel planned to include three of "my father's boyfriends" in the memoir. In a page of notes for chapter 4, she asks, "What is the action of this chapter?" and lists three of her father's relationships, the sense memories linked to them, and her corresponding age (chap. 4, "Under Construction"). We recognize the first two ("Tom/Beach/NYC" and "Bob/Snake/Stripmine"), when Alison was eight and ten, from their later appearance in chapter 4 with other names. But "Rick B.," the culmination of the sequence, when Alison is fifteen, exists only in the archives. The Rick Bowers node is illuminating because it persists in multiple drafts for five years before it vanishes almost without a trace. Like most of the central episodes, this one evolves from a vivid sense memory in a 1999 prose draft that becomes the signature for Rick: "After work we went swimming. The lush summer afternoon, the rank smell of the creek, Ron at the still apogee of a rope's arc for an endless moment before dropping like a smooth stone into the water. Maybe that was enough" ("Stripmine").

Alison is aware, "when my father's inamoratos were my peers," of both her father's interest in the boy and her own "ambiguous sexual position" ("Outline"). Only a single abstract sketch reappears through multiple layout drafts of chapter 7 (fig. 13.2). Spare as the sketch is in each instance, it highlights the triangulation of the father's and daughter's desiring looks converging in the smooth figure of the boy, flying above them, frozen in time "at the still apogee" of his swing. In the moment, he seems endlessly available, and then, as he releases the rope, abruptly gone. A large outline of the father's head in profile is foregrounded at the bottom of the vertical panel, while the daughter's smaller stick figure wades in the shallows at the opposite edge of the creek (chap. 7, layout draft). In early prose drafts, the narrator struggles to define the triangle: "Rick probably did not suspect my father's lecherous gaze, but it's possible he did suspect mine. . . . If it was assessing him, [it] was doing so in a way much more complicated than straightforward desire" ("Outline"). She asks herself,

Fig. 13.2. Sketch from 2004.

in different drafts, if she wanted to look like Rick, or to be as strong as he was, or merely to look at him, but in each instance, she measures her own queer desire intertwined with her father's. Bowers seems to represent what the father cannot legitimately have and, for the daughter at fifteen, what she vainly wishes she might become.

After the sketch in the August 17, 2004, layout draft of chapter 7, the scene shifts abruptly from the afternoon at the creek to undrawn panels of Rick and Alison in her father's class, discussing *The Catcher in the Rye*. As Rick asks about a trusted teacher making a pass at Holden Caulfield, the narrator wryly comments, "Much as Dad admired the 'truth' of *The Catcher in the Rye* he was strangely impervious to its import." Two-thirds of the way down the page in this draft, Bechdel's string of alternative edits in red ink forecasts Rick's disappearance from the narrative: "If there was a similar kind of gratification, invasiveness, intellectual (violation) going on between my father and me, I didn't mind it" (chap. 7, layout draft). The text suggests a parallel between Rick and herself, but she is undecided whether it is gratifying or violating. The juxtaposition of the two scenes is telling. In the classroom scene, desire is everywhere: "I found that not only did I like the books Dad assigned, but I liked Dad . . . and Dad liked me. My own passage into adolescence, it seemed, had rendered me a desirable companion." Desire proliferates across the classroom, including Rick, who "had been rendered suddenly desirable as well," at least to other girls in the class (chap. 7, layout draft). In these crosscurrents of desire, Alison and her father are united in their focus on the text.

In the published memoir of *Fun Home*, the entire incident of Rick Bowers as erotic object of both the father's and daughter's gaze is reduced to a single panel with an unnamed boy sitting next to Alison in class: "Preternaturally handsome football player who was currently hauling junk out of our basement." Alison, who has been peripheral as her father scans his class in disappointment, becomes central. Their looks meet in an intimate, admiring close-up, while other students recede into dark silhouettes. "Sometimes it was as if Dad and I were the only ones in the room. The sensation of intimacy was novel," the narrator comments (*FH*, 199). From 1999 to 2004, the Rick Bowers node explores what Bechdel experienced as an uncomfortable queer sexual rivalry with her father. Ultimately the triangle is erased to focus exclusively on her gratifying intellectual intimacy with her father through literature.

What Comes after the Truck

For Bechdel, juxtaposition—of words and images, and of different time frames—is what makes a graphic narrative "come alive." She explains, "Comics communicate with two different kinds of language. One is symbolic language—words. The other is representational. . . . You're able to show a lot of stuff without the mediating barrier of language. . . . I can show you a picture and I can give you words but if I over-explain either of those things, it kills the tension. . . . I love that juxtaposition, that space for the reader to interpret and connect the wires" ("An Activist Archives"). The technique is particularly striking in her design of the memoir's final page.

To trace the evolution of the ending, we need to return to the graphic book proposal Bechdel worked on for her agent Sydelle Kramer during the summer of 2003. In her synopsis for Kramer, the pages for the last half of the book were largely blank. Bechdel faced the challenge of drawing a compelling conclusion when she had, in fact, by then drawn only the first five pages of three chapters. In imagining the ending in early October, Bechdel knew only that the final panels must include the truck that killed her father. She plans an "image of truck grille" lightly sketched in a tight close-up, implying the instant before impact, for the top panel. Yet her notes for the empty bottom panel move in the opposite direction: "Some image of beautiful things. Flowers, vase, furniture, wallpaper . . . books. Dad napping?" (graphic book proposal). The final page, faxed to Kramer two weeks later, includes most of these elements plus Alison reading in a chair next to him.

Both panels are as elaborately cross-hatched as the photo of Roy. Each wire strand in the grille of the Peterbilt truck is minutely rendered; the massive truck body, darkly detailed, extends in all directions beyond the frame. In the smaller bottom panel, Bechdel draws her childhood self, dreamily lost in a book, sharing her father's literary traits, but unlike the English class, he fails to see her. He naps on the Victorian couch next to her, each scroll of the furniture visible against the densely patterned wallpaper that encloses them both. He is tucked in a fetal position, perhaps prefiguring his final absence, unaware of their likeness. The text box superimposed on the truck focuses on the narrator's regret, either that she caused his suicide by coming out or, even more painful, that she had never touched him: "That his death was not my fault, that in fact it had nothing to do with me at all—is somehow worse." In this ending, the narrator is stuck in the labyrinth of loss, longing for a connection that may be a delusion: "Causality implies connection, contact of some kind, and I'm reluctant to let go of that last tenuous bond" (graphic book proposal). Despite the oblivious peacefulness of father and daughter, the narrator recognizes the daughter's urgent desire that her queerness mattered to her father, even if it precipitated his suicide.

In 2004, when Bechdel was working most intensively on chapter 7, a recurring phrase in her notes is "Dad's sexual shame." She chooses a letter for the most resonant archival artifact of his shame that she first typed when she began the process in the summer of 1999. Bechdel reproduces the typewritten fragments in her own hand, inhabiting, for a second time, the father who wrote them (chap. 7, layout draft). In the published memoir, the temporal gap between her father writing in response to her coming out and her reading his letter is brief but apocalyptic. Before the letter arrives, her mother calls to reveal that her father has had affairs with men. At the top of the page, the mother's call reduces Alison to a fetal curl, while in the excerpt drawn in the bottom panel, her father confesses, "Taking sides is rather heroic and I am not a hero. What is really worth it?" (*FH*, 211). The phrase (faintly highlighted) serves as an apology or rationalization for not acknowledging his homosexuality earlier in his life, and now in this letter to her. As the phrase "I am not a hero" bubbles up in the drafts, the father's rationalization becomes the daughter's accusation.

When she redrafted the final page in December 2004, Bechdel reused the same tightly juxtaposed panels drawn for the graphic book proposal: the close-up of the truck looms midpage, menacing the serenity of the napping father and quietly reading child below it. Repeated three times, "I am not a hero" now dominates the page (fig. 13.3).

At the top of the page, she adds the excerpt from her father's letter; next, in a passage from *Ulysses*, Stephen Dedalus's disavowal: "You saved men from drowning. I am not a hero however. If he stays here I am off." Last, across the grille of the truck that will kill him, Bechdel pastes a banner in a huge typeface: "I am not a hero" (chap. 7, loose pages). The echoing phrase is the brand of his betrayal and her judgment that her father's sexual shame caused his death. Representing a condensed node of tension, "I am not a hero" contrasts what felt like her heroic choice in college with her father's disavowal of his sexuality and disidentification with her. The conclusion to the letter written by Bruce Bechdel, which Bechdel omits in the narrative, makes this explicit:

> What is there I can say. That was the paralyzing first effect. A little was not enough too much is too much. . . . There was a relief. I don't know exactly why. Anything is better than nothing. Knowing something is better than imagining everything. Then there was the old identification. This is probably the scariest. . . . But is it right to talk about it? (Bechdel, letter)

Almost an admission of his queer paternity, his letter finally resists speaking their shared truth aloud. In the published version, Bechdel removes the antiheroic pastiche of her father's letter and the *Ulysses* excerpt from the final page; the narrator also softens her critique of his shameful reticence. The letter is glossed in the published memoir as "the one where he does and doesn't come out to me," a legible equivocation rather than betrayal, and Stephen Dedalus's disavowal is noted as a matter of style, "Joyce's nod to the novel's mock-heroic method" (230).

In the same period in December 2004, Bechdel began drafting an entirely new ending, framed by scenes of herself as a child being ferried across a swimming pool on her father's back. Bechdel tells an interviewer, "I cannot tell you how I got the ending. It just came to me. After sitting in my chair for many years" ("Public," 211). Whatever the source, Bechdel's final images enlarge on the significance of the family photo that becomes the chapter head. The memories that these family photos generate "feel particularly mythic to

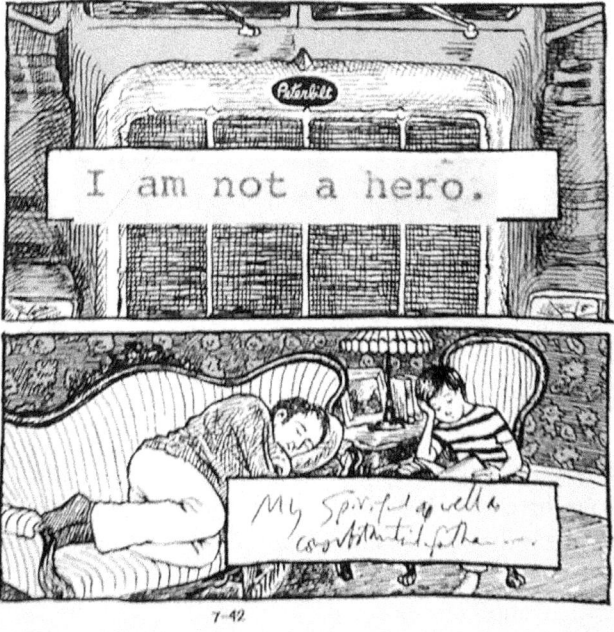

Fig. 13.3. "I am not a hero."

me," Bechdel remarks, and "carry a lot of meaning." She draws them "very realistically," as a strategy to remind readers that "this stuff really happened" (Chute, "An Interview," 1009). The archival photo is taken from a distance, probably by her mother from across the pool. We see Alison, dropping off the diving board, from behind her father, over his shoulders; he stands in the water ready to catch her. In Bechdel's rudimentary first sketches for the diving scene, the figures of father and daughter are seen close-up in three-quarter profile, although, like the family photo, the child still seems awkwardly toppling toward the father's outstretched arms.

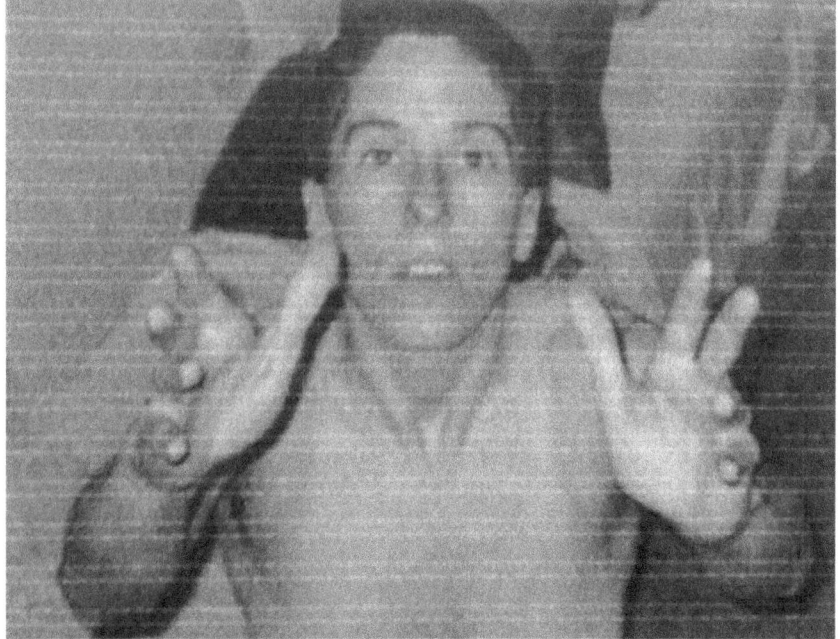

Fig. 13.4. Bechdel posing as her father.

In the final days of December 2004, Bechdel's revised text and new images for the final page seem to have evolved together. In one effort, Bechdel retains the extensively cross-hatched truck from the original ending but shrinks the top panel to half the size of the bottom frame, now empty. In the parenthetical "stage directions" Bechdel used in her layout drafts, she describes what the final frame will contain: "(me, jumping off the diving board as a kid, almost in my father's arms but not quite)." She arrives first at the text: "But in the tricky reverse narration of our entwined stories, he was there to catch me when I leapt" (chap. 7, loose pages). In a handwritten edit, she adds "that impels our entwined stories"; Bechdel's verb underscores the forward trajectory of the memory-work that propels her to imagine her relationship to her father as sustaining rather than a compulsive repetition of what was wounding.

Between her first quick sketch of the diving scene and deciding on her narrator's final words, Bechdel poses as her father in a digital reference photo (fig. 13.4). Shot from the front, Bechdel's naked upper torso and head are framed by her open hands reaching up and out. Her head is lifted, her eyebrows raised in apparent anticipation. The change in perspective is a radical shift. In the finished drawing, we share the leaping child's point of view, looking down into the waiting father's eyes. Bechdel's graphic practice—acting as her father's body double, then translating the digital photo of herself into a rough sketch of him—provides material proof in the archives of how their porous, interactive subjectivities come into being simultaneously through the memory-work of creating this book. The family photo authenticates the gesture of the father being there to catch his daughter; Bechdel the artist provides the close-up. In the visual act of remembering, she creates the father who would embrace her, and simultaneously she becomes the daughter who can forgive him.

NOTES

1. The Alison Bechdel papers consist of 26.75 linear feet of material and are continually being added to; the archives for *Fun Home* comprise 3.5 linear feet. As of winter 2018, the collection is unprocessed, although most of Bechdel's papers are accessible to researchers in the Sophia Smith Collection of Smith College. The Bechdel papers span her professional career as a cartoonist and graphic memoirist from 1985 to about 2011. In addition to the drafts of *Fun Home*, highlights of the collection are a 1988 strip, *Servants to the Cause* (see Galvan in this volume), and the long-running *Dykes to Watch Out For*. Notes for character development, clippings, articles, and ideas for the strip, as well as edited and annotated strips, enable researchers to track Bechdel's creative process as she generated two strips of ten to twelve panels each, within two weeks each month for over twenty years. Reviews, interviews, press releases, correspondence about the syndication of the strip and the publication of the *Dykes* books, and financial records offer insight into the distribution and audience for the strip and its commercial tie-ins. Correspondence with other cartoonists shows the professional context in which Bechdel worked. Later acquisitions include proofs for *Are You My Mother* and letters to her mother, Helen Bechdel, describing early plans for the book.

2. Bechdel tells Hillary Chute that she used reference shots for nearly every panel in the book, which Chute estimates number more than one thousand (quoted in "Gothic," 2).

3. "Daily Progress" is a digital file that Bechdel kept during the first year of composing *Fun Home*, recording her accomplishments as well as her reflections on her work each day. In person she refers to this document as her "work log."

4. I emphasize the separate elements in Bechdel's creative process—transcribing the letters and then responding to them in her work log—to demonstrate the intersections between letter writing and the memory-work involved in composing *Fun Home*. As Liz Stanley describes, letters are dialogic and function to construct a relationship rather than merely reflect on it. Letters also always anticipate a response from the person who receives them, whom Stanley calls a "(writing) self in waiting" (212).

5. These prose drafts, varying from six to twelve pages, are titled "Mud," "Chopin," "That Old Catastrophe," "Strip Mine," "I Was at Stonewall," and "Topography." I have arranged this list to resemble the order of the published memoir.

6. These questions are also raised in several layout drafts in November and December 2003.

7. Notes from Bechdel's telephone conversation with Sydelle Kramer on August 25, 2003, in response to a layout draft of chaps. 1, 3, and 6, sent July 31, 2003 ("Notes").

8. Bechdel adopts several different names in her drafts to protect the boys' identities. In my analysis, I adopt the name she used in the published version, but maintain the name she used in a particular draft in my quotations. "Tom" in the published centerfold is called "Roy" by Bechdel here.

9. Publishers included Viking, Doubleday/Nan Talese, Scribner, Crown, Holt, Pantheon, Houghton Mifflin, Fireside/Simon and Schuster, Workman, and the alternative press Alyson,

which published Bechdel's *Dykes* books, according to her agent, "as a courtesy and a fallback." Houghton Mifflin offered $100,000 as an advance contract on November 12, 2003. Provided to the author, May 27, 2015.

10. Graphic book proposal, chap. 4, November 2003.

11. These revisions of the text for the centerfold occur in a rapid sequence of layout drafts between November 28 and December 2, 2003 (folder for chap. 4 labeled "Under Construction, Summer 2003").

WORKS CITED

Bechdel, Alison. "An Activist Archives." February 3, 2013. Smith College, Northampton, MA. 2018. Accessed February 12, 2018.

Bechdel, Alison. Chapter 4, "Under Construction Summer 2003." Alison Bechdel Papers, Sophia Smith Collection, Smith College, Northampton, MA.

Bechdel, Alison. Chapter 7. Layout draft. August 17, 2004. Alison Bechdel Papers, Sophia Smith Collection, Smith College, Northampton, MA.

Bechdel, Alison. Chapter 7. Loose pages, "discards." December 4 and 31, 2004. Alison Bechdel Papers, Sophia Smith Collection, Smith College, Northampton, MA.

Bechdel, Alison. "Daily Progress." Provided to author, May 27, 2015.

Bechdel, Alison. Graphic book proposal to Sydelle Kramer. August 25, revised October 5–20 and November 2003. Alison Bechdel Papers, Sophia Smith Collection, Smith College, Northampton, MA.

Bechdel, Alison. "I was at Stonewall," dated "10/18/99." Folder for chap. 4, "Under Construction Summer 2003." Alison Bechdel Papers, Sophia Smith Collection, Smith College, Northampton, MA.

Bechdel, Alison. "Notes to a Conversation with Sydelle Kramer." August 27, 2003. Alison Bechdel Papers, Sophia Smith Collection, Smith College, Northampton, MA.

Bechdel, Alison. "Outline Version 3 Proust," n.d. Folder "Under Construction Summer 03." Alison Bechdel Papers, Sophia Smith Collection, Smith College, Northampton, MA.

Bechdel, Alison. Personal interview with author, May 27, 2015.

Bechdel, Alison. "Public Conversation: Alison Bechdel and Hillary Chute." *Critical Inquiry* 40, no. 3 (2014): 203–19.

Bechdel, Alison. "Sketches," chap. 4. Alison Bechdel Papers, Sophia Smith Collection, Smith College, Northampton, MA.

Bechdel, Alison. "Sketches," chap. 7. Alison Bechdel Papers, Sophia Smith Collection, Smith College, Northampton, MA.

Bechdel, Alison. "Stripmine," dated "12/29/99." Prose draft. Alison Bechdel Papers, Sophia Smith Collection, Smith College, Northampton, MA.

Bechdel, Bruce. Letter to Alison Bechdel, February 27, 1980. Provided to the author, May 27, 2017.

Chute, Hillary. "Gothic Revival." *Village Voice*, July 11, 2006, 1–4.

Chute, Hillary. *Graphic Women: Life Narrative in Contemporary Comics*. Columbia University Press, 2010.

Chute, Hillary. "An Interview with Alison Bechdel." *Modern Fiction Studies* 52, no. 4 (2006): 1004–13.

Eakin, John Paul. *How Our Lives Become Stories: Making Selves*. Cornell University Press, 1999.

McCloud, Scott. *Understanding Comics*. Harper Collins, 1993.

Miller, Nancy K. "The Entangled Self." *PMLA* 122, no. 2 (2007): 537–48.

Smith, Sidonie, and Julia Watson. *Reading Autobiography: A Guide for Interpreting Life Narratives.* University of Minnesota Press, 2001.

Stanley, Liz. "The Epistolarium: On Theorizing Letters and Correspondences." *Auto/Biography* 12, no. 3 (2004): 201–35.

Van Dyne, Susan. "'The Slippage between Seeing and Saying': Getting a Life in Alison Bechdel's *Fun Home*." In *Teaching Comics and Graphic Narratives*, ed. Lang Dong, 108–18. McFarland, 2012.

Watson, Julia. "Autographic Disclosure and Genealogies of Desire in Alison Bechdel's *Fun Home*." *Biography* 31, no. 1 (2008): 127–56.

Wolk, Douglas. *Reading Comics.* Da Capo, 2012.

SERVANTS TO WHAT CAUSE

Illustrating Queer Movement Culture through Grassroots Periodicals

MARGARET GALVAN

In the late 1980s, after nearly a half decade of self-syndicating her own comic in grassroots newspapers across the nation, Alison Bechdel took the next step and decided to launch her own periodical. Her creation, the *10% Tribune*, was germinated in phone conversations and written correspondence with Mark Thompson, senior editor of the *Advocate*, a gay magazine with national distribution. The reason that Bechdel's periodical escapes notice is because it was, in reality, a fictional setting for a new comic, *Servants to the Cause*. The contexts surrounding the development of the comic are key because Bechdel integrates them into its plot to theorize the role of periodical production and culture in queer social movements. As she writes to Thompson in a letter dated September 23, 1988:

> How about a comic strip set in the offices of a gay and lesbian newspaper? I collectively run [a] paper in a medium sized city. It would be a perfect context for exploring gay/lesbian relationship dynamics, as well as a natural scenario for covering current events and topical issues.
>
> I've worked in and around the g/l press since I graduated from college, and I'm champing at the bit to do an expose.... My brain is teeming with possible characters and personalities and conflicts. (para. 1–2)

In these paragraphs, Bechdel alludes to her experience as production coordinator of *Equal Time*, a Minneapolis–Saint Paul gay and lesbian newspaper where she worked from 1986 to 1990. She also gestures back toward her years of involvement "in and around the g/l press," which included participating from 1983 to 1985 in the collective of the largely woman-only *WomaNews*, a New York City feminist newspaper, in addition to the perspective she gained through self-syndicating *Dykes to Watch Out For* "in more than two dozen newspapers and magazines in the U.S., Canada and Great Britain" (*New, Improved!* front matter). Arguing that the newspaper provides "a perfect context for exploring gay/lesbian relationship dynamics," she further underlines how her current and prior experience leaves her "champing at the bit to do an expose." Although Bechdel is most known for her lesbian-centered comics, her pitch for a gay and lesbian take on grassroots newspapers reflects an awareness of the *Advocate*'s predominantly gay content and audience.[1] In this context, she wields the knowledge gathered from participating in all these venues to examine the subtleties of gay and lesbian interactions, creating a diverse cast that allows her to investigate these identities in intersectional ways.[2]

Introducing these characters a month and a half later in another letter to Thompson, dated November 11, 1988, Bechdel describes them both as queer social subjects and also in terms of the associated personalities and behaviors that shape the work they do at the *10% Tribune*, for example, Rachel, "an anal-retentive perfectionist who has memorized the *Chicago Manual of Style*" (para. 4) (fig. 14.1). By presenting her six characters textually as well as in sketches alongside the left margin, Bechdel foregrounds their difference. She devotes the most page space to her two protagonists, Eric and Tina (later renamed Liza), who hail from a younger generation than the other characters and represent newer ways of negotiating sexuality in society. While Eric is "a Radical Faerie, a WASP gone amok," Tina (Liza) is a black woman who is a "very hip, free-thinking, sexual libertarian kind of dyke" (para. 3). These characters are balanced by MJ, a white "old-school lesbian-gone-separatist"; Julio, a middle-aged Latino "ad rep, [who is] slightly superficial but charming"; Arthur, an older black man who "tends to be tyrannical"; and Rachel, a Jewish lesbian who "do[es] most of the editorial work" alongside Arthur (para. 4).

I emphasize the generational and racial differences evident through the combination of these textual and visual portrayals because they inflect the interactions of these characters as much as do their personalities, individual expressions of sexuality, and roles on the newspaper staff. After these descriptions, Bechdel concludes, "That's about all I know about them at this point—after I work with them a little more, I will learn more about them" (para. 5). This remark not only points to Bechdel's organic process of character creation but also reflects back on the space of the grassroots periodical office, where one might encounter a range of individuals and "learn more about them" through the process of "work[ing] with them a little more."

These conversations with Thompson set the foundation for *Servants to the Cause*, which ran for nineteen episodes over the course of a year and a half in the pages of the *Advocate* (1989–90).[3] During this time—from the first strip in the March 14, 1989, issue to the nineteenth strip in the August 28, 1990,

Friday, November 11, 1988

Mark Thompson
The Advocate
6922 Hollywood Blvd., 10th fl.
Los Angeles, Ca   90028
871-1225

Dear Mark:

Sorry I took longer than I projected with this. I'm much more punctual when I have a definite deadline.

I ho e you like it. I think 'Servants to the Cause' is a good title because I'd like the strip to apply not just to the newspaper biz but to the whole 'cause'--to all of us working in the community, with other gay folks, for alternative organizations.

It took a while to come up with these characters...they are starting to grow on me. My favorites are Tina, the production manager, and Eric, the guy with the pony tail. Tina's this ver hip, free-thinking, sexual libertarian kind of dyke. Eric's a Radical Faerie, a WASP gone amok. He wears a crystal and does yoga and considers himself a radical feminist.

The other folks are less clear. M.J.'s sort of an old-school lesbian-gone-separatist. Julio is the ad rep, slightly super-ficial but charming. Arthur and Rachel are the heavies--he tends to be tyrannical and she is an anal-retentive perfectionist who has memorized the Chicago Manual of Style. Together they do most of the editorial work.

That's about all I know about them at this point--after xx I work with them a little more, I will learn more about them.

So, I hope this can work out on a semi-regular basis. Here's a couple ideas for possible future scenarios:

o one day in the office the phone keeps ringing--either it's readers complaining, people in the community wanting various kinds of information as if the paper were wsome kind of hotline, xxx or else it's crank/obscene callers. Someone speculates on how it's all worth it if they can be of help to one troubled soul struggling to come out somewhere..then some kind of ironic twist of a punchline..I haven't figured it out yet.

o a collective post-mortem where xkyxxx they thoroughly depress themselves dwelling on all their mistakes and how hard they work, and for what? Not sure what could be funny about this yet.

o They're all sitting around joking about the personal ads, maybe selecting an 'ad of the week' to highlight...then it turns out one of them has placed it.
o Eric & Tina scandalizing MJ with true 'safer sex' stories.

That's all for now... look forward to hearing from you. — Alison

Fig. 14.1. Letter from Alison Bechdel to Mark Thompson, November 11, 1988.
Description: drawings of characters for strip down the side. Creator: Alison Bechdel. Alison Bechdel Papers, Sophia Smith Collection, Smith College, Northampton, Massachusetts.

issue—*Servants* was published alongside Howard Cruse's *Wendel* and Donelan's *It's a Gay Life* and alternated issues with Tim Barela's *Leonard & Larry*. These comics interlocutors, which mainly focused on the gay experience and had largely less diverse casts, further emphasize the radical nature of Bechdel's project. By situating every strip within the newspaper's offices, Bechdel shows how this cast of characters collaborates on production while simultaneously engaging in debates about gay and lesbian life and how that world is shifting around them in the late 1980s. Her episodic, nonserial approach to storytelling means that we encounter these characters at nineteen distinct moments and watch how they mediate long-running and emerging debates, some of which are localized to grassroots periodical production and some of which touch on larger debates in gay and lesbian culture.[4] For example, they argue about the co-optation of Pride celebrations while putting together the annual Pride issue (*Servants* #5), and they all weigh in on the politics of drag when two male staffers dress up for Halloween (*Servants* #9). The office of the *10% Tribune*, the setting for every strip, acts as a place to synthesize these debates, suggesting that all these perspectives inhabit the pages of the periodical as well, making it a venue speaking not just for its own time but also across time.

I position the comic and the newspaper it contains as intersectional spaces to theorize across difference, bringing varying contingents of queer folks together in common cause. Moreover, Bechdel's integration of her own experiences into the strip allows us to reread periodicals in their moment, understanding them not as individual ventures but as an evolving network of activism. These intertwined perspectives—informing the creation of the comics and fueling the characters' interactions—produce queerness. Through this process, Bechdel emerges as a theorist engaging in contemporaneous queer thought. To understand her engagement with, and contributions to, contemporary discourse, I will first put her into conversation with grassroots and academic takes on queerness and then examine how she represents these ideas in the comic itself. Her engagements extend—and presciently challenge—contemporaneous writing about possibilities for coalition within LGBTQ communities.

In the queer periodical press where Bechdel worked, the reality of lesbians and gay men working alongside one another on AIDS activism informed these conversations in the late 1980s and early 1990s. In the editorial for the October 9, 1990, issue of the *Advocate*, editor in chief Richard Rouilard evokes this coalition when he writes: "To be gay in this decade, we feel, one must also be lesbian, since lesbians in the preceding decade, in their participation in AIDS activism, were awfully gay" (6). These remarks are part of an editorial where Rouilard details "a brand-new look" for the magazine, which includes changing its tagline to incorporate lesbians: "the national gay *and lesbian* newsmagazine" (6; italics in original). Over the course of its run, *Servants* directly referenced AIDS activism through the organization ACT UP in three of the nineteen strips (#6, 11, 19). The first two inclusions only reference ACT UP and its actions, while the final strip speaks the words "HIV" and "AIDS" when Liza worries about Eric's status, since he is under the weather and refuses to be tested (*Servants* #19). In the final panel of the comic, a text box instructs us to "Stay Tuned!," suggesting that the following strip would continue this story line, thereby disrupting the nonserial storytelling.

However, Bechdel produced no further strips, as Rouilard's revamping of the *Advocate* included the cancellation of Bechdel's comic and other comics in the publication, except for gay artist Donelan's single-panel cartoons. Thus this moment of recognizing the importance of lesbians to AIDS activism is paradoxically also one of elision that erases lesbian representation and Bechdel's contributions to the conversation.[5] I discuss the reasons behind the cancellation more fully later in this essay, but the move reveals the superficial nature of Rouilard's embrace of lesbian identity, an ethos that Bechdel challenges throughout *Servants*.

Bechdel creates a space for exchange that is not necessarily overdetermined by gay men or by one subset of gay men, as her diverse cast of characters and their interests vis-à-vis the newspaper illuminate. In *Servants*, it is the shared activity of producing a grassroots newspaper that brings the characters together in dialogue. This action produces movement on the local level. Each strip brings us to a different moment in the making of the periodical that unfolds into a larger discussion of gay and lesbian politics from a variety of perspectives. This range is active from the first strip of *Servants*, where all six members of the collective civilly debate the inclusion of a back-cover advertisement featuring a naked gay man (*Servants* #1). When the ad manager, Julio, brings in the salacious ad, Eric quickly recognizes that it "doesn't conform to our guidelines" and calls for a "collective meeting." In this conversation, MJ adds that "naked men upset the balance of gay to lesbian content," while Liza is against "censorship" and Arthur contends that "this is a respectable publication." Because the money from the advertisement is important to sustain the newspaper and the messenger is about to arrive to pick up the finished copy, they quickly have Liza, the staff artist, alter the drawing so that the man is not fully naked, all of them standing behind her in solidarity as she completes the task. This moment of quick processing underlines the range of perspectives that get heard and wrapped into the decision making. In this way, Bechdel imagines the newspaper as the sustaining space that can build deep dialogue around a number of issues.

Through the framework of this grassroots newspaper that centralizes a larger set of perspectives and issues than Rouilard is able to acknowledge,

Bechdel anticipates theoretical work in the early 1990s that would establish the field of queer theory as distinct from gay and lesbian studies. Like Bechdel, these proto-queer theorists acknowledged the important coalition work of AIDS activism but also questioned what perspectives were left out by reductive fusion such as that enacted by Rouilard. In the most quotable axiom with which Eve Kosofsky Sedgwick launches *Epistemology of the Closet* (1990), she observes, "Axiom 1: People are different from each other," following this with a third axiom that more directly pushes back on assertions like Rouilard's editorial position by suggesting that it is not clear whether "it will make sense to conceptualize lesbian and gay male identities together" (22, 36). In an essay widely recognized as naming this emerging field, Teresa de Lauretis meditates on the depth of experiences that continue to separate lesbians from gay men:

> The fact of the matter is, most of us, lesbians and gay men, do not know much about one another's sexual history, experience, fantasies, desire, or modes of theorizing. And we do not know enough about ourselves, as well, when it comes to differences between and within lesbians, and between and within gay men, in relation to race and its attendant differences of class or ethnic culture, generational, geographical, and socio-political location. We do not know enough to theorize those differences. (viii)

At the same time that de Lauretis describes the multifaceted gulf between these identities, she identifies the challenges that enforce this distance. Both Sedgwick and de Lauretis suggest that we need to devote more thought on how to parse these perspectives.

With *Servants*, Bechdel not only demonstrates how one can learn about and acknowledge the differences in the LGBTQ community that de Lauretis outlines but, from this position, also "theorize[s] those differences." *Servants* acts as a model for working across difference and shows how intersectional space can be created and sustained. The image-text form of the comic supports the kind of nuanced representation that can simultaneously examine difference on the visual and verbal axes. Rebecca Beirne and Judith Kegan Gardiner have both written about the evolving viewpoints of Bechdel's long-running strip *Dykes to Watch Out For*, with Beirne specifically tracking how these shifting frameworks parallel theoretical developments—from lesbian feminism to queer theory (Beirne, 178; see also Gardiner and Parker-Hay in this volume). Because of the wider generational range of the characters in *Servants*, older and newer perspectives of what it means to be queer mesh on the page, creating intergenerational dialogue between earlier activisms in gay liberation and second-wave feminism with contemporary movements like ACT UP. Moreover, other forms of diversity—notably gender and race—expand the space between the characters that they must broach in their decision-making processes.[6] Bechdel directs readers to examine these differences through background details and conversational exchange, interrogating how they inform periodical production. Coalition building operates in these everyday moments. In producing the periodical, Bechdel's characters also produce queerness in their exchanges across difference.

A proliferation of recent scholarship has shed light on the role periodicals have played in building the feminist movement at the local level (Beins; Beins and Enszer; Enszer, "Fighting," "Night"; McKinney). In *Liberation in Print*, Agatha Beins constructs a network across individual, local feminist periodicals by examining their interconnections throughout her book rather than treating the history of each individually. Likewise, the field of comics studies has begun to pay attention to comics within queer grassroots periodicals and how the political network of these precarious spaces shapes the comics. In his introduction to *No Straight Lines*, a volume containing a number of queer comics recuperated from such publications, editor Justin Hall remarks how the grassroots context facilitated the "direct political and social commentary" of the comics while also obscuring them from "the traditional comics industry."[7] Hillary Chute contends with how the serialization of *Dykes to Watch Out For* and its treatment of "the present tense" and its "invest[ment] in reflecting the world . . . opened up the door for participation and interactivity, bringing in a population of involved readers . . . eager . . . to see certain kinds of underrepresented lives reflected back at them" (366). Together, this scholarship describes Bechdel's approach to content creation, with the focus on grassroots periodicals reflecting how Bechdel's comic itself echoes the ethos of periodicals by fusing multiple local perspectives into each comic strip. *Servants* is a layered synthesis of Bechdel's networks. In operating as metacommentary on this movement, the strip argues for the periodical as a queer clearinghouse that can recognize difference in a way that other activisms—represented in the pages of the periodical—cannot. It is while producing the periodical that the characters must synthesize how to respect different approaches to queer identity, such as when they discuss how to caption a photo featuring people on a gay softball team who don't want to be publicly outed (*Servants* #7). Among the six characters themselves, movements and positions proliferate, expanding the network that informs their periodicals.

Bechdel explicitly depicts the larger network of grassroots periodicals in addition to implicitly weaving it into the plot. We can read this network as an activist movement and theorize its potential for recognizing difference just as much as those reported in the pages of the periodical itself. These influences are sometimes quite literally named in the comic, as when we see characters reading other gay and lesbian press, whose names are slightly obscured from actual fact: Liza cracks open a copy of the lesbian erotica magazine *Bad Backs* (*Servants* #8) to intentionally shock her colleagues; MJ catches up on the reporting in *Out of It* (#14) and *Gay Community Schmooze* (#16) as the newsroom bustles around her; and Rachel holds a copy of *Weekly Voice* while discussing how a not explicitly out J. T. Chapridge, an analogue for k.d. lang, had done interviews in both that paper and the *Distress* (#17).[8] By including multiple exemplars of, and allusions to, independent publications in the newsroom, Bechdel constructs her characters as connected to other regional outlets about queer folks like them. These periodicals from elsewhere affect discussions about the content and direction of the *10% Tribune*, similar to how all the places where Bechdel published her comics shaped the content of her own representations, including these conversations in *Servants* as well as the narratives in *Dykes to Watch Out For*.

Yet what ends up on the pages of the *10% Tribune* does not always equally represent these perspectives, underlining the inequities present in coalition. When incorporating contemporaneous issues facing both *Equal Time* and the *Advocate*, Bechdel employs her diverse cast of characters to weigh in on how production decisions unevenly affect various constituents. As mentioned earlier, the first strip concerns the newsroom coming to consensus about, and altering an advertisement of, a naked gay man (*Servants* #1). Although the strip ends with everyone huddled together in solidarity, endorsing the change because the original ad violates their collective guidelines, the debate about including sexually explicit ads persists in the fictional newsroom of the *10% Tribune* and in the real production offices of *Equal Time* and the *Advocate*. In *Servants* #15, the comic opens on a collective meeting where Rachel holds up a page spread of a recent issue of *10% Tribune* full of largely gay phone sex ads, acknowledging that "a lot of our readers have been complaining. We have to make a decision" (*Servants* #15). By opening the discussion up to the entire collective, Rachel allows all these different perspectives to have a say in the decision.

While we do not encounter the content of the complaints in *Servants*, we can find them in the surrounding pages of the *Advocate*, encouraging us to compare the handling of this conversation at both periodicals. In a letter printed in the April 11, 1989, issue of the *Advocate*, a reader writes to cancel his subscription, explaining, "I wanted to show an article in a recent issue to a straight friend of mine whom I had come out to, but I realized I couldn't when I saw all the ads for X-rated films, all the pages of personal sex ads, and even an ad for a latex simulation of a certain part of a porno star's anatomy" (Hanscom, 6). The reader further qualifies that this material, which was then concentrated near the back of the *Advocate*, did nothing to dispel stereotypes about "the gay life-style [being] centered around sex." These assertions echo the remarks of Arthur and MJ, the older collective members, especially Arthur, who reveals that he is "embarrassed to show the paper to [his] family and straight friends" (*Servants* #15). The strip's youngest characters and protagonists, Eric and Liza, object to these views, claiming that these ads support "safe sex" and to censor them would be to give in to "what the right-wingers want!" Bechdel interleaves these opposing views, giving each its own panel, so we have pro and con following each other in sequence before Rachel regains the floor, invoking "the voice of reason." In this wider panel showing all six collective members at once, Rachel and Julio hold the financial report as Julio discloses that these ads account for "25% of our total ad revenue." Rachel and Julio are centered in the panel, visually separating the old guard, MJ and Arthur, from the younger generation, Eric and Liza. Visually, Bechdel allows each perspective to be heard in the newsroom even if not all the perspectives make it onto the periodical page, rendering transparent how coalition operates in regard to an issue that has the potential to alienate some members.

Rather than finding a way to resolve the debate and come together in solidarity as everyone did in *Servants* #1, the final three panels show individuals holding fast to their sides. Although this indecision disenfranchises certain collective members and readers, the financial bottom line—and, by default, the younger generation—wins out. In the final episode of *Servants*, MJ is pictured perusing a periodical identified only by the phone sex hotline ad on the back cover (#19). This detail is not part of the main plot for the strip, but it gestures toward the reality that these ads, in part because their revenue stream supports the paper, are here to stay. In including the evolution of this debate in a number of strips, Bechdel encourages her readers to reflect on how the pages of real grassroots periodicals do or do not equally speak to all community members.

Both the *10% Tribune* and the *Advocate* recognize the financial necessity of retaining these ads, and the *Advocate* does so by including them in a removable center section of the magazine. However, the market forces that drive the *Servants* collective to retain the ads are the same as those that compel the *Advocate* staff to reconceive the seriousness of their publication, keeping the ads but ditching the comics.[9] Although we cannot get a behind-the-scenes glimpse of the *Advocate*'s newsroom as its members made their decision, similar to what we witness in *Servants*, Rouilard's aforementioned editorial reflects the role that respectability politics played for this overwhelmingly gay staff. The decision did not escape notice. A reader letter printed in the *Advocate* a few issues after the reveal of the "brand-new look" lamented, "I am dismayed that you have chosen to drop two of the most intelligent, human, and humorous gay comic strips I have ever encountered (namely, 'Servants to the Cause' and 'Leonard and Larry')" (Rouilard, 6; Tate, 11). Bechdel's fellow lesbian comics artist Jennifer Camper more emphatically responded to the cancellation in her write-up of the 1991 Outwrite lesbian and gay writers conference, published in the Lesbian Cartoonists' Network newsletter of spring 1991. Informed by what a staff member from the *Advocate* shared following a panel of cartoonists, Camper opined, "It seems that the image that *The Advocate* is trying to develop is a 'serious' one and that doesn't include comics.... It's a damn shame. Maybe it's time for a posse of leatherdykes to pay a visit to their office?" (3). Together, these lamentations question why the *Advocate*'s new "serious" image did not include "two of the most intelligent, human, and humorous gay comic strips." Although the *Advocate* found a way to balance readers' demands for discretion with the magazine's own need for ad revenue, the decision to cancel the comics reveals that they were deemed out-of-step with the transformation of the *Advocate* into something more mainstream. With this change occurs a compartmentalizing of certain kinds of queer content, along with a complete dismissal of others. In this we see the particular precarity that comics face in grassroots contexts, as they are considered disposable in the ways that other content—especially content that fills, rather than drains, the coffers—is not.

The move toward the mainstream that leaves the comics and, metaphorically, the grassroots newspaper behind is one that Bechdel explores in *Servants*, where she examines not only what but who gets left behind by such a transition. In the comic's penultimate strip, Julio consults an issue of the mainstream magazine *Newstime* (a mash-up of *Newsweek* and *Time*), whose cover story is "The Future of Straight-Looking Professional White-Gay Men in America," as the newsroom erupts into a conversation about assimilation, prompted by the anxiety dream of Eric, who imagines how acceptance for homosexuality ("openly lesbian tennis stars ... on Wheaties boxes") will destroy their community spaces ("gay bars or clubs," "gay churches and synagogues and professional organizations," and "lesbian and gay newspapers or publishers") (*Servants* #18) (fig. 14.2). In retrospective comments on this strip written eight years after its publication, Bechdel expresses "a particular fondness" "because it's so prescient," qualifying that though "everything Eric saw in his dream has already happened," the strip "nicely encapsulates a lot of my own complex feelings about assimilation and identity" (*Indelible*, 191). Although much of what Eric fears comes to pass, by positioning him talking through these fears with only his colleagues of color, Bechdel unpacks how race factors into assimilation.

Although Eric is a ponytailed radical faerie, as the only white man in the newsroom, he is the closest to the identity type that might be seen as the prerequisite for the mainstream acceptance that *Newstime* promises for a small subset of the LGBTQ community, and yet he fears this acceptance and

Fig. 14.2. *Servants to the Cause* #18.

its possibilities more so than do his colleagues of color—Arthur, Julio, and Liza—for whom "the right to be like everyone else" remains a farther-fetched dream. The subtle staging of this exchange reminds readers of the disconnect between the values that gather together a broad-based coalition at the *10% Tribune* and those of a larger public, and how acceptance is not just about sexuality and sexual desire but (as highlighted by the cover story's title) also intersects with gender, gender expression, class, generation, and—further underlined by Bechdel's casting choices—race.

Ultimately, at the end of the comic, Liza joins Eric in his fears about what the mainstreaming of gay and lesbian politics might mean for all their social institutions. This alliance reinforces an intergenerational divide between the two characters and the other members of the collective. By including multiple generations in one newspaper collective, Bechdel suggests that dialogue can bridge this division, representing the possibility through even the smallest of details, including the production of the newspaper itself. Different generations of periodical production coincide as both physical pasteup of the layout and the use of computers are pictured throughout. Notably, characters of different generational positions are shown in relationship to both methods, so we are facing not a moment of obsolescence but one of coexistence that mirrors the material reality of the publication and the relationship of the characters as well.[10]

In *Servants*, Bechdel recognizes how histories of activism challenge intergenerational coexistence, but she posits that it is about making a newsroom—or movement—big enough to respect different histories of, and approaches to, activism. As members of the younger generation, Eric and Liza engage in activism differently from their elders, who were themselves on the front lines, fighting for rights through the movements of gay liberation and second-wave feminism. This divergent perspective is particularly evident in *Servants* #16, when Eric and Liza's loud chants of a new, explicit ACT UP slogan echo throughout the office and frustrate two older members of the collective, MJ and Arthur. An exasperated MJ intones, "They think they're being radical," and Arthur quips, "Radical? It's tasteless, shock-value tactics like that that are gonna set the gay rights movement back 20 years!" (*Servants* #16). Although Arthur's reaction may seem insensitive, we learn in an earlier comic that his partner Bill died—possibly due to AIDS (*Servants* #11). Until this point, the two pairs have been occupying different rooms in the office, but Liza and Eric then enter the other room and attempt to bring MJ and Arthur to their way of understanding. MJ and Arthur are pictured in the foreground and centered as holders of an older perspective being challenged by those coming behind them. Neither side is convinced of the other's position, and they return to different rooms in the office at the comic's end, but we do encounter both sides dialoguing and sharing space, making legible the variety of opinions that queer people hold, informed by their age and histories of activism. Bechdel's ability to facilitate these disagreements positions her comic as one that theorizes differences by creating spaces—like the grassroots newspaper—for proximity.

NOTES

1. As Bechdel relates in her introduction to a compilation of fellow gay cartoonist and mentor Howard Cruse's *Wendel*, which originally appeared in the *Advocate* over the course of the 1980s: "Like lots of women in those days I saw that publication's pink pages as evidence that it was a men-only affair" (Bechdel, "Introduction").

2. I discuss in greater detail how this network of grassroots periodicals shaped and supported the development of Bechdel's *Dykes to Watch Out For* in the "Queer about Comics" issue of *American Literature* (Galvan).

3. In addition to first appearing in the *Advocate*, all of the *Servants* strips were also reprinted three years later in *Gay Comics* #19, an issue devoted to Bechdel's non–*Dykes to Watch Out For* work, featuring three short comics—"Coming Out Story," "The Power of Prayer," "True Confession"—and *Servants*. The three short comics are collected in *Indelible*, 35–54.

4. Bechdel established this storytelling strategy in her first letter to Thompson, dated September 23, 1988, arguing in the aforementioned excerpted paragraphs that the periodical would allow her to "[cover] current events and topical issues" (para. 1). In a later paragraph of the same letter, she further elaborates on this stylistic decision: "And it wouldn't be a serial strip. . . . Each installment would be self-sufficient, given that only one would appear each month" (para. 4).

5. This erasure resonates with Adrienne Rich's meditations on the constant societal erasure of lesbian experience in her landmark essay "Compulsory Heterosexuality and Lesbian Existence" (57). Even more directly, the cancellation, which effaces Eric and Liza's active participation in ACT UP, echoes the problematic recounting of ACT UP's history, where lesbians' participation has been often overlooked, as Ann Cvetkovich details in scholarship that seeks to recuperate their import: "It has seemed all the more urgent to provide a history of ACT UP's lesbians when, with the passage of time, ACT UP is in danger of being remembered as a group of privileged gay white men. . . . Once again lesbians, many of whom came to ACT UP with considerable political experience, seem to be some of the first to disappear from ACT UP's history" (158).

6. The "generational diversity" in *Servants* predates Bechdel's introduction of that facet in *DTWOF*, first through Clarice and Toni's baby, Raffi, and later through a whole host of other characters (*Indelible*, 69). Gender diversity is especially notable, since *DTWOF* was a world populated solely by dykes at this point and contained no major male characters until a few years later. Moreover, among the six major characters, there is an equal 50/50 male/female split, whereas *DTWOF* never reaches that level of saturation. Three years after the end of *Servants*, Bechdel introduced a main male character when Raffi, Clarice and Toni's son, was born in *DTWOF* #171, "Infant Replay," in 1993 (*Essential*, 114). Three more years after that, Carlos, Raffi's caretaker, debuted as the first major adult male character in this near lesbian utopia, in *DTWOF* #232 "A Smidge Too Far" (*Essential*, 155). All told, it took Bechdel roughly a decade from when she introduced recurring characters in *DTWOF* until she allowed a major male character on the same generational wavelength as her main characters to enter the scene.

7. I evoke the same observation by Hall in an *American Literature* article on Bechdel's beginnings, where I contend with how this grassroots publication context kept Bechdel from mainstream renown for decades despite the reach of her subcultural publication networks (Galvan).

8. *Bad Backs* refers to *On Our Backs* (1984–2006), a lesbian erotica magazine that Bechdel occasionally contributed cartoons to and for which she was interviewed by editor Susie Bright in the November–December 1991 issue (Bright). *Gay Community Schmooze* likely denotes the Boston-area *Gay Community News* (1973–92), and *Out of It* refers to the New York City magazine *OutWeek* (1989–91), whose creation during the rise of AIDS activism explains the triangle in the title logo, which Bechdel represents in her rendering. It would take two more years after this comic for k.d. lang to officially come out, doing so in an issue of the *Advocate*, of which she was also the cover star (Lemon). A twenty-year retrospective article in the *Advocate* suggests that "lang became one of the first celebrities to crack open the closet door, laying a blueprint for Melissa, Ellen, and Neil" (Advocate Contributors).

9. During the year and a half that *Servants* appeared in the pages of the *Advocate*, the magazine was in the midst of transforming itself into a more serious publication, shifting from cover images of nearly nude hunks to more clothed, serious portrayals of male cover models that signaled the important feature stories contained within. Later in the year, after the April letter, the *Advocate* moved the ads from the back of the magazine into a separately paginated regional supplement section at the center of the volume that could easily be removed by a reader. These shifts affected the placement of *Servants* and other comics in the magazine, as they were moved around the magazine, sometimes immediately preceding the classifieds and ads and eventually occupying space at the back of the magazine that used to be the domain of the advertisements. That is, the comics experienced a precarity of placement before they were ultimately canceled, in a move that coincided with the finished transformation of the magazine to a broadly respectable magazine at the start of the 1990s, as editor in chief Rouilard detailed in the aforementioned editorial.

10. The computer was reshaping the production of *Equal Time* during this same time frame. In the August 17, 1988, issue of *Equal Time*, Barney Dews begins as the first and only "word processing volunteer" ("Staff Box"). When Bechdel leaves the paper roughly two years later, twelve people are listed in the staff box as "computer volunteers" ("Staff Box").

WORKS CITED

Advocate Contributors. "A Married Life from k.d. lang to Chely Wright." *Advocate*, May 17, 2012. Accessed March 18, 2018.

Bechdel, Alison. Letter to Mark Thompson, September 23, 1988. Alison Bechdel Papers, Sophia Smith Collection, Smith College, Northampton, MA, Accn. #08S-104.

Bechdel, Alison. Letter to Mark Thompson, November 11, 1988. Alison Bechdel Papers, Sophia Smith Collection, Smith College, Northampton, MA, Accn. #08S-104.

Bechdel, Alison. *Gay Comics #19: Alison Bechdel Featuring Absolutely NO Dykes to Watch Out For!* Ed. Andy Mangels. Bob Ross, 1993.

Bechdel, Alison. Introduction to *The Complete Wendel*, 7–8. Universe, 2011.

Bechdel, Alison. *New, Improved! Dykes to Watch Out For*. Firebrand Books, 1990.

Bechdel, Alison. "Servants to the Cause #1." *Advocate*, no. 520 (March 1989): 65. ONE National Gay & Lesbian Archives, Periodicals Collection.

Bechdel, Alison. "Servants to the Cause #2." *Advocate*, no. 522 (April 1989): 62. ONE National Gay & Lesbian Archives, Periodicals Collection.

Bechdel, Alison. "Servants to the Cause #3." *Advocate*, no. 524 (May 1989): 66. ONE National Gay & Lesbian Archives, Periodicals Collection.

Bechdel, Alison. "Servants to the Cause #4." *Advocate*, no. 526 (June 1989): 84. ONE National Gay & Lesbian Archives, Periodicals Collection.

Bechdel, Alison. "Servants to the Cause #5." *Advocate*, no. 528 (July 1989): 66. ONE National Gay & Lesbian Archives, Periodicals Collection.

Bechdel, Alison. "Servants to the Cause #6." *Advocate*, no. 530 (August 1989): 42. ONE National Gay & Lesbian Archives, Periodicals Collection.

Bechdel, Alison. "Servants to the Cause #7." *Advocate*, no. 532 (August 1989): 38. ONE National Gay & Lesbian Archives, Periodicals Collection.

Bechdel, Alison. "Servants to the Cause #8." *Advocate*, no. 534 (September 1989): 38. ONE National Gay & Lesbian Archives, Periodicals Collection.

Bechdel, Alison. "Servants to the Cause #9." *Advocate*, no. 536 (October 1989): 38. ONE National Gay & Lesbian Archives, Periodicals Collection.

Bechdel, Alison. "Servants to the Cause #10." *Advocate*, no. 538 (November 1989): 40. ONE National Gay & Lesbian Archives, Periodicals Collection.

Bechdel, Alison. "Servants to the Cause #11." *Advocate*, no. 540 (December 1989): 73. ONE National Gay & Lesbian Archives, Periodicals Collection.

Bechdel, Alison. "Servants to the Cause #12." *Advocate*, no. 542 (January 1990): 81. ONE National Gay & Lesbian Archives, Periodicals Collection.

Bechdel, Alison. "Servants to the Cause #13." *Advocate*, no. 544 (February 1990): 73. ONE National Gay & Lesbian Archives, Periodicals Collection.

Bechdel, Alison. "Servants to the Cause #14." *Advocate*, no. 546 (March 1990): 73. ONE National Gay & Lesbian Archives, Periodicals Collection.

Bechdel, Alison. "Servants to the Cause #15." *Advocate*, no. 549 (April 1990): 73. ONE National Gay & Lesbian Archives, Periodicals Collection.

Bechdel, Alison. "Servants to the Cause #16." *Advocate*, no. 551 (May 1990): 77. ONE National Gay & Lesbian Archives, Periodicals Collection.

Bechdel, Alison. "Servants to the Cause #17." *Advocate*, no. 553 (June 1990): 77. ONE National Gay & Lesbian Archives, Periodicals Collection.

Bechdel, Alison. "Servants to the Cause #18." *Advocate*, no. 556 (July 1990): 81. ONE National Gay & Lesbian Archives, Periodicals Collection.

Bechdel, Alison. "Servants to the Cause #19." *Advocate*, no. 558 (August 1990): 89. ONE National Gay & Lesbian Archives, Periodicals Collection.

Beins, Agatha. *Liberation in Print: Feminist Periodicals and Social Movement Identity*. University of Georgia Press, 2017.

Beins, Agatha, and Julie R. Enszer. "'We Couldn't Get Them Printed,' So We Learned to Print: *Ain't I a Woman?* and the Iowa City Women's Press." *Frontiers: A Journal of Women Studies* 34, no. 2 (2013): 186–221.

Beirne, Rebecca. *Lesbians in Television and Text after the Millennium*. Palgrave Macmillan, 2008.

Bright, Susie. "The *On Our Backs* Interview: Alison Bechdel." *On Our Backs* 8, no. 2 (December 1991): 20–22, 41–43.

Camper, Jennifer. "Outwrite '91." *Lesbian Cartoonists' Network* #3, Spring 1991, 3. Jennifer Camper Personal Archives.

Chute, Hillary. *Why Comics? From Underground to Everywhere*. Harper, 2017.

Cvetkovich, Ann. *An Archive of Feelings: Trauma, Sexuality, and Lesbian Public Cultures*. Duke University Press, 2003.

de Lauretis, Teresa. "Queer Theory: Lesbian and Gay Sexualities; An Introduction." *Differences* 3, no. 2 (1991): iii–xviii.

Enszer, Julie R. "'Fighting to Create and Maintain Our Own Black Women's Culture': *Conditions Magazine*, 1977–1990." *American Periodicals* 25, no. 2 (2015): 160–76.

Enszer, Julie R. "Night Heron Press and Lesbian Print Culture in North Carolina, 1976–1983." *Southern Cultures* 21, no. 2 (2015): 43–56.

Galvan, Margaret. "'The Lesbian Norman Rockwell': Alison Bechdel and Queer Grassroots Networks." *American Literature* 90, no. 2 (2018): 407–38.

Gardiner, Judith Kegan. "Queering Genre: Alison Bechdel's *Fun Home: A Family Tragicomic* and *The Essential Dykes to Watch Out For*." *Contemporary Women's Writing* 5, no. 3 (2011): 188–207.

Hall, Justin. "File under Queer." In *No Straight Lines: Four Decades of Queer Comics*. 1st ed. Fantagraphics, 2013.

Hanscom, Alan. "Opinions: No Sex, Please—We're Gay." *Advocate*, no. 522 (April 1989): 6. ONE National Gay & Lesbian Archives, Periodicals Collection.

Lemon, Brendan. "k.d.: A Quiet Life." *Advocate*, no. 605 (June 1992): 34–41.

McKinney, Cait. "Newsletter Networks in the Feminist History and Archives Movement." *Feminist Theory* 16, no. 3 (2015): 309–28.

Rich, Adrienne. "Compulsory Heterosexuality and Lesbian Existence." In *Blood, Bread, and Poetry: Selected Prose, 1979–1985*, 23–74. Norton, 1994.

Rouilard, Richard. "Comment." *Advocate*, no. 561 (October 1990): 6. ONE National Gay & Lesbian Archives, Periodicals Collection.

Sedgwick, Eve Kosofsky. *Epistemology of the Closet*. University of California Press, 1990.

"Staff Box." *Equal Time*, no. 166 (August 1988): 4. ONE National Gay & Lesbian Archives, Periodicals Collection.

"Staff Box." *Equal Time*, no. 217 (August 1990): 4. ONE National Gay & Lesbian Archives, Periodicals Collection.

Tate, Robert. "Letters: No Laughing Matter." *Advocate*, no. 564 (November 1990): 11. ONE National Gay & Lesbian Archives, Periodicals Collection.

FRAMING COMMUNITY FROM INSIDE OUT

The Information Worlds of *Dykes to Watch Out For*

DON L. LATHAM AND JONATHAN M. HOLLISTER

Alison Bechdel's groundbreaking comic strip *Dykes to Watch Out For* had an important effect on representing and shaping the LGBTQ+, especially the lesbian, community in the latter decades of the twentieth century and the first decade of the twenty-first, a time of great change for that community. Within the world of the comic strip, information, information behavior, and the exchange of information play key roles in helping build and maintain community among the (mostly lesbian) characters. In turn, the evolving community shapes the identities of its individual members.

Numerous examples of the importance of information and information exchange can be seen in the strip over the twenty-five years it was published. For one thing, various characters are intimately associated with institutions of information dissemination. Mo, the strip's central character, and several other characters work at bookstores, initially at the independent feminist bookseller Madwimmin Books, then at the corporate behemoth Bounders Books and Muzak; Mo eventually enrolls in a library science program. The importance of information and information behaviors can also be seen in the characters' participation in various rallies, Pride parades, political events, and so on. On a more personal level, the nuances of information exchange can be seen in the characters' regular participation in the community "grapevine," sharing information about one another's lives.

This essay uses Gary Burnett and Paul T. Jaeger's theory of information worlds as a framework for examining how information and information behaviors help to form and maintain the information world of the lesbian community depicted in *Dykes to Watch Out For*. We examine the various aspects of information worlds in relation to four recurrent themes in the series: the grapevine, gender identity and membership in the community, mainstreaming, and the role of Madwimmin Books.

Information Worlds

Gary Burnett and Paul Jaeger's theory of information worlds provides a useful and flexible framework for analyzing the social context(s) of information use and behavior within and across communities. Drawing on the work of Elfreda Chatman and her concepts of small worlds and theory normative behavior (see Burnett et al.), as well as the work of Jürgen Habermas and his concept of the lifeworld, Jaeger and Burnett define five aspects of information worlds: social types, social norms, information behaviors, information value, and boundaries.

Social types refer to the "ways in which individuals are perceived and socially defined within the context of their small world" (Jaeger and Burnett, 22). This is partly a matter of how individuals want to present themselves, and partly a matter of how others view them. Social norms refer to the generally agreed on, but not necessarily articulated, acceptable forms of observable behavior (22). Social norms can range from formally established laws and regulations to informal rules, guidelines, or taboos.

Information behaviors are the potential normative behaviors regarding the use or nonuse of information that a world's members might exhibit (Jaeger and Burnett, 23). Information is typically sought from a variety of traditional and new media, as well as through other people in the community. Information value is an information world's "shared sense of a scale of the importance of information" (8). Certain sources and types of information may have different levels of importance to different information worlds, and even for different social types within an information world.

Finally, boundaries are "the places at which information worlds come into contact with each other and across which communication and information exchange can—but may or may not—take place" (Jaeger and Burnett, 8). As individuals interact with others within and outside their immediate community, they have the potential either to share or not share information. The interplay between information and individuals within and across boundaries can impact the characteristics of the community itself.

Information Behavior in Literature

There is some precedent for using information behavior theory as a way of analyzing literature. Rhiannon Gainor, for example, reports that the success of protagonists in detective fiction often depends on their ability to effectively seek, process, and evaluate information. Gainor goes on to argue that while the narratives are fictional, the activities related to finding and using information are not. She even suggests that narrative fictions could be used for information literacy instruction (3–4). Michelle Kazmer also focuses on information behavior in detective fiction, specifically in Agatha Christie's Miss Marple novels. Using the theory of information worlds as a theoretical lens, Kazmer argues that the information behaviors of Miss Marple can be characterized by the aspects of access, tactics, and value (4). As one reliable tactic, for example, Miss Marple undervalues herself when sharing information to gain further information and to strengthen her case for or against the culprit (8, 13). She also values critical thinking and thorough assessment of the information she collects and uses (14). In a previous study, we explored the depictions of information and media literacy in Suzanne Collins's *The Hunger Games* trilogy, a popular series of dystopian young adult novels, in which the protagonist, Katniss Everdeen, uses a variety of information and media literacy skills to survive the Hunger Games, interpret and manipulate media messages, and ultimately outsmart the totalitarian government (Latham and Hollister, 45). As each of these studies demonstrates, fiction often provides detailed accounts of information behavior; consequently, theories of information behavior can provide a useful framework for analyzing such works.

Literature Review

Scholars who have written about *DTWOF* have not taken an information behavior approach, although Gary Burnett and his coauthors do use Madwimmin Books as a source for examples to illustrate how normative behavior can be seen in the (real-world) communities of feminist bookselling (542). Most scholars have focused on the importance of community building and maintenance in lesbian and queer culture and have discussed the role of *DTWOF* in both reflecting and facilitating that process. In a 2001 interview with Marny Hall, Bechdel acknowledged this role, sharing an email she had recently received from a young woman. Hall reports, "The young dyke wrote that 'the kind of community that's shown in Madwimmin books' had inspired her to start a gay-straight alliance in her high school. Such a supportive group, she was sure, would help others like herself come out" (21). Kathleen Liddle frequently references *DTWOF* and Madwimmin Books in her article on the continuing importance of feminist bookstores despite economic and social changes. Through surveys and interviews, Liddle found that "far from being outdated, feminist bookstores hold great relevance in contemporary society, particularly for the establishment and maintenance of lesbian community" (147).

Just how *DTWOF* accomplishes the feat of helping define lesbian identity and community is the subject of several scholarly essays. Carol Guess notes that while *DTWOF* assumes lesbian identity can, in fact, be depicted, it also actively subverts the notion of an essentialist lesbian identity (28). Adrienne Shaw looks at the work of four comics artists, including Bechdel, and argues that all four reflect and contribute to the concepts of lesbian identity and community through three interrelated themes: visibility, self-reflexivity, and the process of defining identity and community (93). One important strategy in helping define identity and community, according to Robin M. Queen, is the creation of a unique lesbian language through "the recontextualization and reappropriation" (242) of four stereotypical stylistic tropes: women's language, working-class urban male language, gay male language, and lesbian language (239–40). Queen notes that the lesbian characters in *DTWOF* represent different types and, as such, are marked by different linguistic traits (242). Another strategy for creating lesbian identity and community is, according to Tuula Raikas, as well as Janet M. Bing and Dana Heller, the use of humor, especially the "inside joke." Bing and Heller see *DTWOF* as one exemplar of this kind of humor, including humor that resists categorization, distinguishes between lesbian humor and feminist humor, and reflects a shared culture (158; Raikas, 15). In a thoughtful analysis of the humor in *Fun Home* and *DTWOF*, Judith Kegan Gardiner argues that Bechdel uses humor in *DTWOF* to bend genres, eschew happy endings, and destabilize gay and straight identities. In doing so, Bechdel creates "a queer community of multiple identities" (206; see Gardiner in this volume).

Bechdel also foregrounds how the lesbian and queer community is impacted by, and defines itself in relation to, the larger political and social sphere. She herself has described *DTWOF* as "half soap-opera, half editorial cartoon about how politics shapes daily life" (quoted in Thompson, 84), and as "half op ed column and half endlessly serialized Victorian novel" (quoted in Garner, C1). Susan Kirtley sees *DTWOF*'s interest in how politics intersect with the personal as really an interest in "dual domesticity." In other words, Bechdel shows again and again how US domestic policies "permeate personal, intimate domestic lives and situations on a daily basis" (Kirtley, 41). Rebecca Beirne identifies three key political and social themes in *DTWOF* that impact community: the relationship between queer theory and lesbian-feminist thought (179), the acceptance (or lack thereof) of transsexual people into the lesbian community (182), and the mainstreaming of lesbian identity and culture (185).

Not everyone has found the lesbian and queer community of *DTWOF* reflective of her real-life experiences. Esther Rothblum reports that only 55 percent of the sixty women she interviewed, including thirty-one lesbians, said that they had experienced social support from their community in times of need ("The Costs," 72). Although neither this study nor a follow-up study ("Where Is the Women's Community?") focuses on *DTWOF* per se, both reference Bechdel's comic strip, arguing that its diverse characters who live in physical proximity and form a supportive community do not reflect the experiences of many lesbians and genderqueer women ("The Costs," 69; "Where," 461). Gabrielle Dean acknowledges that Bechdel attempts to portray a diverse community by including characters of different races, ethnicities, and body types, but complains that none of the characters is well developed, with the result being merely the representation of stereotypes (212). Kathleen Martindale, though more sympathetic to the portrayals in *DTWOF*, also sees the characters as stereotypes and notes that though the characters possess racial and ethnic diversity, they present far less sexual diversity in the form of "leather dykes, butch daddies, or femme tops" (63). During an interview with Eva Sollberger, Bechdel herself admits that the community in *DTWOF* does not reflect reality, saying, "I created these characters to be my community, to be my fantasy community that I never quite felt that I had."

The Grapevine

The significance of information exchange as a theme in *DTWOF* is announced at the outset by the cover design of *The Essential Dykes to Watch Out For*. The collection's cover depicts a dozen pairs of characters, and in each pair the character on the left is clearly giving the character on the right a juicy bit of information. The grapevine begins with Mo telling Clarice something, who in turn tells Toni, who in turn tells Carlos, and so on, until the final pairing shows a clearly perturbed Sydney confronting Mo, presumably about whatever it is Mo told Clarice. As this cover suggests, the grapevine represents an important type of information behavior that helps provide cohesion—and comedy—to this community.

The efficiency of the grapevine is seen in all its glory in "Communique" (#26; *Essential*, 24). In this strip, Mo and Harriet have spent their first night together, and Harriet talks Mo into calling in late to work at the bookstore. Mo calls Ariadne, and the information quickly makes its way along the grapevine. When Lois teases Mo about it, Mo's exasperated response is "**Great**, Lois. **Great**. I'm really **impressed**. I think this community just set the land speed **record** for **gossip mongering**!" (*Essential*, 24). In "The Line" (#247; *Essential*, 166), Sydney, who is trying to get Mo to go out with her, tells Mo that her "sources" tell her that neither Lois nor Clarice is speaking to Mo because she's "such a rigid, self-righteous **prig**" (*Essential*, 166). In both strips, we see not only the information behavior known as the grapevine but also the fact that the information that is valued is information about relationships, whether recent sexual encounters or long-term friendships. Valued sources are other people in the community, who give information authenticity by virtue of being members of the community, and give it life by passing it along.

Sometimes the grapevine proves to be even more intertwined than anyone might imagine. In "Gossip Failure" (#307; *Essential*, 217), Mo is ready to share some juicy news when she arrives for her shift at Madwimmin Books. She has seen Sparrow buying a home pregnancy test at the drugstore, so when Toni and Clarice come into the store to, as Toni says, "hear the latest dish," Mo replies, "Well, have I got some news for you. Guess who was recently spotted purchasing a home pregnancy test!" (217). She is flabbergasted when Toni says, "Harriet! I know! Isn't it wonderful?!" (217). Although it has been seven years since she and Harriet broke up, Mo can't help but gasp, "**Harriet? My Harriet?**" (217). The grapevine works quite effectively in this community and is clearly a valued source of information and a frequently employed type of information behavior.

Gender Identity and Membership in the Community

In the "Cartoonist's Introduction" to *The Essential Dykes to Watch Out For*, Bechdel alludes to her struggles in representing the diversity of identity and ideology within the lesbian community (xvi–xviii). These themes often manifest as discussions and debates among the characters and the depictions of gender identity and, as such, are recurring topics and themes throughout *DTWOF*. The concepts of social types, social norms, and boundaries thus offer a lens through which to explore these themes.

Mo's opinions and actions cast her as a champion of lesbian feminism. Her restrictive or perhaps more "traditional" views often clash with those of her friends and lead to disagreements. One recurring thread throughout *DTWOF* is Mo's views on transgender members of the community. An early example of this is found in "Au Courant" (#193; *Essential*, 125), where Mo is reviewing submissions for the "Madwimmin Read" series she is organizing at the bookstore. In this strip, Mo receives a submission from Jillian, a potential presenter who self-identifies as a transsexual lesbian, who also requests that the bookstore consider renaming the reading series to be more inclusive toward bisexual and transgender women writers. This irritates Mo, and she complains to Lois, "I'm still trying to adjust to lesbians using dildos! What am I supposed to make of a man who became a woman who's attracted to women?!" (125). Lois rebukes Mo, saying that "love is a many gendered thing, pal. Get used to it"

(125). Mo reluctantly allows Jillian to participate but complains that she still doesn't understand what transgender means. Lois then explains and provides Mo with further information on the topic, which she has received from a local lesbian group. This "teachable moment" between Mo and Lois also serves as dissemination of information to readers, who may, in turn, be inspired to learn more about the topic or discuss it with their friends. The discussions, experiences, and lessons learned by the characters in *DTWOF* can vicariously contribute to the community beyond the pages, too.

The social norms to which Mo subscribes enforce specific rules about which social types are allowed in the lesbian community (cisgender lesbian women) and those that are not (bisexual and transgender lesbian women). Lois's encouragement of Mo to permit bisexual and transgender women to participate in the readings can be interpreted as an attempt to ease the rigid boundaries around the lesbian community created by social norms restricting membership to certain social types. Allowing bisexual and transgender women to participate in the reading also facilitates information flow among different social types. As Lois remarks, "Why not? I'm sure they'd have a unique perspective on the topic" (*Essential*, 125). In this case, Lois sees the perspectives of other social types as valuable information and seeks to include rather than exclude them. Information values that encourage inclusion may eventually alter social norms or shift boundaries.

In the next strip, "Lime Light" (#194; *Essential*, 126), while "schmoozing" with guests after the successful event, one attendee misgenders Jillian and complains to Mo about allowing a man to present. While Mo mistakenly misgenders Jillian at first, she corrects herself and defends Jillian's participation, saying, "First of all, he's not a man, he's a lesbian. I mean, **she's** a lesbian. And second, I want this series to be inclusive, and not some private club. I mean, who am I to question someone else's identity?" (126). While Mo's response only infuriates the presumably transphobic attendee, a different audience member comes up and thanks Mo for including Jillian's work, saying she is going to recommend that one of her own transgender friends submit work for a future event. And still another attendee is more concerned about having vegan hors d'oeuvres at the next event than about anyone's gender identity. "Lime Light" illustrates the interconnected nature of social types and social norms in the community: Jillian's participation is not acceptable for some, a welcome inclusion for others, and a nonissue for still others.

Although the first installment of "Madwimmin Read" is a successful, inclusive event, readers find out later that Mo still holds conflicted feelings about transgender people. The topic reappears in a long-running dispute between Mo and Lois, in which Lois pretends to pursue a female-to-male transition to teach Mo a lesson for being transphobic. This story arc reaches something of a conclusion in "Girls! Girls! Girls!" (#367; *Essential*, 262). In this scene, Lois finally admits that she is not taking hormones and is not actually transitioning at all. At first, Mo seeks clarification by trying to confirm Lois's social type: "So if you're not doing hormones, that makes you, like, a **no-ho tranny**, right?" (262). Before revealing that she is not actually transitioning, Lois expresses her surprise that Mo has "been doing her homework" on the issue. Frustrated and confused, Mo then accuses Lois of being in denial about her identity or suffering from internalized transphobia.

This episode also demonstrates the importance of information value. Mo, obviously conflicted, appears to have been seeking out and reviewing information on transitioning because she cares about her friend despite reservations she may have. Mo trusts Lois, as her friend, as a source of information. As mentioned earlier, Lois shares some of the information she gained from attending a local progressive lesbian group with Mo in "Au Courant"; perhaps this is a sign that Mo actually read the information she was given. Moreover, Lois often serves as an emissary of inclusive social norms to Mo and others in the community; she is also a role model, parental figure, and champion of Janis, her partner's transgender teenage daughter (see Thalheimer in this volume). The information sought provides affective and ideological value and may ultimately alter social norms and shift boundaries on social types in the lesbian community. Consequently Mo may potentially be influenced by Lois's social norms, information values, and information behaviors. However, this is subject to debate, as Mo is often critical and less than welcoming, at least initially, of alternative social types in the community.

Similar relationships between social norms and social types with regard to the community's acceptance, inclusion, and support (or lack thereof) of bisexual women are evident in the series as well. For example, in "Cultural Exchange" (#155; *Essential*, 99), Mo is bothered that Naomi, one of her coworkers at the co-op, frequents the bookstore despite sleeping with a man. Again, here Mo is attempting to reinforce (or enforce) a social norm: it is not appropriate for the social type of bisexual women to frequent the bookstore, which she seems to believe is only for lesbians. Relatedly, Sparrow's relationship with Stuart and unexpected pregnancy cause Sparrow a great deal of distress because she feels internal confusion and external judgment because of her identity as a "bisexual lesbian" (her term). In "Same as It Ever Was" (#397; *Essential*, 281), Sparrow vents to Ginger that she has not "felt this lonely and confused since I **came out**" (281). Ginger recommends that Sparrow do what she did then, to which Sparrow sarcastically replies, "Right. I'll move to the **bisexual** neighborhood and start volunteering at the coffeehouse for unintentionally pregnant bi-dykes with over-zealous male partners" (281). Sparrow's remarks reveal her own difficulties in understanding or identifying herself, as well as perceptions that she is no longer feeling comfortable or welcome in the lesbian community because of her bisexuality and pregnancy.

The multiple story arcs focused on the experiences of bisexual and transgender women demonstrate an information world dealing with internal conflicts among communities with different social types and social norms. Through the lens of information worlds, the lesbian community depicted in *DTWOF* can be seen as being in a state of transition from only including and welcoming members who are lesbian to including additional social types—bisexual and transgender women.

Mainstreaming

A key issue related to community is the perceived threats and opportunities represented by mainstreaming. Throughout *DTWOF*, a growing sense exists among some of the characters that mainstreaming—that is, acceptance by, and inclusion in, mainstream society—comes at a price, namely, the dissolution of a strong lesbian community through which the characters gained both support and identity. In some cases, mainstreaming is portrayed as occurring because of choices the characters make, such as choosing to have commitment (and, later, marriage) ceremonies. In other cases, mainstreaming is shown to be a result of heteronormative society's co-opting of lesbian and gay culture for profit. In both cases, though, information behavior plays a vital role.

The issues surrounding marriage emerge in an early strip titled "Altared States" (#87; *Essential*, 56), in which Toni and Clarice have a commitment ceremony in their backyard. Their friends, representing different social types within the community, offer support and best wishes while at the same time articulating what the ceremony means to each of them. Lois, ever the proponent of sexual freedom, says, "Personally, I can't really get behind the monogamy thing, but I wish you luck. And if it doesn't work out, you both have my number, right?" (56). Tanya, the radical lesbian feminist, offers a backhanded affirmation: "I just wanna say I love you both like **sisters**. Maybe that's why I give you so much shit about being **yuppie sellouts** and why I sincerely hope that in your wedded **bliss** you don't abandon the struggle of radical lesbians of color against the **imperialist patriarchy!**" (56). Jezanna, the levelheaded proprietor of Madwimmin Books, provides a counterpoint to the notion of marriage being a sellout: "Well I am hard-pressed to think of a more **radical** act than two courageous women challenging the powers that be by publicly celebrating their lesbian relationship. Here's your **golden anniversary!**" (56). These differing viewpoints reveal not only the various social types in the community but also contested social norms. For everyone, though, the commitment ceremony has information value in that it is a public declaration filled with meaning—negative for some, positive for others.

The threats that come from outside the community represent the boundaries of information worlds coming into contact with one another. The issue of co-optation of lesbian and gay culture by mainstream society emerges several times throughout the series, often in relation to changing attitudes toward the Millennium March and Pride celebrations. In "Balm Blast" (#294; *Essential*, 206), for instance, Mo and Sydney are enjoying a day at home when Mo starts venting about the upcoming Millennium March, which has been planned "unilaterally." Aside from being annoyed by the "closed-process, top-down executive decision," Mo is offended by the theme "Faith and Family." When Sydney suggests that the theme might represent a good strategy for winning support for the movement, Mo explodes: "**What** movement? This isn't a movement anymore, it's a @#i*! **closely-held corporation**, run by a bunch of white, power-hungry **marketing strategists** who're packaging our lives into a commodity they can sell to pay their salaries!" (206). Sydney counters, "One soundbite on CNN's worth a hundred sweaty, weekend-long consensus-building mass meetings" (206). In this scene, we see information behavior in the gleaning of information from periodicals, the source of the story that leads to Mo's rant. Note that what she questions is not the value or veracity of the information but the value of the strategy itself. We also once again see the boundaries of communities, both external and internal, coming into contact, as well as the debate about what the social norms should be within the community—resisting the commodification of lesbian (and more broadly LGBTQ+) culture versus being grateful for an opportunity to move into the mainstream. A few years later, Mo is still protesting the co-optation of gay and lesbian culture, explaining to Sparrow and Stuart that she is going to Gay Shame rather than Gay Pride, "to protest how Pride has gotten so corporate" ("Shameless," #442; *Essential*, 311). Mo plays the role of self-appointed guardian of the boundaries in response to the fact that social norms, and lesbian culture, are clearly changing around her.

The Role of Madwimmin Books

Another key issue for the community throughout *DTWOF* is the economic viability of Madwimmin Books. Madwimmin Books is a source of valuable, relevant information and a dedicated space that provides social support and promotes political awareness for both the lesbian and the greater feminist community. The bookstore is a major setting throughout the series; several of the characters are employees, and their friends and family members are frequent patrons, stopping by to pick up a book or share the latest gossip. Despite the store's critical role in the lesbian community, Madwimmin Books faces tough competition from large corporate bookstores, such as "Bunns & Noodle" and "Bounders Books and Muzak," as well as monstrous online retailers, such as "Medusa.com." The community's, and Madwimmin's, responses to mainstream encroachment are mixed, signaling differences and changes in information values, social norms, information behaviors, and boundaries.

Signs of struggle for Madwimmin Books occur throughout the series. In "Loyalty" (#182; *Essential*, 121), a customer wishes to purchase a book that has just gone out of stock at Madwimmin Books. Jezanna says they have more copies coming in, but the customer says she will just pick up a copy at Bunns & Noodle. After wishing the customer a nice day, Jezanna snaps a pencil and vents, "I sold that woman her first lesbian sex book fifteen years ago, and now she's taking her business to those **cutthroats!**" (121). Here Jezanna implies a social norm, namely, that community members should feel obliged to buy locally from feminist booksellers, and when looking for information, the community should value the source of the information—locally owned feminist bookstores—rather than convenience or lower prices.

As Jezanna walks sullenly back to her office, trying to keep her blood pressure in check, Clarice asks Mo why Jezanna is so upset. Mo explains that Jezanna has worked hard for years building her business and is upset because Bunns & Noodle is "luring folks away with their massive selection and big discounts" (*Essential*, 121). When Clarice lets it slip that she thinks that Bunns & Noodle has good coffee, Mo is flabbergasted and argues, "Books are just a commodity to them, like small appliances, or . . . **health insurance!** They don't care about literature, or ideas, or community. How can you shop there?!" (121). Here Mo attempts to reinforce the social norm of buying from locally owned feminist bookstores and also articulates the information value that such stores offer: unique, relevant literature and ideas that support and are representative of the community. However minor Clarice's transgressions may be, competition and consolidation in the bookstore industry continue to escalate and impinge on the community. In "Gossip Failure" (#307; *Essential*, 217), Jezanna warns Mo that "you can say goodbye to books by risky or unproven authors, like the ones I've been handselling to our customers for years. We'll all be up to our **cerebral cortexes** in Celine Dion's **'Titanic Cheesecake Recipes'!**" (217). Jezanna's argument is that the information in the form of books provided by her store, coming from authors who are not likely to have their books carried or sold at the large corporate stores, has unique value, and losing access to this kind of information would be detrimental to the community.

Madwimmin Books continues to lose customers to both brick-and-mortar and online competitors, and in "Same as It Ever Was" (#397; *Essential*, 281),

Jezanna reveals that she will close the bookstore. Mo sullenly remarks, "Jeez, I thought we were gonna make the world safe for feminism" (281). Morosely, and perhaps resentfully, Jezanna replies, "We did. To be packaged and sold by global media conglomerates" (281). Here it seems that Madwimmin Books is another victim of mainstreaming, and the loss is one of a clearly defined space (read "boundary") where information valuable to lesbians and other feminists could be promoted and exchanged. Jezanna's lament also implies a broader concern that while some of this information may be more widely available to the general public through corporate bookstores than it may have been otherwise, the information will be less accessible to, and representative of, the lesbian community. Without such dedicated spaces, which provide essential access to both information and community, the identity of the lesbian community itself and the power to curate and disseminate valuable information may be lost or transferred to the mainstream. Ironically, Mo ultimately violates the social norms and transgresses the boundaries she so adamantly defends, later becoming an employee of Bounders Books and Muzak. The general mood of despair and guilt reflects betrayed social norms and changing information values. Ultimately these changing social norms and information values result in a change in information behavior: it becomes a socially acceptable, hence normative, information behavior to seek and buy books at corporate bookstores and on online markets rather than solely at locally owned feminist bookstores.

While Madwimmin Books serves as a crucial community hub as well as a source of inclusive, representative information throughout most of the series, it is able to survive neither the competition nor the slow creep of changing social norms and information values. Even the community that revered it has, ironically, surrendered to convenience and better deals, accelerating the demise of one of the community's few remaining dedicated spaces.

Conclusion

Information worlds theory provides a useful theoretical lens for examining how the community in *DTWOF* functions, changes, and continues to thrive. The multiple story arcs demonstrate an information world in a state of flux owing to pressures from within and without. As the series progresses, the community it depicts changes to include additional social types and social norms. These changes, in turn, impact information behavior, values, and boundaries. As more diverse social types are welcomed into the community and their perspectives become valued, greater information transfer occurs between two previously separate groups, making boundaries more permeable.

This process connects, expands, and, potentially, unites the information worlds of lesbian women with the information worlds of a larger, more inclusive LGBTQ+ community.

But at what price? Some characters fear that the inclusion of more social types, while increasing diversity, may also dilute the identity of the community. Similarly, some characters worry that mainstreaming, whether because of choices made within the community or pressures from without, may result in the loss of community through absorption and assimilation. *DTWOF* demonstrates that these threats are real—but also that, in spite of such threats, the core community of *DTWOF* remains intact, not just surviving but thriving amid the vicissitudes of contemporary life. Understanding the dynamics of the information worlds represented within the series provides valuable insight into how that process occurs. In the final strip reprinted in *The Essential Dykes to Watch Out For*, Stuart has converted the backyard into a vegetable garden in his quest to be food self-sufficient, Lois is planning to protest at both political conventions, and Sydney is going on sabbatical to write a book on modern leisure. Although the strip is titled "Sing, Cuccu" (#527; *Essential*, 390), it could have taken its title from an earlier strip (and Talking Heads lyric), "Same as It Ever Was" (#397; *Essential*, 281). There is great comfort in that thought.

WORKS CITED

Bechdel, Alison. Interview with Eva Sollberger. *Seven Days*, December 13, 2008. Accessed August 8, 2018.

Bechdel, Alison, and Marny Hall. "Ordinary Insurrections: Alison Bechdel Interviewed by Marny Hall." *Journal of Lesbian Studies* 5, no. 3 (2001): 15–21.

Beirne, Rebecca. *Lesbians in Television and Text after the Millennium*. Palgrave Macmillan, 2008.

Bing, Janet M., and Dana Heller. "How Many Lesbians Does It Take to Screw in a Light Bulb?" *Humor: International Journal of Humor Research* 16, no. 2 (2003): 157–82.

Burnett, Gary, Michele Besant, and Elfreda A. Chatman. "Small Worlds: Normative Behavior in Virtual Communities and Feminist Bookselling." *Journal of the American Society for Information Science and Technology* 52, no. 3 (2001): 536–47.

Burnett, Gary, and Paul T. Jaeger. "Small Worlds, Lifeworlds, and Information: The Ramifications of the Information Behaviour of Social Groups in Public Policy and the Public Sphere." *Information Research* 13, no. 2 (2008): n.p. Accessed July 7, 2019.

Dean, Gabrielle. "The 'Phallacies' of Dyke Comic Strips." In *The Gay '90s: Disciplinary and Interdisciplinary Formations in Queer Studies*, ed. Thomas Foster, Carol Siegel, and Ellen Berry, 199–223. New York University Press, 1997.

Gainor, Rhiannon. "The Relevant Clues: Information Behaviour and Assessment in Classic Detective Fiction." *Proceedings of the Annual Conference of CAIS/Actes du Congrès Annuel de l'ACSI*, 2013.

Gardiner, Judith Kegan. "Queering Genre: Alison Bechdel's *Fun Home: A Family Tragicomic* and *The Essential Dykes to Watch Out For*." *Contemporary Women's Writing* 5, no. 3 (2011): 188–207.

Garner, Dwight. "The Days of Their Lives: Lesbians Star in Funny Pages: Books of the Times." *New York Times*, December 3, 2008.
Guess, Carol. "Que(e)rying Lesbian Identity." *Journal of the Midwest Modern Language Association* 28, no. 1 (1995): 19–37.
Habermas, Jürgen. "Further Reflections on the Public Sphere." In *Critical Social Theory: Culture, Theory and the Challenge of Difference*, ed. Craig Calhoun, 421–62. Blackwell, 1992.
Jaeger, Paul T., and Gary Burnett. *Information Worlds: Social Context, Technology, and Information Behavior in the Age of the Internet*. Routledge, 2010.
Kazmer, Michelle M. "'One Must Actually Take Facts as They Are': Information Value and Information Behavior in the Miss Marple Novels." In *The Ageless Agatha Christie: Essays on the Mysteries and the Legacy*, ed. J. C. Benthal, 114–29. McFarland, 2016.
Kirtley, Susan. "The Political Is Personal: Dual Domesticity in *Dykes to Watch Out For*." *Inks: The Journal of the Comics Studies Society* 1, no. 1 (2017): 40–55.
Latham, Don, and Jonathan M. Hollister. "The Games People Play: Information and Media Literacies in *The Hunger Games* Trilogy." *Children's Literature in Education* 45, no. 1 (2014): 33–46.
Liddle, Kathleen. "More than a Bookstore: The Continuing Relevance of Feminist Bookstores for the Lesbian Community." *Journal of Lesbian Studies* 9, nos. 1–2 (2005): 145–59.
Martindale, Kathleen. *Un/popular Culture: Lesbian Writing after the Sex Wars*. State University of New York Press, 1997.
Queen, Robin M. "'I Don't Speak Spritch': Locating Lesbian Language." In *Queerly Phrased: Language, Gender, and Sexuality*, ed. Anna Livia and Kira Hall, 233–56. Oxford University Press, 1997.
Raikas, Tuula. "Humour in Alison Bechdel's Comics." MA thesis, University of Jyväskylä, 1997.
Rothblum, Esther. "Finding a Large and Thriving Lesbian and Bisexual Community: The Costs and Benefits of Caring." *Gay and Lesbian Issues and Psychology Review* 4, no. 2 (2008): 69–79.
Rothblum, Esther. "Where Is the 'Women's Community'? Voices of Lesbian, Bisexual, and Queer Women and Heterosexual Sisters." *Feminism and Psychology* 20, no. 4 (2010): 454–72.
Shaw, Adrienne. "Women on Women: Lesbian Identity, Lesbian Community, and Lesbian Comics." *Journal of Lesbian Studies* 13, no. 1 (2009): 88–97.
Thompson, Tulia. "Queer Attachments: Alison Bechdel and the Shifting Relationship between Queer Selves and Heteronormativity." *Women's Studies Journal* 28, no. 1 (2014): 83–87.

CONTRIBUTORS

Michelle Ann Abate is professor of literature for children and young adults at The Ohio State University. She is the author of the forthcoming critical book *Funny Girls: Guffaws, Guts, and Gender in Classic American Comics* (University Press of Mississippi, 2019). Michelle has published articles on a wide array of comics and graphic novels, including *Calvin and Hobbes, Garfield, Terry and the Pirates, Little Lulu, In the Shadow of No Towers*, and *Drama* by Raina Telgemeier. She is also the coeditor (with Gwen Athene Tarbox) of *Graphic Novels for Young Readers: A Collection of Critical Essays* (University Press of Mississippi, 2017).

Leah Anderst is associate professor of English at Queensborough Community College, CUNY, where she coordinates the Writing Program and teaches writing, literature, and film courses. She is also an affiliated faculty member of the MA Program in Liberal Studies at the CUNY Graduate Center. Her work has appeared in *a/b: Auto/biography Studies, Narrative, Orbis Litterarum, Senses of Cinema, Teaching English in the Two-Year College*, and *Quarterly Review of Film and Video*. She is the editor of the essay collection *The Films of Eric Rohmer* (Palgrave, 2014), and she is a co-guest editor on a recent special issue (14, no. 1) of the *Basic Writing e-Journal* focused on acceleration in basic writing pedagogy.

Alissa S. Bourbonnais holds a tenure-track position in English at Spokane Falls Community College, where she serves as faculty liaison with Washington State University in a partnership to help CC students successfully transfer into four-year degree programs. She completed her PhD at the University of Washington, and she has won numerous teaching awards. Her teaching and research explore the relationship between memory, performance, and embodiment in composition studies and in contemporary American literature.

Tyler Bradway is assistant professor of English at State University of New York–Cortland and author *of Queer Experimental Literature: The Affective Politics of Bad Reading* (2017), coeditor of *After Queer Studies: Literature, Theory and Sexuality in the 21st Century* (2019), and editor of "Lively Words:

The Politics and Poetics of Experimental Writing," a special issue of *College Literature*. His essays have appeared in venues such as *GLQ, Mosaic, Stanford Arcade*, and *American Literature in Transition, 1980–1990*.

Natalja Chestopalova is part of the PhD in Communication and Culture Program at York and Ryerson Universities in Toronto, Canada. Her research is informed by the study of phenomenology, popular culture aesthetics, and psychoanalysis and focuses on the transformative sensory experience and multimodality in film, the graphic novel medium, and immersive site-specific performances. She has presented at multiple Canadian and international events, including roundtables and panels on new media archives, visual storytelling, and preservation of ephemeral cultural narratives. Her recent works include papers on archives-of-trauma in nonfiction comics and theoretical developments in the Lacanian concept of the voice and voicelessness, as well as publications in the *White Wall Review, Dialogue, Canadian Journal of Communication*, and *The Routledge Encyclopedia of Modernism*.

Margaret Galvan is assistant professor of visual rhetoric in the Department of English at the University of Florida. She is at work on a book, *In Visible Archives of the 1980s*, under contract with the University of Minnesota Press, which traces a genealogy of queer theory in 1980s feminism through representations of sexuality in visual culture. Her published work, which analyzes comics through intersectional approaches, can be found in journals like *Australian Feminist Studies, WSQ: Women's Studies Quarterly, Archive Journal, American Literature*, and *Journal of Lesbian Studies*. See margaretgalvan.org for more information.

Judith Kegan Gardiner is Professor of English and of Gender and Women's Studies Emerita at the University of Illinois at Chicago. Her publications on modern and contemporary women writers include the book *Rhys, Stead, Lessing, and the Politics of Empathy* and essays on Doris Lessing, Christina Stead, and Alison Bechdel. Her edited collection *Approaches to Teaching Bechdel's "Fun Home"* was published by the Modern Language Association in 2018. Other publications discuss feminist theories, masculinity studies, popular culture, and pedagogy. She is a member of the editorial collective of the interdisciplinary journal *Feminist Studies*.

Katie Hogan is a professor of English and faculty affiliate of women's and gender studies at the University of North Carolina, Charlotte. Her book *Women Take Care: Gender, Race, and the Culture of AIDS* was a finalist for the CGS Gustave O. Arlt Award in the Humanities. Katie is also coeditor of *Gendered*

Epidemic: Representations of Women in the Age of AIDS and *Over Ten Million Served: Gendered Service in Language and Literature Workplaces*. Her current project, *All Over the Place: Environmental Belonging in Queer and Trans Literature*, explores how LGBTQ+ literature engages spatial and environmental justice issues. Her research and teaching interests include LGBTQ+ literature, queer and trans ecologies, the literature of environmental justice, and girl cultures.

Jonathan M. Hollister is an assistant professor in the Department of Library, Archives, and Information Studies at Pusan National University. His research focuses on the depictions and uses of digital literacy skills and social information behaviors in recreational, popular media, such as online games, graphic novels, and young adult literature. He is also a founding member of 3 J's & a G, a research group dedicated to continuing development of the theory of information worlds. Please visit https://jonathanmhollister.com for more information about his work.

Yetta Howard is associate professor of English and comparative literature at San Diego State University. Howard is the author of *Ugly Differences: Queer Female Sexuality in the Underground* (University of Illinois Press, 2018) and the editor of *Rated RX: Sheree Rose with and after Bob Flanagan* (forthcoming Fall 2020, The Ohio State University Press).

Katherine Kelp-Stebbins is an assistant professor of comics studies at the University of Oregon, Department of English. Her work examines comics and visual media as tools for rethinking world literature and remapping transnational media flows. She is interested in decolonial and feminist methodologies for research and teaching. Her work has been published in *Feminist Media Histories*, *Media Fields*, *Studies in Comics*, and a number of anthologies. She received her PhD in comparative literature from UC Santa Barbara.

Don L. Latham is a professor in the School of Information at Florida State University. His research focuses on information literacy and information behavior of young adults. He has published extensively on information literacy, young adult literature, and graphic novels in a variety of journals, including *Library and Information Science Research*, *Library Quarterly*, *Journal of Research on Libraries and Young Adults*, *Children's Literature*, *Children's Literature Association Quarterly*, and *Children's Literature in Education*. His most recent book is *Literacy Engagement through Peritextual Analysis* (ALA/NCTE), coedited with Shelbie Witte and Melissa Gross.

Vanessa Lauber is completing her PhD at the University of Wisconsin–Madison, writing a dissertation on contemporary queer literature, and currently pursuing her JD at Harvard University.

Katherine Parker-Hay specializes in late queer studies, affect, temporality and minor genres. She is a CHASE-funded PhD candidate in English and teaches at University of Sussex. She has a master's degree in women's studies from the University of Oxford and is a peer reviewer for *Excursions* and the reviews editor at *Encounters*.

Anne N. Thalheimer is a professor in the Postgraduate Seminar for International Students certificate program of Yale Summer Session, where she has been a faculty member since 2012. Anne completed her PhD at the University of Delaware and her undergraduate studies at Simon's Rock College of Bard, and her research interests include popular culture, feminist and gender theory, and comic books. She is also a roller derby official and is based in western Massachusetts.

Janine Utell is Distinguished University Professor and Chair of English at Widener University. She is the author of *Engagements with Narrative* and *James Joyce and the Revolt of Love*. She is also editor of the journal *The Space Between: Literature and Culture, 1914–1945*.

Susan R. Van Dyne is Professor of Women and Gender Emerita, Smith College. Her research examines how archives provide windows into the creative process and yield richly textured social histories. Her publications based on archives include *Revising Life: Sylvia Plath's Ariel Poems* (1993), and a microhistory of female friendships, "'Abracadabra': Intimate Inventions among Early College Women in the U.S." (*Feminist Studies*, 2016). Her research on *Fun Home* is based on the Alison Bechdel papers, held by the Sophia Smith Collection, Smith College. "Entering the Archives: Reading *Fun Home* Backward" appears in *Approaches to Teaching Bechdel's "Fun Home"* (MLA, 2018).

INDEX

Advocate, xxi, 214–18, 221–26
AIDS, 177, 217–19
archive, the, 16, 48–50, 82–83, 92, 122, 195, 197–213, 214–29. *See also* Cvetkovich, Ann; memory
Are You My Mother?, xxii–xxiii, 121–28, 135–47, 148–64, 187–90
Autography, xx, 7–9, 92, 105–18, 132–33, 197

Bechdel, Bruce. See *Fun Home*
Bechdel, Helen. See *Are You My Mother?*
Bechdel Test, xviii, xxvin5, 23
Beech Creek, xv, 167–80. See also *Fun Home*; maps
body, the, xxiii, 89–104, 111, 116, 137–41, 142–43
Butler, Judith, 6–7, 37–39, 91–92, 148–49, 152

Camper, Jennifer, xiv, 24, 27, 223
Cartography. *See* maps
Chute, Hillary, xxvin3, xxvin7, xxviin8, 5, 8–9, 72, 92, 162, 168, 186, 203, 211n2, 220
Crumb, R., xvi, 72
Cruse, Howard, xiv, 72, 217, 226n1
Cvetkovich, Ann, 40, 82, 92, 122, 226n5

DiMassa, Diane, xiv, 24, 25, 34
Disability, 137–41
Dykes to Watch Out For, xiii–xiv, xv–xix, 9–16, 22–35, 36–51, 52–67, 68–83, 230–43
  characters:
    Clarice and Toni, xvii, xviii, 12–13, 63, 226n6, 234–35, 238; Ginger, xvii, 28–31, 33–34, 45–48, 58; Lois, xvii, 22, 25–29, 31–34, 43–45, 59, 63–66, 234–38; Mo, xviii, 68–83, 234–37; Sparrow, xvii, 27–29, 34, 58–59, 237; Stuart, xvii, 25–34, 57–62, 237, 242; Sydney, xviii, 13, 32, 63, 234, 239, 242

Embodiment, 64–65, 89–92, 98–99. *See also* body, the

Feminism, xvi, 40–45, 218–21, 225–26, 235–38
Freud, Sigmund, 127–28
Fun Home, xix–xxii, 16–19, 52–67, 82–83, 89–104, 105–18, 128–32, 167–80, 186–87, 192–94, 197–213
Fun Home, the musical, xix–xx, 105–18; "Ring of Keys," xvi–xvii; "Telephone Wire," 113–16

Gay Comics (#19), xxi–xxii, 117n3

Halberstam, Jack J., 61, 64–65, 140, 168–69, 185
Hothead Paisan. *See* DiMassa, Diane

Intimacy, xiii, xviii, xxi, xxiii, xxvi

Joyce, James, xx, 208

Kinship, 148–64, 169–74
Kron, Lisa, 109–10, 111–12

Lacan, Jacques, 119–34
lesbian comics, xiv, xvi, xxvin3, 22–35
life writing. *See* autography

maps, 168–70, 177, 181–96
masculinity, 52–67, 169–74
McCloud, Scott, 8, 24, 41–43, 97–99, 190–91, 203
Memoir. *See* autography
Memory, 17, 39, 82–83, 89–104, 119–34, 197–213
Musical (genre), 106–9, 115–16

Narrative, 103, 107–8, 148–50, 161–62

Peanuts, 68–83; Linus, 77–80; Peppermint Patty, 76–77
Pekar, Harvey, 72
Performance, 105–18
Performativity, 89–104

249

photographs, Bechdel's use of, xx, 89–104, 110, 158–60, 198, 209–11
"Play Therapy," 105–7
Proust, Marcel, xx, 117
Psychoanalysis, 119–34, 135–47, 148–64

queer theory, 7–8, 16, 32–33, 36–51, 161–62, 218–20

Rich, Adrienne, xxiii, 136, 142–43, 183–84, 226n5

Schulz, Charles M. See *Peanuts*
Secret to Superhuman Strength, xxiii, 89–90
Sedgwick, Eve Kosofsky, xxviin11, 32, 47, 151, 156, 219
Servants to the Cause, xxi, 214–29
Spiegelman, Art, 72

Trauma, 119–34

Winnicott, D. W., 119–34, 135–47, 148–64, 187–90
WomaNews, xvii, 24, 214
Woolf, Virginia, xxiii, 136, 142, 146, 158, 187–90

www.ingramcontent.com/pod-product-compliance
Lightning Source LLC
Chambersburg PA
CBHW052047220426
43663CB00012B/2473